Five Years, One Kata

Putting kata back at the heart of karate

By Bill Burgar 6th Dan

Martial Arts Publishing Limited

1st Edition 2003

(v1.3)

Published by
Martial Arts Publishing Limited
www.MartialArtsPublishing.co.uk
email: enquiries@MartialArtsPublishing.co.uk

ISBN 0-9544466-0-7

Important Notice

The author, publishers, printers and distribution agents will not accept any responsibility for any proceedings or prosecutions brought or instituted against any person or body as a result of the use or misuse of any techniques or information described in this book or any loss, injury or damage caused thereby.

The information in this book is distributed without warranty and is only presented as a means of preserving a unique aspect of the heritage of the martial arts. All information and techniques are to be used entirely at the reader's discretion. While every precaution has been taken in the preparation of this book, neither the author nor publisher shall have any liability to any person or entity with respect to liability, loss or damage caused or alleged to be caused directly or indirectly by the contents of this book or by the procedures or processes described herein. There is no guarantee that the techniques described or shown in this book will be safe or effective in any self-defence, or otherwise. You may be injured or injure a 3rd party if you apply or train in the techniques described in this book. Specific self-defence responses illustrated in this book may not be justified in any particular situation in view of all of the circumstances or under applicable national, federal, state or local laws.

Dedicated
to my parents

Acknowledgments

Emma - my wife, for her full support of my karate endeavours and for patiently taking more than 1000 photos for this book.

Rick Clark - for opening my eyes to the painful reality of vital point manipulation and showing me the elegance therein; for being a first class mentor; and for planting many seed ideas.

Patrick McCarthy - for his pioneering work in the study of karate history, principles and technique; for bringing to public attention the Habitual Acts of Physical Violence.

Vince Morris - for being a tireless force applying unstoppable common sense to karateka around the world.

Steven Webster and **Gerry O'Dea** - for being the best peers and co-conspirators a man could wish for; for their constant encouragement; for their inspirational ideas; for their constructive criticism of the drafts of this book; and for their help in proofreading - without them this book and many of the ideas herein would most probably never have happened.

David Margree - for providing valuable feedback as a great training partner; and for his patience posing for many hundreds of photos for this book.

Tracey Harte and **Ravi Khanna** - for their many years of friendship and making karate a joy to practice.

Malcolm Phipps - for his teaching on the first part of my karate journey.

Steve Rasmussen - for his first-class book cover design.

Nicholas Heath - for his excellent work in proofreading the text.

ADK members and leaders - In particular Rick Clark, Ken Tucker and Steven Webster for coming up with a progressive and challenging grading framework. Also to the many ADK members who have influenced and challenged me.

Peter Consterdine and Geoff Thompson - for their leading part in exploding many martial arts myths.

The other martial artists too numerous to mention individually by name - Over the years I've been influenced by the ideas of a great many martial artists both in person and through their work presented as books and videos; to you all: thank you.

Table of Contents

Section 1 - Theory

Section 2 - The Example of Gojushiho

Section 3 - Your Own Single Kata Study

Section 4 - Where To From Here?

Foreword by Rick Clark

Bill Burgar, with his new book *Five Years, One Kata,* has undertaken a unique exploration of kata. The father of modern Japanese Karate, Gichin Funakoshi, believed true Karate required a deep understanding of the various kata. He understood if the practice of kata were nothing more than moving your hands and feet and jumping up and down like a puppet, learning karate is not very different from learning to dance. Funakoshi felt that an individual would never reach the heart of the Karate, and would not be able to grasp the quintessence of Karate-do if they had not studied in-depth.

Taking to heart the words of Gichin Funakoshi, Bill Burgar began a long and intensive study of a single kata, Gojushiho. Forsaking the practice of the other kata, Bill Burgar pursued a course of study few individuals have the temperament to undertake. By delving deeply into the practice of a single kata Bill Burgar sought to develop an understanding of Karate few have been able to achieve.

In this book Bill Burgar has been able to organize and codify the knowledge he has gained over his years of study and has written this book to share his hard-gained knowledge with others willingly; and make it possible for anyone to to the same. Without question, this book adds to the body of knowledge in the study of Karate. Bill Burgar has become one of those rare individuals who go before and then lay down a path for others to follow.

Rick Clark
Ao Denkou Kai
www.Ao-denkou-kai.org

Foreword by Patrick McCarthy

"There, in the middle of the journey of life I found myself astray in a dark woods where the straight road had been lost." Dante's quote from Inferno seems appropriate when trying to portray what most traditional karateka must experience when faced with uncertainty. How many yudansha are challenged to explore the ambiguous depths of this ancient tradition but remain unknowingly trapped inside the proverbial box? Myth, misunderstanding and a narrow mindset, all too often disguised as a way to preserve the "purity" of this or that style, have led to hypocrisy, fragmentation and isolation in karate. In our modern age of politics and protectionism, it is truly a rare occurrence to find budoka capable of thinking outside this box, much less making the important contributions Bill Burgar has.

Unsatisfied with the defensive inadequacies espoused in the modern interpretation of kata, and unable to get the answers he needed within traditional karate circles, Bill Burgar decided to conduct his own independent study. Cultivating influential liaisons with like-minded colleagues who helped him nurture the understanding he now commands, this young researcher acted on his instincts and trained diligently. Reaching deeply into the abyss of this tradition he has brought forth important discoveries, and the work that lies before you is a testament to this effort.

A member of our research group for many years, I have long been impressed with his genuine passion for this tradition, respect for its heritage, and pragmatic deductions. If ever there were an insightful publication by an open-minded and progressive researcher, then this must be it. For those with the eyes to see, I believe that his book will help break down the many preconceived yet erroneous barriers that otherwise impede learning how to understand what defensive secrets lie hidden with kata. Culminating his lengthy study, this publication brings new meaning to otherwise inflexible rituals, while also revealing why it is important to make the obligatory paradigm shift and learn to think outside the box. I sincerely urge the reader to look beyond the techniques and labels displayed in this book, and use it as an opportunity to examine kata from a functional point of view.

I doubt a single foreword will do justice to the depth and breath of his work, yet I am convinced that *Five Years, One Kata*, may very well be the best book on kata I have ever read. Based on its insightful messages, *Five Years, One Kata* is certain to become a timeless classic valued for generations to come. In fact, I believe that the overall value of this publication might also compel us to look beyond kata and more closely at ourselves. I am sure that is what the original pioneers wanted.

I am pleased that my own research has had such a positive influence on Mr. Burgar and I am very grateful for the opportunity to voice my recommendation.

Patrick McCarthy
International Ryukyu Karate-jutsu Research Society
Brisbane
www.society.webcentral.com.au

Foreword by Vince Morris

I was very pleased when Bill Burgar asked if I would contribute a few words in way of an introduction to his work on the kata Gojushiho.

In particular, I remember Bill from many years back when he began attending seminars I had arranged by George Dillman, and then my own.

It was obvious that here was a martial artist who was fully committed to gaining a true appreciation of all the elements which go into a proper understanding of the kata, the so-called 'bedrock' of the martial arts.

Since then I have met with him from time to time and been quietly delighted by the continual and single-minded progress that Bill was making.

Never satisfied with the obvious, he has dug deep into what really matters: not the outward form, but the inner meaning of the kata. He realised that winning medals in the performance of that which was not even understood was a poor criterion of success.

In this book, Bill has laid before the reader a paradigm for both practice and understanding which should be studied carefully.

His method of considering the situations from one of real combat, rather than as choreography, is one I heartily endorse as, in my often-stated opinion, the very basis of a martial art is self-defence; all else follows that, no matter how commendable.

The reader should note that due to the obvious constraints of book size it has not been possible for Bill to go into more depth on the important factors that I call 'Rules of Combat'. I feel sure that the discerning reader will want to further his or her knowledge in this area once he or she has understood the importance of the method of study Bill presents here.

No martial artist serious about gaining a true understanding of kata should miss this work.

Vince Morris, 7th Dan. Feb. 2003, New Jersey USA.
Kissaki-Kai Karate-Do
Director: Law Enforcement Training Services International.

Section 1 - Theory

This section introduces the historical and theoretical background necessary to get the most from the study of a single kata.

Initially, the subject matter may seem varied and unrelated; however, all of the threads are woven together by the kata. Subject matter covered includes:

- Some history and background on the evolution of kata and its original purpose.
- My probability theory which provides a guide as to what to practice.
- Imagery (visualisation), which is a key component for achieving the maximum in any activity and especially kata practice.
- The psychology of confrontation and how this, along with probability theory, feeds into ideas on habit and how to build habits which are beneficial during confrontation.
- Vital points: where to find them, how to use them and why.
- Bunkai and Oyo (the breakdown and application of kata movements) are discussed and the use of and understanding of bunkai through the different periods of history is examined.
- Detailed explanation of the skills and knowledge required for the understanding (reverse engineering) of kata movements is given.
- An area ignored by most karateka who work on bunkai is that of applying some objective measure to the quality of the bunkai. Suggested measurement criteria are given and a method of step-wise refinement of applications is proposed.

With the knowledge contained in this section you will be better able to appreciate the example of Gojushiho and will be in a good position to start your own study of a single kata.

Introduction

Purpose

There are two objectives for this book; the first is to show that it is possible to study a single kata for a period of years and from that kata create a detailed self defence training regime. This is illustrated by detailed examples from my own more-than-five-year study of Gojushiho kata. The second objective is to give guidance to enable the reader to recreate this experience for him- or herself using a kata of their own choice so that more karateka can appreciate the great depth and meaning of kata.

Intended audience

This book is aimed at the experienced karateka, who has gained a strong grounding in a traditional style of karate and who is now ready to embrace the wider concepts that karate and other martial arts have to offer. The intended audience is, therefore, karateka who have attained the rank of approximately nidan or higher. The mindset of the reader should be one of open enquiry, curiosity, and the desire to delve deeper into the art that is their passion. The reader must be prepared to challenge received wisdom, evaluating all information on its merits rather than from an emotional perspective.

Introduction

Funakoshi Gichin[1] wrote “In the past, it was expected that about three years were required to learn a single kata, and it was usual that even an expert of considerable skill would only know three or at most five kata”. He further notes that he studied for ten years to learn the three Tekki forms properly.

To the vast majority of modern karateka studying a single kata for many years is a concept so foreign that most would not even know where to begin. This book tells you how to do it. It shows that a single kata can be a magnificent training tool that, when properly and thoughtfully implemented, may facilitate a full and efficient training regime. Kata may indeed have become a “classical mess”[2] but it doesn’t have to be that way. We can, should we choose, restore kata to their former glory as the heart and soul of karate.

This book is the fruition of my more-than-five-year study of a single kata. It presents my new understanding of the lost knowledge of deep kata study that I have painstakingly recovered. I sincerely hope that many karateka will find inspiration from my experience and will view their karate kata in a new light. At the very least this book contains many training concepts that can be used in any training regime - single or multiple kata or even with no kata at all!

Over the years, I have often studied a single kata for three or four months at a time but this was taking place alongside my standard Shotokan dojo training. In 1994 I left the comfort zone of the standard Shotokan dojo that I had trained in for 15 years to the level of 4th dan and

1 Page 38. Funakoshi Gichin; Karate-do Kyohan; Kodansha 1973; ISBN 0 7063 1996 6

2 Bruce Lee

cross-trained for about 18 months. In 1996, mainly due to pressures of work, I could no longer attend a dojo regularly so I decided to start a singular study of kata where I could control when and how I practised. I determined that I would study only one kata exclusively for a period of one year. It was an experiment to find out what it was like studying narrowly and deeply as I had so often read that the old masters of karate had done.

And so started the process that over five years later affords me the opportunity to write down some of my discoveries and to share some of what I have found. It has taken me five years to make a vast shift in mindset, made painstakingly step-by-step over the days, months and years. In presenting the information here I am aware that for the reader the material may present a culture shock. You will absorb the information in a much shorter time frame than I experienced. As such you will need to be flexible in your thinking and I ask that you read with an open mind; or to use that hackneyed old martial cliché - "empty your cup".

The first section of the book sets down the key information, the tools of the trade, upon which an in-depth study of a single kata can be built. These include probability theory, habitual acts of violence, the skill sets or habitual behaviours and the tools that can all be applied to the study of a martial art and, by implication, a kata. Also presented are some objective metrics for ensuring that the resulting applications of the kata movements are within the parameters that define useful techniques.

The second section of the book shows how I have applied the tools in the analysis of Gojushiho kata over the last five years. It should be borne in mind that this book is the culmination of many years of study. Had I known more of the information presented here earlier I believe I could have greatly reduced the amount of time required for a full, in-depth study of the one kata. Section three shows how to build a complete training regime using just one kata as the mnemonic device for that training schedule. Finally there is a description of the recommended process you should follow in order to make your own long term in-depth study of a single kata.

Overview

This section gives a brief overview of how kata can be used during practice.

The key difference from the modern norm is that, for the most part, karateka tend to practice the performance of the kata rather than practising the self defence techniques contained therein.

So make a paradigm shift for a moment, if you will, and imagine that the performance is completely irrelevant; i.e. going through the whole sequence without pausing, hesitating or making mistakes is simply not important. Just imagine this for a moment - you make a mistake during the performance of the kata what is the reaction of your instructor, your peers and juniors, competition judges and grading examiners? Will they commend you or condemn you? The whole of the karate kata landscape is set up to rate people on their ability not to make mistakes. Some groups are introducing testing on oyo (the application of kata movements) but in the main kata are judged on performance, not content.

Now think about this: kata is a solo practice. It is designed to be done on your own. If you had a partner you would be practising the techniques of self-defence with them, wouldn't you?

Many karateka will argue in favour of the fringe benefits that practising kata performance brings like balance improvement, body control, and so forth. Well there may be fringe benefits but you could improve those aspects of karate more directly than with kata. That is to say, kata is not the optimal tool for those things. So what is kata optimal for?

My view is that kata gives the knowledgeable karateka (i.e. the karateka who understands what each individual movement in the kata means) a mnemonic to facilitate solo practice of his repertoire of techniques and skills. The sequence of the kata is easy to remember (maybe not at first for beginners, but a capable dan grade should be able to learn the movements for a new kata in an hour or so). Now having learned the sequence gives you the ability to practice each movement individually without missing any out, i.e. it gives you a training regime. You start at the beginning and work to the end but for each technique you practice it on its own, visualising what you are doing to an opponent. The techniques, strategies and tactics will deal with the habitual acts of violence and also there will be some "in the thick of it" techniques for use when things have kicked off as well as some general purpose techniques for crash and bash. Maybe you spend one or two minutes per technique, maybe you do one technique per day. Any capable dan grade could practice bassai-dai, for example, one technique per day and never have to write down where he got to: you remember it and it is easy to remember - that's a good mnemonic.

Let me describe how I practice kata in my dojo at home. I'll vary what I do from day to day but one day I may go through each technique spending some time on each one. I'll go through the sequence but to the observer it would not look like kata, it would look like shadow-boxing practice of numerous techniques. The observer may wonder how I remember them all and the answer is simple: I'm "reading" them from my mnemonic which is the kata. On other days I may play "linkage"; that is, for each move in the kata there will be a probable outcome (i.e. me and my opponent will finish in a certain position). Playing "linkage" means that you follow the movement immediately with another appropriate movement from the kata. So for example if one technique deals with a lapel grab and I deal with it by striking the grabbing arm to bring the opponent into range for a head strike, after the head strike the opponent's head may be tipped back and he may be off-balance to the rear. I would immediately go to another technique later in the kata to capitalise on my advantage to put him on the floor. I would work through each move in the kata stringing them together as appropriate. The purpose of this exercise is to ensure that should I need to use this for real I will be able to flow from one technique to the next without hesitation. I do various other types of practice but this gives you a flavour. They all use the kata to ensure that I practice my techniques but I rarely/never do the kata all the way through as a performance.

Each technique is only applicable to one person. If I'm in a multiple-attack scenario I can only really deal with one person at a time. Maybe by positioning sensibly I can do it from a position of advantage but generally if I'm hitting I can probably only really hit one person at a time. I have no reason to believe that kata are deliberately constructed to deal with a set sequence of attacks. I have a probability theory (see The Probability Theory on page 41) one part of which deals with the (un)predictability of sequences of techniques. Essentially, you cannot predict long strings of techniques - the longer the string the less predictable it becomes. If an application of a movement in kata relies on the opponent doing two things in sequence then it must be flawed, because how could you have chosen your defence based on the first technique when you cannot be sure that the others will follow in the required sequence? The problem is exacerbated for multiple attackers. It seems a bizarre thing to spend time practising low probability event sequences at the expense of more likely scenarios. If they represent the techniques that are most likely to be used against us then we should be spending most of our time practising to defend against them.

Terminology

The terminology used in this book includes some mainstream Japanese karate words, which reflects the main target audience of the book. Usually these words accompany a picture so the meaning should be clear.

Other terms used include Bunkai, Oyo and Henka which are defined here in order to be clear about their meanings.

Bunkai: This is simply the analysis of a kata movement; working out what it means.

Oyo: This is an application of a kata movement and is the result of having done bunkai i.e. analysing the movement and working out what it could be used for.

Henka: This is simply a variation. When we are doing bunkai to create oyo we have to ask ourselves what are the most likely variations on this theme. The resultant variations are the henka.

Pictures

Pictures in a book which attempt to show something as dynamic as karate will never be able to capture accurately what is happening with a particular technique. The photographs in this book have been posed to show the essential elements of a movement. As a result they are not always "practical". The reader should take this into account when trying to put the techniques into context.

History and background

History

The karate history books are replete with evidence that shows that before the modern era each karate master knew only a small number of kata, and often only one or two. John Sells writes[1] that "A student could spend up to three years on just one kata. The term 'hito kata san nen' (three years - one kata) grew out of this traditional methodology". Funakoshi wrote[2] "...it was usual that an expert of considerable skill would know three or at most five kata". Indeed the words "kata" and "style" are synonymous in some texts. For example Choki Motobu[3] uses the words kata and style interchangeably and mentions that "A Master usually only had one kata in his style".

To most modern karateka it seems almost incomprehensible that anyone could possibly find one or two kata sufficiently absorbing to enable their long-term study. Most karateka are required to perform at least seven kata (and often a great many more) in order to reach the shodan level which many regard as merely the start rather than a sign of mastery. Indeed it is not unusual that by 3rd or 4th Dan levels the karateka may "know" between 15 and 30 kata.

The emphasis today is on the performance of kata rather than its practice. To most practitioners today the performance of and the practice of the kata are the same thing. What is really meant by "practising a kata" is "practising the performance of the kata". In contrast, a deeper practice of a kata involves:

- the full break down of the kata into its constituent applications;
- the individual practice of those applications, both alone using powerful visualisation techniques, and with a partner in training drills;
- putting strings of applications into tegumi or flow-drills;
- and also practising the individual principles that pervade all of the techniques.

Regardless of how things stand today, the fact is that before circa 1880 it was the norm for karateka to know a small handful of kata. We also know that each master of karate was capable of defending himself. Therefore his one, two or three kata contained all of the knowledge that he would have needed to achieve that goal. This means that each kata (or small group of kata) was a "style" in its own right.

Japan began a radical period of modernization at the start of the Meiji period and in the thirty years between 1880 and 1910 karate, swept up with these changes in society, changed almost beyond recognition. Funakoshi remarks[4] that "The karate that high school students practice today is not the same karate that was practised even as recently as ten years ago, and it is a long way indeed from the karate that I learned when I was a child in Okinawa."

1 Page 204, Unante, John Sells, Hawley Publications 1996 ISBN 0-910704-89-9
2 Page 38, Karate-do Kyohan, Gichin Funakoshi, Kodansha 1973 ISBN 0-7063-1996-6
3 Page 17, Okinawa Kempo: Karate-jutsu on Kumite, Oyata transalation 1997.
4 Page 36, Karate: My way of Life, Gichin Funakoshi, Kodansha 1975 ISBN 0-87011-463-8

This transformation of karate from jitsu to do, a fighting art to a sport, merely followed what was happening in the other martial arts. The fighting applications were no longer required and fell into disuse. The objective of the new karate was to create fit, healthy and courageous young men who would serve in the military forces of the Japanese empire. The civilian self defence system (te or tode) that karate had been did not fit well with the new objective, and new practices evolved from the old to meet better the requirements of the new military drilling practice.

The kata did not escape the tide of change and the practice of studying a small number of kata was replaced by the callisthenic practice of many varied kata. After all, if you are not going to teach in-depth you need more things to teach and multiple kata fit the bill nicely. Funakoshi embarked on a programme of importing many varied kata from other sources to supplement the small number of kata he knew. This rush to learn more kata was not confined to Funakoshi, and it was not long before the norm was to learn many kata and in a reasonably short period of time.

Prior to the Meiji era the way kata were used was almost unimaginably different from the "tradition" we recognise today. Recent work, principally by Patrick McCarthy among others, has created the hypothesis that karate was originally a civilian art of defence as opposed to a martial (battlefield) method. This civilian method of defence was constructed to defend against the most common instinctive techniques of combat.

When viewed in this light each kata represents a well thought out method that covers the defences for a number of the most common habitual acts of violence and a sufficient number of techniques and skills required for fighting. The kata is simply a mnemonic device[5] that enables the practitioner to practice the full system of his karate without any written reference. Modern man has become lazy with the use of his memory. The modern prevalence of written and pictorial material has put a huge gulf between us and our ancestors of only a hundred years ago in understanding the power of mnemonic devices. Calling a kata a library of techniques merely scratches the surface of its potential as a mnemonic device.

History of Gojushiho kata

Readers may be surprised to learn that I have not taken much interest in the history of the Gojushiho kata, instead preferring to work on what was available to me rather than tracing the various versions of the kata back in time. Nevertheless it is interesting to understand a little of the history of the subject matter at hand.

The old Okinawan name of the kata is Useishi and it can be traced back to Matsumura's era. Useishi literally means 54 in the Okinawan dialect. Gojushiho also means 54 but is the standard Japanese pronunciation. There are many Okinawan kata named simply by various "magic" numbers. Examples are shown in the following table.

5 A "mnemonic device" is anything that aids the memory. Specifically the sequence and pattern of kata form a mnemonic device which helps the karateka to accurately recall many movements (typically about 50 or more for advanced kata).

Kata Name	Number
Seisan	13
Seipai	18
Niseishi	24
Nipaipo	28
Sanseiru	36
Useishi	54
Suparinpei	108

Nobody can say for sure why these kata were so named nor can any definitive statements be made about why the other kata were given more esoteric names. We do know that numerology was very important in the Okinawan and Chinese cultures and that many of the numbers shown above do appear to have had spiritual or mystical relevance.

There is speculation that the numbers related simply to the number of techniques or steps or principles. I cannot see any substantial evidence to support this theory. Until there has been a more thorough study of the historical origins of karate we will not be able to draw any definitive conclusions.

For our purposes of single kata study the name is not relevant, except when comparing notes with other karateka where there is a requirement for common terminology.

It is likely that Gojushiho is one of the older kata or, more correctly stated, kata bearing the name Gojushiho or Useishi have been practised since the time of Matsumura and probably for some time before then. Most versions in use today trace their history through Itosu or Kyan. The kata was brought into Shotokan by Nakayama (according to Nakayama) after being asked by Funakoshi to learn the kata from Mabuni. Actually the kata was being practised before then within Shotokan. Several versions of the kata have been merged in modern Shotokan to form a sho/dai pair of kata. In most styles of karate it is considered to be one of the more advanced kata although my study of the kata suggests that comparisons of "advanced" and "less advanced" kata is a dubious practice due to poor comparison metrics being laid out. Most modern practitioners compare the level of difficulty of the performance of the kata – something which has little use beyond the competition mat.

It should be noted that Funakoshi attempted to rename the kata Hotaku (meaning woodpecker) for obvious reasons during his mass renaming of kata in order to help gain acceptability in Tokyo. For some reason the name failed to stick.

The common contemporary view of kata

We cannot say with any certainty how kata were used prior to the Meiji period in Japan, nor can we make large deductions about the time period from 1880 through to 1940 as there is not an enormous amount of reliable written testimony, particularly about the earlier part of the period. However, we can make some statements about what kata has become. It is probably true to say that there are millions of practising karateka through out the world. The vast majority of them broadly experience a similar practice of kata.

John Sells[6] gives a pretty standard interpretation of most karateka's experience of kata: "Kata practice seeks to develop the skills of power, balance, focus, coordination and technique. Kata are both a form of exercise and an active meditation."

Mr. Sells then goes on to explain the next level of kata usage i.e. that of extracting the meaning of the movements so that their application is understood. The kata is used as a reference to the various techniques – a mnemonic tool. Although the practice of bunkai is now growing in popularity it is not widespread, and the applications that are widely taught (presented in many of the major styles' standard texts) leave much to be desired as self defence techniques and are rarely taken seriously by practitioners.

Finally, others suggest that, in addition, there is a further level to kata that is the "spiritual" or meditative practice of kata.

These are the generally accepted views of kata. In this book, I would like to present another view. I believe that kata can form the foundation of a karate-training regime. The kata acts as a mnemonic to facilitate the entire training regime rather than just a small insignificant part of it. It also acts as a powerful mental rehearsal training tool.

Personal responsibility

Modern karate is highly organized. From his first day in the dojo the karateka is told how to behave, how to act, how to move and when to move. The karateka progresses along the conveyor belt that is the rank system. The objective of the system is to produce replicas of the stylised ideal. The karateka willingly buy into this system and strive to become as close a replica of the ideal as possible no matter how futile the attempt may be. The measurement of the karateka is against the yardstick of the idealized form. From day one this conformity is continually emphasized so that the product is lines of automaton. In short, the art is being taken out of karate due to the mass production system.

The system has the effect of reducing personal responsibility to an absolute minimum and it encourages each karateka to abdicate original thinking in exchange for repeating received 'wisdom'. The tale-tale sign of a karateka firmly imbued in this thought process is the words "My sensei said…" with the implication that "Sensei said it so it must be true".

A prerequisite for studying a single kata is that the karateka take responsibility for his own progress. Ultimately each karateka must decide which direction to take in their study of the art.

Personal responsibility covers all of the decisions about what to learn, how, when and what to practice, and how the training regime is practised. Can junior karateka be expected to make these kinds of decisions? Possibly not, but as time moves on the instructor should be not only giving the student techniques to practice but should also be showing methods of original

6 Page 204, Unante, John Sells, Hawley Publications 1996 ISBN 0-910704-89-9

thinking. We all move through various stages of maturity in our training. As in life we all mature at different rates. The maturity spectrum is described in karate circles by the term "Shuhari". This represents three stages. First is Shu: this is where the student obeys tradition, does as he is told and has decisions made for him. Ha is the second stage where the student begins to break the bonds of childhood and makes the transition to adulthood. It is where a greater level of freedom needs to be given to the student and where the student needs to take more personal responsibility in order to benefit properly from those freedoms. The third stage is Ri, where the student has attained independence and takes full responsibility for themself.

The expectation in the karate fraternity is that we are pursuing a lifetime study. The false assumption that many make is that we have to be perpetual students stuck in the first stage of immaturity. This is not so, our goal should be to reach maturity in our studies. Taking personal responsibility is the first step in the process.

The environment for study

How can we possibly practice full personal responsibility in a modern dojo? Is it possible to have each karateka making their own decisions about what and when they should be practising? The modern sensei has to maintain control and set a syllabus in order to satisfy the needs of the majority. The health and safety of the practitioners is paramount, and having large numbers of karateka doing what they want could lead to accidents and claims of professional negligence.

The best environment for undertaking practice of a single kata is in the informal setting of one's own dojo or back yard. Indeed, practising in an informal setting either alone or in very small groups makes single kata study possible. As soon as we move karate to being practised by larger groups we necessitate a change in the way we practice to the more formal end of the spectrum.

The implications of this are that in order to study a single kata properly it is necessary to step outside the current "traditional" karate scene. This is perhaps the most difficult situation to face for the karateka. There is a social and political comfort zone in the dojo and the thought of stepping outside is for most karateka a challenging prospect and not a nice challenge at that. Fortunately, complete separation from the standard dojo is not a requirement and the serious in-depth study of a single kata can take place alongside regular attendance at a dojo. The kata study is undertaken as "homework".

It is for each karateka to find the most conducive environment to suit personal needs.

Kata-centred karate[7]

It is interesting to track the development of karate with respect to how the central theme of practice has changed. Originally, the heart of karate was individual kata training with one-on-one instruction being a central feature. However, when karate was introduced into the school system on Okinawa (in the early 1900s) the emphasis started to change. Instruction

7 Page 11, Pressure Point Fighting, Rick Clark, Tuttle, ISBN 0-8048-3217-X

became one-to-many and classes took the form of performing kata synchronized by count. The use of training kihon (basic techniques) in lines advancing up and down the dojo then became widespread. By the time karate was introduced into Japan from Okinawa this practice was already well established and was then built upon.

In the late 1950s and the early 1960s with the introduction of competition with rules the emphasis again began to change and through the 1970s to the 1990s sport karate was very much at the centre of our thinking. The purist karateka may claim that they never practised sport karate and that they always maintained their tradition. Although many of us would like to think that, the evidence is against us. So all-pervasive is the competition ethic, and so deeply it is ingrained in practice methodology that it is difficult to distinguish it from what we aspire to, namely the practice of the art of karate.

The competition thought-process manifests itself most obviously in use of combat range or engagement distance (maai). Most contemporary karateka are comfortable at long range (also called competition range). All modern Kumite practices are designed to operate at this long range, and by continual exposure to it the karateka finds his comfort zone. Changing back to short range upsets the average karateka's level of comfort and puts him in unfamiliar territory.

So, the contemporary karate experience is generally that of kihon-centred long-range training. This means that the basic techniques of karate form the central core of practice from which the rest of the art is practised. The basic punches, kicks and blocks practised making long steps up and down the dojo floor, set the scene and form the thought boundaries for the way we define our karate.

Karate has not always been taught in this way. Travelling back in time we can see that originally karate was taught in a kata-centric manner. The kata was taught and from that the basic techniques and concepts were practised, and also the short-range self-defence techniques which are the building blocks of the kata sequence.

Looking further back to the creation of the kata, we see that the kata are the culmination of training rather than the start[8]. That is to say, that before kata existed there were only fighting techniques that were gathered by karate's pioneers. In order to remember and practice those techniques, and not having access to recording media such as videography, photography or even the low-cost abundant availability of writing materials, those pioneers used the most natural media available: their memories. Mnemonic techniques were perhaps more commonly known in that era than today and they would have easily been able to construct kata to remember their fighting principles and techniques.

Should we so choose we can change what we practice, and return to a kata-centred approach that was the original legacy of the originators of karate. Taking a kata-centred approach has the potential to change us back from a competition focus to concentrate on self defence at short range. It is for each of us to decide what our aims and objectives are in the study of karate.

8 See Patrick McCarthy's work for more detail.

Aims and objectives

The Chinese cliché much used in martial arts circles says that the longest journey starts with a single step. What it fails to mention is that if that step is in the wrong direction the overall journey just become two steps longer.

Knowing where you want to get to is fundamental. As Steven Covey says in his book *Seven Habits of Highly Effective People*, [paraphrased] "Everything is created twice, first in the mind and then in reality". Until we understand what we are trying to achieve it is futile to take action. Once we know what we want to get to then we must take the *right* action to get there.

We can make a distinction between an aim and an objective. The *aim* or purpose is usually a loose description of roughly where we want to get to. It is akin to a mission statement used in many companies. Mission statements rarely have specific measurements. They usually set direction and describe values.

For the most part beginners come to the martial arts with fairly clear mission in mind; "I want to learn to defend myself", "I want to get fit", "I want to be superhuman!"... As the months and years roll by this sharp focus becomes gradually blurred, until by 1st dan the karateka is often confused as to what it is he is trying to achieve. There are many messages and propaganda pushed into each karateka and someone who originally went to the dojo to learn self defense may start to quote other reasons for continuing practice. For example, self development, health and fitness, self confidence, balance and coordination and so on. By the time the rank of 3rd dan is reached (usually after some 8 or 10 years training) the reasons for continuing are murky and often very different from when the karateka first entered the dojo.

Therefore, the first task before starting any training regime, whether that be a single kata or otherwise, is to have a clear understanding of what the end result of that training should be. If we are fully to understand the nature of kata and appreciate its depth then it helps to know what we are trying to achieve. When I started my long-term study of a single kata I didn't know what I wanted from the kata. With hindsight I can now appreciate that having clear goals is the best way to derive maximum benefit from single kata training. In order to set these goals it is advisable to have a mentor who can wisely guide your choices. In section 3 of this book there is some general advice on how to approach a single kata study.

Borrowing from the field of management we can start to clarify our objectives. All objectives should be SMART that is:

Specific	We must make clear and unambiguous statements about what it is we are going to achieve.
Measurable	There must be some way to determine when the objective has been met. We therefore make a statement that describes how we will measure success or failure of the objective.
Achievable	It must be possible to reach the objective. It is important to understand in advance whether or not the objective is achievable. It is important to remember however that many tasks when first approached seem insurmountable, so it is important to be optimistic and to take on a challenge.
Reward	The objective should bring sufficient reward that it is worth undertaking. There is always a cost / benefit ratio to consider. Every prize has its cost or as the old saying goes "you don't get owt for nowt", in other words you don't get something for nothing. It is always important to consider what the cost and benefit will be before initiating a task.
Time limited	There should be a clear time frame set out for when the objective will be met. Many things of worth are not achieved quickly and it is important to approach tasks consistently rather than sporadically. Breaking the task down into sub-tasks and estimating time frames is essential if we are to understand the cost of the task.

Understanding and writing down our objectives in karate is surely one of the most difficult tasks we can undertake. It is very rare that these objective-setting skills are taught in traditional dojo. It is particularly difficult for karateka who have been practising for a good number of years or where the karateka has many, often conflicting reasons for continuing to train.

Setting objectives is so vital to our success in our endeavours that we must ensure we spend sufficient time creating and reviewing them, lest we head off in the wrong direction and waste our valuable time and energy.

In studying a single kata the overall aim is to create a training regime, using the kata as the central tool which has mnemonic value and which facilitates practice of useful skills and techniques.

Difference between learning, practising and drilling

There are, broadly speaking, three stages in assimilating new techniques and concepts. First we have to gain an understanding in our heads, and then we must practice until we are satisfied that we have the technique correct. Finally we must repeatedly practice (drill) until the technique is second nature. The sequence can be defined as learning, practising, drilling[9].

Not all of our techniques will be at the same stage of development. We will always be learning new techniques while we continue to drill old techniques. Often we will learn how to enhance a technique, which means that we have temporarily dropped that technique back to the first stage. We then build back up again through practising and into drilling.

This much is fairly obvious and it is mentioned here because it is often taken for granted. Being conscious of the learning stages and being acutely aware of where we are with each technique can enhance our productivity during training.

It is recommended that for each activity undertaken in the dojo the student makes a conscious note, which phase he is in.

Think in training, do not think in battle

There are times for thinking and times for doing. In the heat of battle there is no time to think. Therefore, if we are forced into a thinking cycle by unfamiliar circumstances during time of conflict we are necessarily hindered by the extra time required to come to a solution.

In order to reduce the thinking required during conflict it is essential to get the thinking done ahead of time, i.e. during the learning and practising phases. Drilling techniques and principles should require no thought. There should be a simple stimulus-response loop in action.

There are two phrases often quoted in martial arts circles: "The battle plan rarely survives contact with the enemy" and "train hard, fight easy". What are these two simple expressions telling us?

First, we have the fact that things do not always go the way you would have liked them to. That is, you can make your plans but the fact that there is some other "thinking" person involved means that you cannot have thought of everything in advance. However, that is not to say that it is not possible to minimise the deviations from plan that are possible and thereby increase the probability of staying mostly on the battle plan.

So, second, we come to the idea that in order to minimise the chances of deviating from plan we need to work harder to cover the eventualities and to train sufficiently that we can adequately deal with them as they arise. This then comes down to a simple trade-off – harder work is better prepared, easier work not so well prepared. It is for each of us to decide how much effort is required to meet our objectives. Obviously, having clearly identified goals is

9 c.f. NLP: unconscious incompetence, conscious incompetence, conscious competence, unconscious competence.

imperative here, so that we know how much work is required and in what areas to bring the desired results. It's no good being very well prepared for a battle plan that has little chance of being put into action, and being poorly prepared with a battle plan that is very likely to be required.

Negotiation skills

A confrontation can be viewed as a negotiation in which both sides are trying to get what they want, and sometimes that will mean that talking has run its course and violence will follow. That means that if you are good at negotiation you can avoid violence and still get what you want. There are many management texts available on negotiation skills that go into far more detail than space allows here. However, the key notion as far as we are concerned is that of knowing what you want. Often fights start because neither party really understands what they want from the negotiation, pride becomes a factor and fighting is the inevitable outcome. Many fights could be avoided if one party to the negotiation gave way on one thing that was not important to them in order to achieve their goal.

Our goal (usually) is to minimise injury to ourselves, our family and friends. Nothing else matters.

Observation skills

Gerry O'Dea and Steven Webster coined the phrase "having the eyes". This refers to the way we watch our instructors and learn from them. Much of the time we do not *really* watch. When we are beginners we only see the gross macro movements, and over time we begin to see the more subtle nuances. However, all too often we stop watching because we take for granted much of what we see.

It is essential we ensure that we observe more closely what is really happening when we are in the presence of someone more skilled – whether it be in person or on video. In other words, we have to educate ourselves to "have the eyes" and start to see ever more subtle detail.

A key thing to note here is that the real action is often not where your eye is naturally drawn.

A major enemy of good observation skills is complacency. I was embarrassingly reminded of this only recently when the person that really taught me observation skills in the first place (Rick Clark) put me on the spot in a seminar. Having asked me to make the point about observation skills he proceeded to show the point to the rest of the class. I made the embarrassing error of saying what I saw rather than really taking the trouble to observe carefully. Having just given a lecture about how important observation was I'd actually been about the worst observer in the room. This episode, though embarrassing, did make me consider what was involved in observation a little more, and so I offer the following tips to help you in structuring the way you observe in order that you can see more.

1. Have the person performing the technique do it as many times as it takes you to get a proper understanding.

2. View from as many different angles as possible.

3. Have the person perform the technique on you - feeling is as important (more so actually) than seeing.

4. Force your eyes away from the obvious scene of action and look at other things that are going on.

5. Don't be complacent; having seen something 100 times you can often see something more on viewing for the 101st time.[10]

6. If you can get something on video, do so because you can watch it again and again.

Climbing out of the box

Thinking out of the box is a crucial skill that is closely related to observation skills. It is important for the advanced karateka to be able to put to one side all of the knowledge he has gained and see a technique or a concept from an entirely different and often unexpected angle.

In order to think out of the box we have to climb out of it first. Sometimes that climb can take a long time. Once we have made the climb out of the box and can think from that new perspective we realise that we didn't necessarily climb an optimal path.

When we are out of the box we can then pull people up to stand with us and they don't have to make the climb following the winding route that we took. To those people looking at the path we took they may be confused as to why it is so illogical and tortuous. It is like watching a mouse in a maze looking for the cheese. The first route goes down many dead ends and wrong turns until the cheese is found. On the second time through the maze the mouse will take a more direct route. The casual observer who comes not understanding that there have only been two runs may question why the mouse took such a poor route on the first. It is the path that makes us what we are.

Getting help from a mentor

A mentor is someone who has trodden the winding path and can advise on how to straighten the path for the student. However, it is also the job of the mentor to allow the student enough leeway to experience the full lessons offered by the student's own path.

In Rick Clark's Ao Denkou Kai we have pioneered a system of rank advancement by a framework of peer review and mentorship. This experience has shown that it is essential that we seek out several mentors to help our development in various areas. The modern invention of blind loyalty to a single instructor is quite limiting to the individual student. The practice that was widespread in Okinawa was to seek instruction from specialists in various fields and then integrating the new knowledge into the student's personal system (the essence of cross training).

10 With thanks to Rick Clark!

The student is encouraged to identify areas of weakness and to address them by getting help from people in that area who have some expertise. In today's flooded martial arts market these skills are usually fairly close at hand.

The important thing to bear in mind here is that karate is supposed to be an individual experience. Creating clones (which can never match up to the most talented karateka) is not a worthwhile exercise. Each individual must find their own way and not only be encouraged to do so but should have the environment placed around them to allow this to happen.

The strategy of karate

Karate is a punching and kicking art. There are many who claim that there are all manner of other skills to be found in the kata for example, grappling, throwing, locking and so on. Indeed if you look you can certainly find these things. Also it is impossible to know if these things were in there originally or are we just reading these things into the kata when they were not there originally.

It is my contention that karate's strategy is that of primarily striking skills and the supporting skills to enable one to continue striking. Therefore the grappling skills to be found in karate are sufficient escapes to remove any grip and get back to hitting. So principally we learn to kick and strike; we learn to get up from the ground quickly to continue kicking and striking; we learn to escape any grip quickly so we can continue to kick and strike. This means that the grappling such as it is in karate need only be sufficient to escape these situations. It does not have to be as sophisticated as other arts that specialise in finishing confrontations by remaining at that range and employing specialist skills.

Probability theory

Introduction to probability

The mathematics of probability can be complex, but for our purposes we do not need to delve into the realm of academia. We will use what might be termed natural probability or common sense probability. It is the type of probability each of us weighs up every minute of every day in every decision we ever make. It is what lies behind our determination of possible outcomes given current information at our disposal. We all have a natural feel for what are more likely outcomes and what are less likely. These are based on our common experience.

Normal distribution curve.

The normal distribution curve is extremely important to give us a feel of how things are in general. Again, we don't use the normal distribution curve in the strictest mathematical sense but merely to help guide our thinking in how we set up our optimal training regime.

This is a typical shape of a normal distribution curve which is often called a bell curve, for obvious reasons. There are many natural phenomena which when plotted will conform to the bell curve shape, for example, the height of people in the adult population.

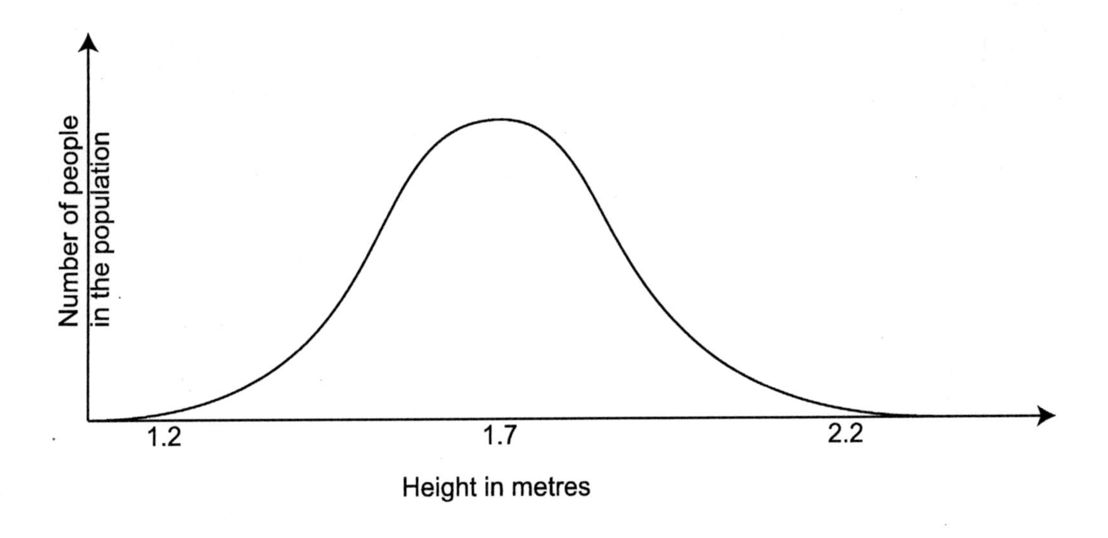

As you can see there are a few people who are short and a few who are very large, but most of the population is gathered around the average height.

Why is this useful?

Examining probability theory through vital points

To illustrate, let us take the example of the various levels of response that people display to the manipulation of vital points (vital points are discussed in detail starting at page 87). There are a few people to be found who have little or no response to vital point manipulations. Conversely, there are a few people who are ultra sensitive to the merest touch. Most people have a moderate to reasonable response. If we were to plot the level of response to vital point manipulation we would find a bell curve similar to the one shown below.

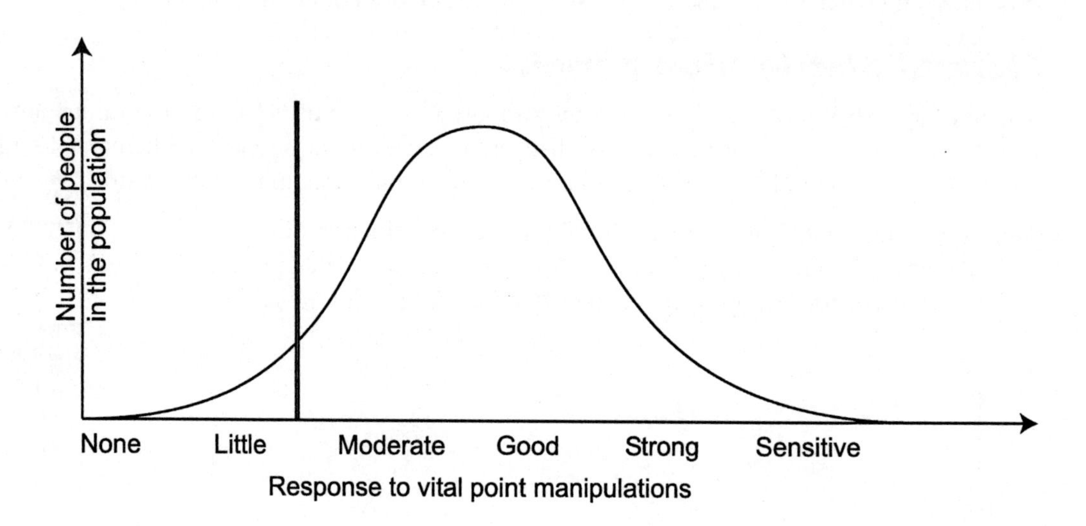

Practical experience experimenting with low power manipulations shows this graph to be a reasonable picture of what we could expect. To put this into some meaningful numbers we could say that one out of every hundred would have little or no response, 5 or 10 may have little or moderate response. Most would be moderate, good or strong responders and one or two would be ultra sensitive.

From a martial perspective we only need concern ourselves with the none or little responders i.e. all those to the left of the vertical line shown in the above figure. Viewing the information in this way shows us that a thorough understanding and good skill set for manipulating vital points is not sufficient to cover the entire population. We must build some redundancy into our techniques so that we are not reliant on the effects of vital point manipulations. The techniques we choose must have some mechanical and/or mental effect too.

Predictability of assault techniques

We can use probability theory to focus our training further. If we were to run a survey in the street asking respondents to rank the likelihood of being attacked with the following techniques:

1. Spinning jump kick
2. Round swinging punch
3. Head lock

They would probably rank them 2,3,1. i.e. the round swinging punch is the most likely, followed by the head lock followed by the spinning jump kick.

Using probability to define training time

Probability Theory uses the fact of the instinctive and cultural confrontational behaviours - also called the habitual acts of violence (HAOV[1]) - to help us in the way we think about HAOV and how we construct a training regime to take advantage of it. There are also numerous side effects that are of use.

Probability Theory simply states that out of all the possible techniques that we may have thrown at us in an encounter some are more probable than others. Specifically the HAOV are more likely to happen than, say, specific martial arts techniques. Some HAOV are more likely to happen than other HAOV. It is possible, given any two techniques, to rank them as most likely and least likely (however slim the margin). It is therefore possible to rank all techniques into a spectrum of most likely to least likely. Note that compound techniques, for example a double punch, fall further down the list because the more techniques you add to the compound the more difficult it becomes to predict the entire sequence. The rank order of probabilities will change with different environments around the globe, depending on local laws with regard to weapons licencing etc. The unarmed, untrained HAOV will not vary by a significant degree. Highest probability HAOV vary for men and women.

A common sense view shows us that it would be most sensible to expend most of our training time practising to defend against the most probable attacks. Thus there ought to be a direct relationship between practice of defensive tactics and the likelihood of their occurrence. There is a current historical hypothesis (mentioned earlier) which states that karate is a civilian form of self defence designed specifically for the use against the HAOV and is not a battlefield system. This means that the kata were designed as a mnemonic for remembering and practising the techniques designed to combat the HAOV. We will use this reasoning later.

Another outcome of probability theory is that if some techniques occur more frequently than others there is a spectrum of predictability that surrounds the possible techniques one may encounter. In order to go to the uppermost extent of that spectrum one must look at pre-emptive techniques. These give us the maximum predictability, as they do not allow our opponent to lead the conflict. We can therefore put our pre-emptive techniques at the top of the list of HAOV probabilities.

1 The phrase HAPV Habitual Acts of Physical Violence is a term coined by Patrick McCarthy from which the other acronyms such as HAOV, HAV etc., which are in common use, have been derived.

Possibility sets

At any given moment in a confrontation there are a number of things that may happen; a set of possibilities. In the next moment, one of those possibilities will be happening and it is our ability to read the situation to anticipate which it will be that decides the outcome of the encounter.

In traditional karate, ippon kumite is the principle method for teaching skills for dealing with particular attacks. The most normal arrangement is to have a possibility set of size one i.e. you know exactly which technique your opponent will attack you with. Later on we make a jump to a much wider possibility set when we start free sparring. This larger possibility set is limited by the range and the rules of the sparring and so, although it may seem that the exchange consists of an unlimited number of techniques, this is not actually so. However, it would seem sensible deliberately to build up the skill of anticipation gradually rather than trusting to luck that people will cope.

Therefore the idea of possibility sets is useful. Initially, the size of the possibility set should be increased from one to two, so for example, instead of just having to defend against a right hand round punch you may extend the possibilities by adding a right hand push to the chest. When confidence has been built add further habitual acts.

You will note that habitual acts will naturally fall into groupings. This is convenient for practice, so for example you may group all ballistic and semi-ballistic techniques into one possibility set for practice (e.g. Punches, kicks and pushes). You will probably also find upon grouping them that they fall naturally into ranges and angles of attack so that, for example, if you are at talking range there will be a possibility set that you would use to practice at that range because the attacker would not be able to attempt other techniques at that range.

Other areas of application of probability theory

Probability theory can also be usefully applied in the following areas to optimise your training regime: reflexes, ability to move, ability to balance, natural fighting spirit and many others. In each of these areas you could look at where you are under the bell curve and see what extra work would be required to elevate you abovet a significant proportion of the population.

Mental rehearsal

Introduction to visualisation

Visualisation: certainly the most important of skills for the kata practitioner and yet it may seem that it is difficult to test it in a grading, or have any concept of how well or badly it is being done by any particular karateka. But when it is *right* it is so obvious to the observer – there is no mistaking what the intent of each move is. Visualisation is *the* essential skill to learn and do well. Funakoshi wrote[1], "...your opponent must always be present in your mind...".

How many people really take the time to develop this skill? Not many; there are many reasons for this, ranging from poor understanding of each movement through to the speed that the kata are executed in modern dojo. The predominance of performance values over practical issues means that aesthetic points are emphasised. This means that concentration on making the kata flow, to look right, not to make mistakes in sequence, and to keep precision all conspire to take the practitioner's mind away from the application and visualisation of the opponent.

On the other hand, using the kata as a mnemonic tool means that the performance issues are removed and we can return to a more paced practice. To give an example, it can take me between five and fifteen minutes to execute a single practice of my Gojushiho kata depending on the focus of the practice session. Think on that for a moment – *fifteen* minutes for a single execution of a kata!

The lack of understanding of visualisation can be seen easily in many dojo. When the instructor explains a technique many of the students will not be able to recreate that technique unless they have a real opponent in front of them. Having a real opponent in front of you greatly simplifies the mental process; you only have to do the thinking for one person. Indeed it is apparent that many karateka have nonexistent visualisation skills – that is, they are unable properly to recreate techniques without an opponent in front of them.

The question then is, what constitutes good visualisation?

Someone who is good at visualisation will be able to imagine in perfect detail all aspects of the opponent and the surroundings on a moment-by-moment basis, so as to be able to create realistic scenarios within the mind. The good visualiser will be able to see, hear, feel and smell everything about the scenario in clear detail and will be able to run the scenario in real time or, better still, faster than real time. Good visualisation will have a physiological effect: adrenaline should be dumped with all the resulting physical reactions. This can be measured for example by the use of heart rate monitors that are now available at reasonable cost. During and after the visualisation you should feel the effects of the adrenaline release. Good visualisation will also take account of how the opponent will react to techniques and the range of variability therein. It will also allow the branching of scenarios given different opponent

1 Page 105, Karate-do My Way of Life, Funakoshi Gichin, Kodansha International, ISBN 0-87011-463-8

reactions and environmental conditions. The visualisation can be performed as a mind exercise only or with body movement (as per kata or shadow boxing).

By contrast, poor visualisation has little detail there is no sound, no touch, certainly no smell. There is no background setting or scenery. The attacking limb may be visualised but it is disembodied i.e. the visualisation only sees the immediate threat, without awareness of the body position of the opponent or the range of following continuation scenarios.

How good is your visualisation?

Take for example the simple karate lunge punch aimed at face height. Visualise yourself stepping back and blocking with a standard rising block (i.e. a standard ippon kumite technique common to nearly all styles of karate). Just visualise the terminal position and then turn the page.

Now check what you saw in your visualisation against the following list to see how complete it was.

Did you visualise:

1. The opponent's:

   a) Fist at (relative location and distance from you, overall speed)

   b) Forearm (angle in relation to you and to the opponent's shoulder)

   c) Elbow (direction of bend and degree of flexion)

   d) Upper arm and shoulder (degree of rounding and degree of rise)

   e) Left arm at hip including (height of fist in relation to belt, degree of elbow inclination to the body, degree of Hikite)

   f) Head (inclination forward, tension in muscles around neck, teeth showing, general expression, wrinkled or flat brow, hair colour, overall height)

   g) Trunk (inclination and angle, shape)

   h) Hips (inclination and angle)

   i) Right leg (inside or outside your own, relative distance from you, degree of bend, foot angle)

   j) Left leg (degree of bend, angle to you, degree of support to opponent's structure, angle of knee and foot)

   k) The sound of expulsion of breath on completion of the technique (possibly a kiai)

   l) Colour of karate-gi and obi.

   m) Smell

2. Your own:

   a) Blocking arm (fist angle, forearm angle, degree of tension, contact point and speed, feel at the contact point including direction of pressure against your limb)

   b) Withdrawing hand (fist/elbow/arm position, angle and inclination)

   c) Head (inclination and direction, location with respect to the opponent's fist)

   d) Trunk (inclination and angle, direction and location with respect to opponent's body)

   e) Left leg (relative position to opponent, degree of bend, feel of the floor)

   f) Right leg (relative position, degree of bend, foot position on floor, feel on floor)

   g) The sound of expulsion of breath and the clash of arms.

h) The feel of the opponent's arm on yours (pressure, friction).

3. The scene:

   a) Floor type and level (for this scenario probably level, polished wooden floor)

   b) Background scene type (for this scenario probably your normal dojo, pictures on wall, wall bars, kick bags, mirrors, makiwara, door etc. as appropriate)

   c) Smell

The above is not an exhaustive list by any means and it only described the last moment of the technique as if it were a photograph in a book. Did you visualise all of the above? Did you visualise the entire movement from start to finish with all of the above at every stage? Exactly how good is your visualisation?

Sufficient vs. complete visualisation

Although the example of visualisation given above was very detailed and in many respects complete it was more than sufficient for the purpose. In fact, it could be argued that in the example of the simple rising block in ippon kumite the only visualisation that is required is that of the self and of the attacking limb. The more subtle points of visualisation are not required. This shows that complete visualisation is not always necessary and that visualisation only needs to be sufficient for the purpose (a recurring theme in this book i.e. optimal input for a given goal).

The key is that the visualisation must be *at least* sufficient to attain the goal of a realistic scenario. If we aim for complete visualisation then we expend extra energy (more than is necessary) to create the more detailed picture. It is sensible to concentrate on the key points of the scenario.

Finally we should note that insufficient detail in a visualisation can dramatically reduce the effectiveness. This includes a proper visualisation of the effects of what you are training to do. This can be compared with the kill-rate variances noted by Grossman[2] between World War II and Vietnam which was attributed to the training differences one of which was the change from the bullseye target to one with human shape.

How to develop good visualisation skills

Improving visualisation skills is about practising imagination. We all have the potential to be perfect visualisers; our minds think in pictures. It is simply a matter of exercising the mind so that it gets better at the task.

1. Start with simple movements that you are used to performing with a partner. Perform the movement slowly with the partner and then without the partner, just visualising how he moved. Start with just the attacking limb and then expand the visualisation to include the limb on the other side, followed by the other limbs, torso and head.

2 On Killing, Lt. Col. Dave Grossman, Back Bay Books ISBN 0-316-33011-6

2. Build up on the number of compound movements required in the overall technique. For example, move on from a single block to a block/counter. Then possibly an exchange of techniques.

3. When practising pre-arranged kumite, arrange with your partner to pause before attacking so that you can visualise the movement first. Build in as much detail as possible in the visualisation so that when the attack does come it is just as you imagined it.

4. Learn some grappling skills and practice visualising them. Grappling visualisation is generally more difficult than that for blocking, striking and kicking.

5. Learn the purpose of the movements in your kata and ensure that when you practice those techniques you visualise your opponent correctly.

6. Whenever you practice karate alone, always visualise your opponent (c.f. the quote from Funakoshi earlier in this chapter).

7. If you want a real visualisation challenge then go ride a horse and then try to visualise how four legs move in walk, trot (seated and rising) and canter along with the way the saddle movement is co-coordinated with the leg movements.

Instinctive confrontational behaviours

Introduction

Intraspecific conflict (conflict between members of the same species) takes many forms throughout the animal kingdom. It is characterised by varied displays and posturing before the two combatants make any kind of physical contact. Indeed the majority of conflicts are decided without real physical danger (although threat of serious injury is very much present in the minds of the combatants) and many others with merely mild cuts, scrapes or minor bites.

The method of display and posturing is very predictable for most species. It is instinctive and the animal does not have to learn the behaviour although it is often practised during play. It does not take too many hours for an interested observer to understand the level of conflict between two animals, what the next stage is, who is dominant, and so forth. The same is true for the great apes of which the human is a member. These "instincts" have been built in over many thousands of generations by evolution or survival of the fittest.

The human displays a common set of posturing rituals and fighting techniques that we could call instinctive confrontational behaviours. (For a more detailed description see texts such as *The Naked Ape*[1] and *People watching*[2] by Desmond Morris, *The Gift of Fear* by Gavin De Becker[3], *Chimpanzee Politics* by Frans de Waal[4], *Natural Conflict Resolution* edited by Filippo Aureli and Frans de Waal[5], *Demonic Males* by Richard Wrangham & Dale Peterson[6] and *On Killing* by Lt. Col. Dave Grossman[7]). These posturing behaviours have been evolved to minimise the chance of actual violence between people. They escalate from verbal threats and calls through displacement activity to what we might call low-level violence (e.g. pushing and shoving) and up to full-force blows and use of weapons to render the opponent non viable. No training is required beyond normal childhood play to make most people capable of an average level of defensive skill.

The skills that are learned from other members of the community are referred to as cultural confrontational behaviours. These are usually based on instinctive confrontational behaviours and are adaptions or enhancements.

The verbal stage of confrontation is accompanied by attempts to appear larger than one is in reality. Our chimpanzee cousins show an example of this where the alpha male of the group always appears larger than the other members of the group. This is achieved by his permanently having his hair stood on end, which makes him appear larger. The other chimps in the group only have their hair elevated during conflict and then to a lesser degree than the

1 The Naked Ape, Desmond Morris, Vintage Books, 1967 ISBN 0-09-948201-0
2 People Watching, Desmond Morris, Vintage Books, 2002 ISBN 0-09-942978-0
3 The Gift of Fear, Gavin De Becker, Bloomsbury Publishing, 1997, ISBN 0-7475-3835-2
4 Chimpanzee Politics, Frans de Waal, Johns Hopkins University Press 1989 ISBN 0-8018-3833-9
5 Natural Conflict Resolution,University of California Press, 2000, ISBN 0-520-22346-2
6 Demonic Males, Richard Wrangham and Dale Peterson, Bloomsbury Publishing plc, 1996, ISBN 0-7475-3301-6
7 On Killing, Lt. Col. Dave Grossman, Back Bay Books, 1995, ISBN 0-316-33011-6

alpha male. Humans tend to use other ploys in order to appear larger than the opponent. The face is also contorted to take on a fiercer visage. These intimidation displays may be enough to make the other combatant back down and so resolve the conflict. It is that certain something that just seems to cry out "don't mess with me".

If the conflict is not resolved by simple posturing then gesticulation and displacement activity will start. This is where the opponent's space is intruded upon, arms and fists are waved, fingers poked towards the opponent giving emphasis to the verbal assault. The opponent may be approached rapidly in pseudo charges. The displacement activity is where the air or inanimate objects are struck in a display of the striking power that the protagonist possesses, for example fists struck into open hands, fists waved at the opponent, slapping the hand onto a nearby object, or stamping the feet. Again, these behaviours appear naturally at a subconscious level i.e. by instinct.

The next level is where physical contact is made. Fingers are poked at the chest, hands push the opponent or attempts are made to control the arms of the assailant. Grabs at clothing are common, for example taking hold of lapels or grabbing the upper arms.

From here, if one opponent has not yet backed down, blows and kicks may be exchanged. In any untrained person there are instinctive and cultural attacks that are used. The most common attacks are easy for anyone to list from common experience and observation. They are the things that we have all seen in fights over the years. There are wild swinging punches, soccer-style kicks, rushing tackles, simple wrestling and so forth. An example list of these common attacks and techniques is presented below. These are the instinctive techniques of combat that will appear from the untrained human. They have evolved over the millennia as an optimal compromise of defence.

Patrick McCarthy has coined the phrase "habitual acts of physical violence" (HAPV), and this term has passed into common usage among many martial artists as a result of Mr. McCarthy's tireless and excellent work. The author wishes to acknowledge the huge body of excellent work completed by Mr. McCarthy, without which many of the ideas presented in this book may not have materialized. An almost equivalent term for HAPV is "habitual acts of violence" (HAOV) which is also in common usage. The two are often used interchangeably, however, I feel that the term HAOV also covers the pre-physical stage of conflict and as such is a useful broadening of the concept. This broader thinking allows us to further widen the approach to list "habitual acts of verbal violence", "habitual acts of weapon violence" which can be further subdivided to "habitual acts of knife violence", "habitual acts of stick violence" and so on. Making lists of these acts gives us the opportunity to study them in a structured way, using the probability theory to guide our training to the most likely scenarios that we could face.

An example list of the confrontational behaviours

Presented below is a list of some of the instinctive techniques you may expect. This list also includes some techniques that are more than instinctive but are in common usage i.e. cultural. They are presented in an order with photos and explanatory text.

Body space invasion

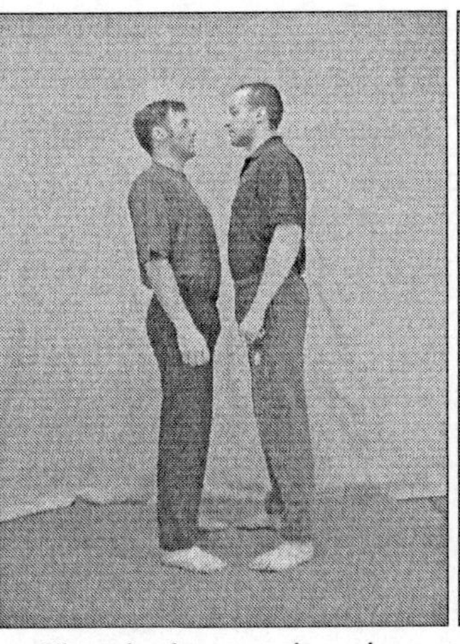

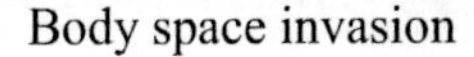

Body space invasion

Close body space invasion (aka chest butt)

Opponent tries to intimidate using height and close proximity

Invading the personal space of another person is a highly threatening act and the usual reaction of the person being threatened is to try to re-establish control over the interpersonal space or to match or best the aggressive action. The aggressor will naturally expect you to try re-establishment actions such as retreat or fending off with the arms. When arms are used to fend off, the aggressor will often either just continue to push forward (that is where his mind-set is) or will in turn attempt to remove your hands from him, often using short phrases like "Hands off the f***ing jacket". Notice how in the second photograph there is a temptation to puff up the chest and match the aggressive action but the face is pulled back which gives away the submissive feelings of the victim.

If the aggressor is allowed to remain at this distance and he does decide to physically assault you (which given the aggressive body language you would be entirely reasonable to expect or fear) it is likely that you will have been hit before you can react - most probably by a head butt, a knee to the groin or, at a lower probability, a short round punch to the head.

Geoff Thompson has coined the term "The Fence"[8]. The concept is in essence that we keep the aggressor at bay by fending off with the arms and attitude; we create a *perimeter fence* which the aggressor is not allowed to move inside. Stepping inside the fence along with other actions or intent will trigger actions on the defender's part which are designed to resolve the situation. It is important to assume the fence position in an (initially) non threatening way, which does not give away the fact that you are a martial artist (which in itself could fuel the dispute) - the intent being to defuse the situation calmly without violence whilst at the same time putting yourself in a position of best advantage. Actually, the idea is not new (although the "fence"

8 The Fence, Geoff Thompson, Summersdale, 1998, ISBN 1-84024-084-9

terminology is unique and is an excellent metaphor to use) and has been present in karate back into the mists of time - the concept is kamae or combat posture.

The concept behind kamae is to maximise your offensive potential whilst neutralising the aggressor's offensive potential. Ideally, you should be positioned in such a way as to remove the opponent's most obvious weapons. The opponent must *feel* like there is no point launching a particular attack because it will probably not work. The aggressor will only launch an attack if he truly believes that it will succeed, the only exception being a feint.

The "fence" position

Longer range fence

If your body space is invaded then immediately try to re-establish the fence, or if you are sure he will initiate, then pre-emption may be the only course of action available.

Round punch

Round punch
(initiation)

Round punch
(before impact)

Round punch
(impact)

Round punch
(initiation - telegraphed)

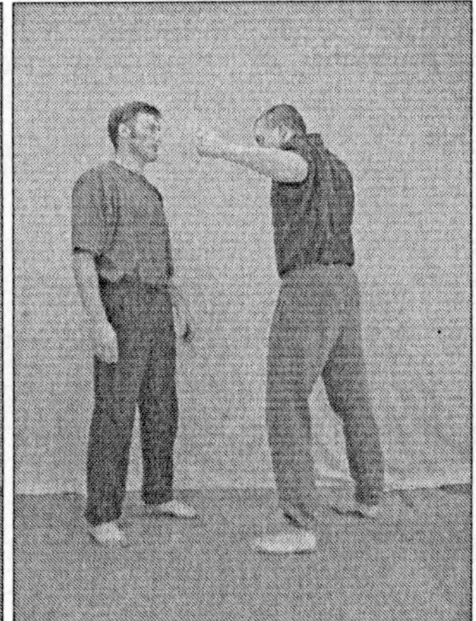
Round punch
(flight path)

Round punch
(impact)

Head shots are probably the most common instinctive assault technique used by both trained and untrained combatants. The majority of head shots follow an arc rather than a straight line.

The aggressor will always have to do something prior to launching the attack in order to satisfy himself that it will succeed. This pre-action can be as simple as stepping into range or may be a more complex setup such as a psychological disarm (a simple question will usually do the trick, or a physical unbalancing tactic such as a grab followed by the punch).

Most probable follow-up techniques are the continuance of punching and kicking (as that is the established mindset) unless circumstances change - for example a range change i.e. going to grappling.

Single-handed lapel grabs

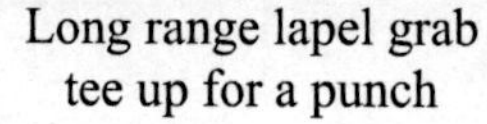

Long range lapel grab
tee up for a punch

Close range lapel grab
tee up for head butt or knee

The lapel grab is one of the most common control and threat mechanisms. Its main objective is to steady the victim's head (by controlling the position of the torso) ready for striking it or to make the threat of striking. It also has the advantage of giving some measure of control over the victim's balance. Instinctively, a very powerful non-verbal message is conveyed to the victim - his movement is restricted with a primary target made more vulnerable, compromise of balance is felt immediately in the soles of the feet - in short, being grabbed by the lapel sets instinctive alarm bells ringing.

The most probable next attacking technique will be a head punch. Other less probable next attacks are punches to the body and, depending on distance of the lapel grab, head butts and knee to the groin.

Throat grab

Bent arm throat grab

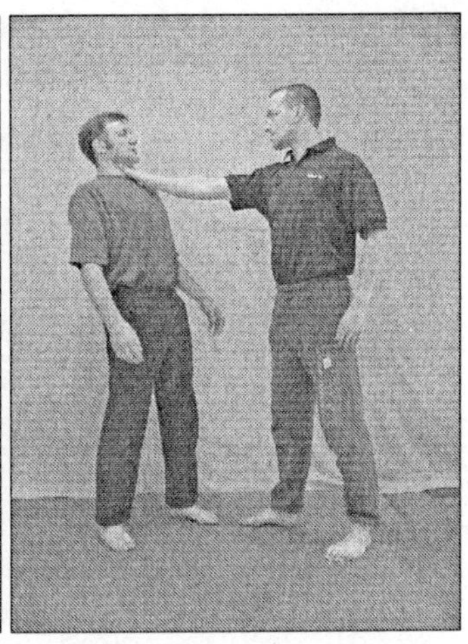

Straight arm throat grab

Being grabbed by the throat puts you in a similar position to the lapel grab. From the aggressor's point of view he has better control of your head in order to strike it, however you have better freedom of movement going backwards. If you have a solid object behind you then this gives the aggressor more advantage.The aggressor is likely to follow up with a punch.

Pushes

Tail end of a one-handed push

Tail end of a two-handed push

The push is at once a threat, a control and a displacement act. The first two are clear, however the third is not obvious as displacement is usually associated with an entirely displaced action.

However, in the case of the push it is a displaced punch. The psychology behind the act is that the aggressor cannot yet justify to himself that higher-impact acts are justified or that they would work.

Note that for a push to work it must be initiated from a range significantly shorter than the length of the arm.

Straight punches

Straight punch — Jab punch — Chest punch

Straight punches need less preparatory motion than most and so have greater capability to take the victim by surprise. They are often a precursor to other, higher-impact shots and to a certain extent are more cultural than instinctive.

Uppercut

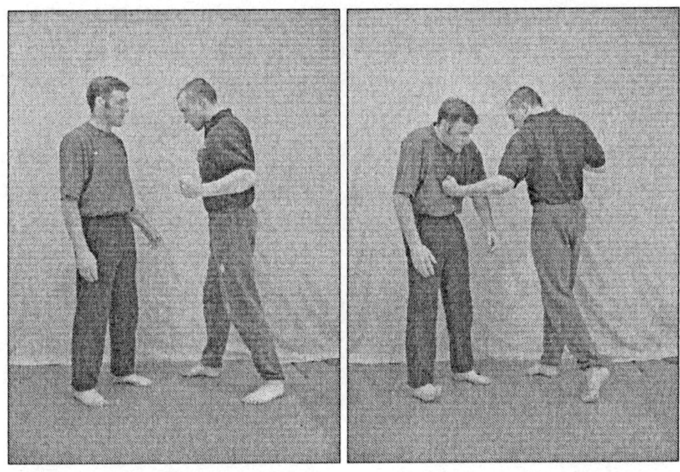

Flight path of the uppercut   Uppercut impact

Usually delivered from very close range under the cover of some psychological or verbal distraction. Once a confrontation has reached ballistic techniques then it is unlikely to be defused by verbal or posturing means. Expect a flurry of punches and kicks as a follow-up if you are not already on the ground with no wind.

Argumentative gestures

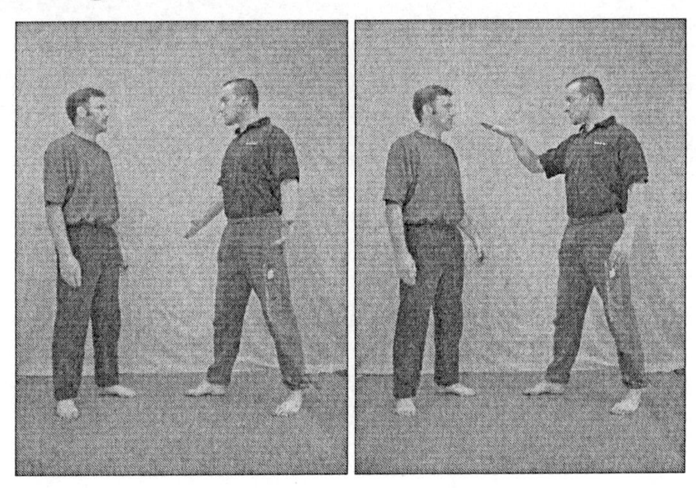

When you watch a film or a play you can instantly see when one of the actors is angry even if you cannot hear the dialogue. The actor knows how to make angry or argumentative gestures and we all instinctively and culturally know how to decode the gestures. The gestures and body language have encoded within them threat and displacement activities. The way we read these gestures, is important to the outcome of a confrontation. We have the possibility of fight, flight, posture or submit. Most confrontations are decided by the latter two of these rather than by fighting or running. Flight implies that one of the combatants has departed the scene quickly, however most confrontations don't happen that way. The submitting party usually leaves rather slowly and often loudly making an attempt to not lose face as they go (often reassuring their mates all the way home that "I could have taken him, easy, no problem - just wasn't worth my while bothering").

The essential point here is to try to understand the underlying emotion and desires of the other party. By trying to understand their motivation we maximise our chance to negotiate a peaceful settlement to the situation. As with any negotiation it must be entered into from a position of maximum strength (i.e. from a good kamae or fence posture).

Grabs from behind

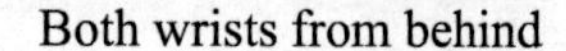

Both wrists from behind

Both elbows from behind

Both shoulders from behind

Being grabbed from behind is likely in scenarios where you are engaged in a confrontation with one person and one of his friends tries to pull you away (or worse still one of your own friends!) Being grabbed by the wrists from behind is not a particularly likely scenario but being grabbed by the upper arms is. Likely successive actions from this are that you will be thrown or pushed off balance to one side or the other, or held in place while the first opponent attempts to strike you.

One shoulder from behind

One elbow from behind

One wrist from behind

Other grabs from behind tend to be used most often when you are moving away from someone and they want to stop you or to pull you around into a strike. Follow ups from these grabs are strikes or grappling.

Arm grabs

All combinations of arm grabs (anywhere from the wrist to the shoulder) on the same side, cross side or both hands.

Same-side wrist grab

Same-side elbow grab

Same-side shoulder grab

The photos show sterile versions of the grabs for clarity but the grabs usually happen in a more dynamic fashion. It is important to understand the intent behind a grab. It is designed to exact a measure of control on the victim and to expose other targets. Therefore follow-up actions will be consistent with the intent and further control and dominance will be sought.

Opposite side wrist grab

Opposite side elbow grab

Opposite side shoulder grab

Two-handed wrist grab

Two-handed elbow grab

Two-handed shoulder grab

Two-handed upper arm grab

The two-handed upper arm grab is common when the grabber is being punched with a flurry of strikes. In order to stop the punches uke grabs the arms in an attempt to control them.

Finger pointing

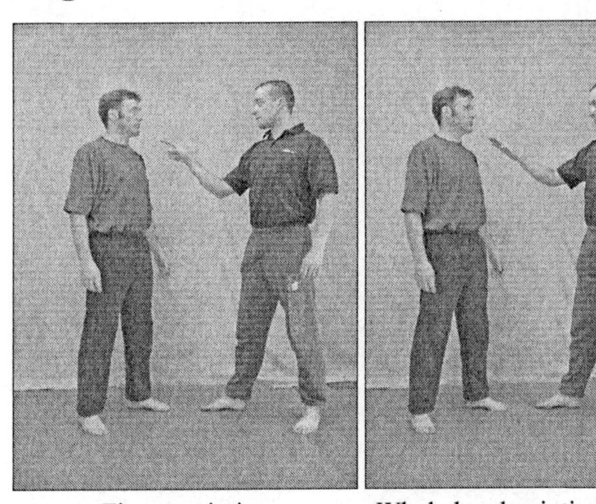

Finger pointing Whole hand pointing / poking

Finger pointing is a dominance and threat behaviour. It is usually used to emphasise a lecture. Any escalation from this point will often be of the form of pushes and punches but could also include a peaceful outcome.

Football kicks

Groin kick initiation | Groin kick completion | Natural flinch avoidance

Most people can kick reasonably quickly and accurately - football practice ensures that much. If someone starts off by kicking, expect multiple kicks and punches as a follow up. Note that it is very natural for men to flinch away from the kick - an instinctive defence against this type of attack.

Chancery head lock

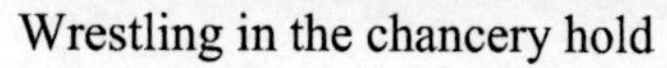

Wrestling in the chancery hold | And being... | Hit - repeatedly.

A very common fighting technique: grab round the neck, pull down and punch into submission.

Reverse chancery head lock

Held...

Hit with the knee

With the reverse chancery instead of expecting punches to the face (as in the chancery) expect knee kicks to the groin and chest.

Bear hugs

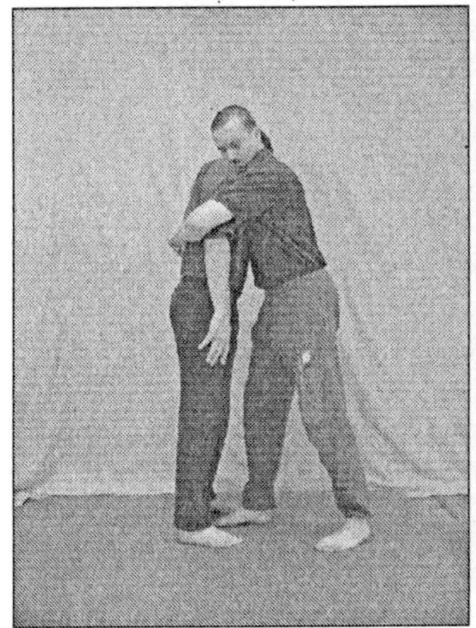

Over-arm front bear hug

Under-arm front bear hug

Under-arm front bear hug

Back over-arm bear hug Back under-arm bear hug

There are four variants with the bear hug: front and back, under and over arms. You should expect to be thrown off balance, thrown to the floor or be rammed into a nearby obstacle, or to be held to be attacked from the front by an accomplice of the first attacker.

Rugby or running tackle

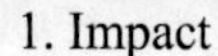

1. Impact 2. And thrown off balance to the rear

Many people are good at this technique on account of practising it every week playing rugby. If it is successful you should expect to be taken to the ground, sat upon and pummelled with punches using the old school-ground favourite of kneeling on your arms.

Head butt

Lapel grab to pull into a head butt

Head butt from a lapel grab

The head butt may be delivered assisted by arms or not. Expect follow-up techniques of further head butts, knee to the groin and grappling.

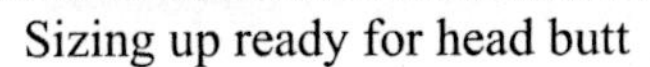

Sizing up ready for head butt

Head butt without grabbing

Habits built upon instinctive behaviour

Habit is habit and not to be flung out the window by any man,
but coaxed downstairs a step at a time.

Mark Twain

What is a habit?

Habit is defined in the dictionary as: ordinary course of behaviour: tendency to perform certain actions.

Good habits can save us and bad habits can kill us. It is our job as karateka to build on our good habits and reinforce them, and to eradicate our bad habits.

It is karate folk-law that says that the object of kata is to perfect technique so that it becomes second nature and we react to certain stimuli instinctively without the need for conscious thought. In short, we need to make our responses habitual.

These habits are the internalisation of the "principles of karate" or "the rules of combat". It is essential not only to understand these principles but also to put them into practice. I have used techniques from project management which help take an essentially passive knowledge (i.e. Knowing what the principles are) and turning it into an active knowledge (i.e. Putting it into practice)[1].

Habit and instinct

Over the millions of years of human evolution we have acquired powerful survival instincts. Even without specific training our natural fighting ability, when unleashed, has the potential to be formidable. We all have lightening fast reflexes, the ability to move and balance without thought, the ability to strike, kick and grapple. There is a range of ability in these things which takes a normal distribution (see Probability Theory on page 41).

When our martial habits and our martial instincts are aligned we will have optimal fighting potential. That is to say, if we take our instinctive response to a situation and build upon that with good habits of response we can maximise our effectiveness.

However, if we train in techniques that are in opposition to our natural inclinations, we will have to put in extra training and drilling effort to overcome our natural response. Even with the extra drilling time behind us there is always the strong possibility that we will revert to type when under stress.

This fact must be borne in mind when deciding which techniques are to be selected for drilling into habits.

1 For a comprehensive explanation of rules of combat see "Rules of Combat", Vince Morris, ISBN 09539325 0 8

Log-jam

A phrase coined by Geoff Thompson and Peter Consterdine in martial arts circles is "log-jam"[2]. This refers to the problem that can happen to experienced karateka who have drilled too diverse a number of techniques for dealing with the same situation. As the situation develops the karateka does not act quickly enough because he has to select from the wide variety of techniques at his disposal. Due to the effects of his adrenal dump his decision-making capacity is diminished, and by the time he has selected an appropriate response it is too late. In short, his mind was "log-jammed".

In order for us to ensure that we do not suffer the effects of log-jam it is imperative that we drill a minimum number of techniques (preferably only one) for certain scenarios. In this way we can minimise the log-jam effect and make our response to the stimuli a habit.

Habit change

It is possible to change habits; throw out the bad and replace with the good. In order to build excellent habits we must devise drills that specifically isolate and improve them. We must find ways to identify poor habits and ways to shed them.

One of the simplest methods for noticing a bad habit is to set trigger reminders[3]. This is something that you associate with the bad habit which, when it occurs, reminds you of the bad habit bringing it to your conscious mind. Once the adverse behaviour can be readily identified as or just before it occurs, it can be changed.

Predominant side

One in ten people is left-handed. For some reason evolution in its wisdom has decided that humans should favour one side over another. More than that it has dictated that most of us be right-handed. Curiously, when a lefty talks about being left-handed many of them claim to be "mixed" in that they do some things right-handed and others with the left, others claim right-footedness while being left-handed. Paradoxically, we never hear right-handed people defining themselves as partially left-handed. Why is this? Is it possible that there are pure left-handed and pure right-handed people but in an effort to conform in a right-handed world the left-handed people get a little mixed up?

Further questions spring to mind: what evolutionary factors so strongly favour right-handers? If being right-handed is so favourable why are there left-handers in the population at all? These are complex questions that, no doubt, science will unravel in the fullness of time.

In martial arts many people are of the opinion that we should train to be equally proficient on both sides of our body. However, for a great many of the karateka who claim to have this as an objective, close scrutiny of their training methods shows that their practice does not match their goal. Modern kihon training (advancing up and down the dojo) is done by 3 or 5 steps – the right side is predominantly trained in a ratio of 2:1 or 3:2 respectively. Modern ippon

2 Page 203, Streetwise, Peter Consterdine, Protection Publications, ISBN 1-873475-527

3 Page 97,NLP & Sports, Joseph O'Connor, Thorsons 2001, ISBN 0-7225-3671-2

kumite practice favours the right side with the left practised less frequently. Three and five step sparring favours the right side. The basic kata are reasonably well balanced but still have a slight right-side bias. The advanced kata are decidedly one-sided with many techniques only being performed on the one side.

Regarded in this light it seems that the underlying cultural background upon which karate rests is one-sided. Again the more curious karateka will have to ask the question – Why?

Let's go back to examine our instinct. When we perform actions we have what we might term an active hand and a passive hand. While the passive hand holds objects in place the active hand manipulates the object. Hold the nail; hit it with a hammer. Hold the food; cut it with the knife. Steady the paper; write on it with the pen.

The fact of our active / passive hands is so deeply assumed that we simply don't notice it in our everyday lives. However, as soon as we do notice it we naturally seem to jump to the conclusion that one hand is not as good as the other. This is an unthinking conclusion and out of the box thinking is required; actually both hands are just good at different jobs. They are complementary. Once we see this it opens up a valuable range of training options. We immediately see that both hands need to work in unison to achieve a goal.

An examination of the more ancient kata shows this idea in practice. These kata favour the right hand as the active hand and choose the left hand as the passive hand. In other words the kata are hinting to us that we should accept our active and passive sides, and build upon the strength that is the two working in harmony.

Finally, it really boils down to what your objectives are. If we are trying to optimise our self-defence skills then we can accept having an active and passive side. If our goal is physical fitness and equal dexterity and muscular balance, then practising some of the kata which were designed for that purpose (e.g. the Heian or Pinan kata) would be more appropriate.

Identifying, practising and drilling habits

There is a three-stage process to building good habits.

1.Identify the good habits to incorporate (and the bad habits to be eradicated).

2.Create practice regimes that cause the habit to become ingrained.

3.Drill the habit on a regular maintenance programme so that it is continually reinforced and further ingrained.

Kata is an ideal tool for the practice and drilling of the habits. It is important to note that simply performing the kata over and over again without a mindful awareness of the habit-building process will not have the desired effect. It is essential to engage the brain fully to practice each habit, both isolated and in tandem with others. When drilling the techniques, the habits that have been ingrained will be expressed without thought. It is at this stage that we need to ensure that we continually weed out any bad habits that form. Bad habits will only form unconsciously so they tend to be very hard to spot until it is too late. This is where we need either an instructor, a mentor or a tool such as a camcorder to watch and identify bad habits.

There are many drills (both solo and with a partner) in karate that we assume are all good because that is the way we practice our art. However, it is essential to be ever-vigilant for the bad habits that can be formed due to either the bad design or by the careless execution of the drill.

Take for example a flow drill. A flow drill is a sequence of exchanged techniques between a pair of karateka. First one attacks and the other defends using a set of techniques. Then at a predetermined point the roles are reversed and the flow continues. These types of drill are very popular. They are fun to practice and each karateka feels like he is getting practice at, for example, defending against a HAOV. However, the weak point of the exercise is the change over from defender to attacker. There is an unwritten consent that you will let the opponent off the hook so that the roles can be reversed. Continually practised, this can form a habit of not fully prosecuting a counter attack in a fully proactive way. Further, in any situation where full-contact blows cannot be exchanged (i.e. most training sessions) we are forming the habit of pulling our strikes. Again this is a bad habit, and we should be mindful of it. There are numerous other examples of the deficiency of partner drills. Yet it is essential to do partner work to build implicit understanding of the tactile part of our art. The important point to remember here is that we should be ever-aware of the purpose of the drill and beware of the poor habit that can be formed as an unwelcome side effect.

The habitual behaviours

Introduction

As noted in the previous chapter, it is important to identify the habits we wish to build and then set out to form practice methods and drills to ingrain them. For each habit we should identify how well aligned it is with our instincts and then decide the level of work that will be required to implement and maintain the habit.

Many of the habits are applicable to all techniques (*ubiquitous habits*), the rest only apply to some techniques (*specific habits*).

The ubiquitous habits can be trained "horizontally". If we take a grid, and label the axes with the ubiquitous habits on the Y axis and the techniques in our arsenal on the X axis, we can build a tool for a careful and methodical training regime.

	Technique 1	Technique 2	Technique 3	…	Technique n
Breathing					
Centre					
The Zone					
…					
Mindset					

By following any horizontal line on the grid we can train any ubiquitous habit for all techniques. By taking any vertical line we can train each habit for a given technique.

By isolating these habits and giving practice time to each one, for each technique we can train our use of the habit to be more instinctive. The reason this method is effective is that during training we are conscious of the particular aspect we are trying to ingrain, which commits it more effectively to the subconscious mind. Mindful, concentrated training simply makes better use of the time than just hoping that these habits will develop of their own accord.

For each of the various habits it is important to know how to understand them intellectually, how to practice each skill and finally how to drill each one until it becomes a natural part of each technique.

Breathing

The oxygen bank account

Breathing in martial arts is an interesting subject. In most cases the literature is confined to describing when to breathe in and when to breathe out. For the most part these are artificial prescriptions that are the first to be lost when the adrenaline starts to course around the body. Many thousands of generations of evolution have given us a finely-tuned survival system; anything we do which works contrary to that system is both hard to develop as a skill and also hard to maintain. That's not to say that it is not a good thing to do, it's just more difficult. The optimal path is to work with the body so that we allow it to work at its most efficient.

Correct breath control can make an enormous difference in all aspects of our lives. Few people are in the habit of breathing deeply and steadily, instead, we perpetually engage in shallow breathing. Poor breathing is often accompanied by poor posture in a chicken and egg relationship. The calming effect of deep, controlled breathing is well documented. However, instinctually, under the influence of adrenaline we tend to take rapid shallow breaths, or in many cases we tend not to breathe at all for short periods of extreme stress.

There is a simple balance that has to be maintained in the body. We need just the right amount of oxygen to sustain the level of effort we require at any particular time. As the oxygen is burned to make energy in the muscles, more oxygen is being supplied in the blood via the lungs pushed around the body by the heart. As more oxygen is required the heart pumps faster and the breathing rate increases to ensure that the demand is met. Under normal operating conditions this is fine and reasonably high levels of exercise can be maintained for long periods. This is called working aerobically i.e. the body can supply sufficient oxygen to power the muscles on an ongoing basis.

However, the heart and lungs have their limits and can only work at a maximum rate before they lose efficiency and they can no longer supply sufficient oxygen for all of the active muscles (including the heart and the diaphragm). There is a point where we are teetering on the edge of aerobic and anaerobic work. As soon as the muscles are demanding more oxygen than can be supplied, the body starts to borrow – to run up an overdraft which has to be paid back (one of my favourite sayings is "you don't get owt for nowt"). In situations where we make immediate explosive demands on our bodies the debt starts to build immediately. Any positive oxygen balance is drained from the account far faster than it can be paid back. The lungs and heart have to mobilise to produce at a faster rate and the body switches into anaerobic work within a few short seconds.

Anaerobic means working without sufficient oxygen present to fuel the muscles. The body starts to burn its less efficient reserves, and waste product (lactic acid) starts to accumulate in the body and cannot be removed quickly enough. This borrowing cannot be sustained and eventually we have to slow down and return to aerobic work rates. The price we pay for working anaerobically is that the body needs to work at far less than peak aerobic levels in order to recover.

Let's look at a typical fight timescale. Generally, fights are pretty quick, some lasting just a few seconds; others go for as long as 30 seconds; others (generally those which have degenerated to grappling) may go on longer. Other scenarios include frantic activity for very short periods followed by more posturing and then another round of violence.

The reason that fighting is limited to that kind of time frame is that it is a frantic activity and everyone involved will be working anaerobically for all but the first few seconds of the fight. After 15 or 30 seconds of anaerobic work the fight drains out of most people.

The fact is that for the most part of an active fight your body will go quickly into anaerobic mode and that's where it will stay until the fight finishes.

The question, then is, can we do anything to enhance our performance? i.e. ensure we can go longer anaerobically than most people we are liable to meet.

The first thing is to understand that we can raise our anaerobic threshold. We can undergo specific training drills that increase our anaerobic fitness so that we can perform better over short, frantic time frames.

The second thing is that we can do training drills that help us to control our breathing under stress.

Anaerobic threshold training

The body is a marvellously adaptive organism. Push it a little and it compensates appropriately. Work it a little harder and it gets stronger. All, of course, within reason. We can look to probability theory to understand the amount of work required to raise our combat fitness to an appropriate level. The various levels of fitness of the people who may cross our path will be determined on a normal distribution curve. Some will be very unfit, others at the other end of the scale will be highly fit. To be highly fit and at the far right edge of the curve you need to put in the time and the effort. Most martial artists don't have the time to devote simply to being fit; they have other skills to maintain and so there can only be a limited time available to devote to raising and maintaining fitness levels.

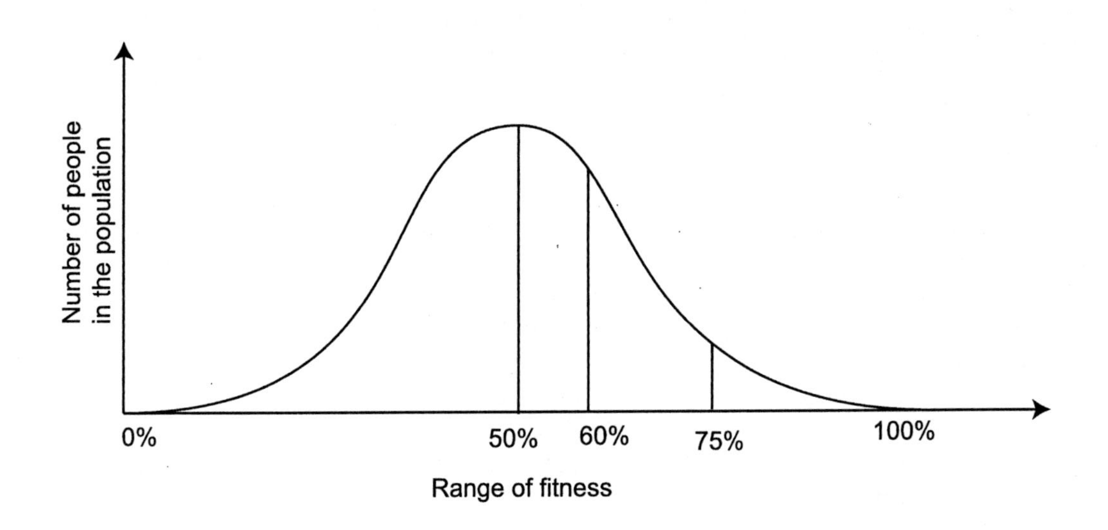

Consider this, if you are exactly of average fitness, you are grouped with the majority of people. Most people are at, just above or just below average fitness. You only have to improve by a very small amount and you will be fitter than most people. If you say that people who are totally unfit are at 0% and people who are totally fit are at 100%. The average is at 50%. If you can move yourself to say 60% on the scale (see diagram above) you can see that already the area under the curve to the left contains around 75% of the population. If you can do a little more work to move yourself to 75% on the fitness scale you can see that 95% of the population are less fit than you. Put in simple terms if any one of those 95% were to attack you, you would be fitter than them. That leaves the question of the other 5%. Put simply how much work are you prepared to put in to be fitter than them? There has to be an appropriate level of work that you are prepared to put in for a particular gain. (This is the "reward" part of your SMART fitness objective).

Of course it is not easy to know how fit you really are in comparison with the rest of the population, but if you do just a small amount of exercise each week you will be fitter than most of the population. Probably the best way to measure your fitness level for combat is how long you can go flat out before you have to stop.

When all technique is stripped away it comes down to who can keep going longest, therefore it is important that we raise our anaerobic threshold as far as possible in order that we can have that extra edge. So how do we do that?

Specificity is important in any training, i.e. you must construct a training regime that is as close as possible to the real activity. Burst work on the bag is probably one of the best fitness level raisers. This is where you go flat out hitting and kicking the bag (a burst of activity) for a set amount of time, for example 30 seconds, then rest for a short period and go again. Over time you build up the intensity of your assault on the bag and the duration.

An excellent tool for burst work is kata. The duration of kata is a bit longer than a normal fight particularly if you work the techniques on the bag. Remember, kata is simply a mnemonic device for efficiently recalling your set of techniques. You do not have to do the embusen (set pattern), you just have to do the techniques in turn to aid recall. With bag work you can also repeat the same technique for the burst duration.

Autogenic breath control

Raising the anaerobic threshold is an important pre-fight consideration, but during a confrontation breath control can ensure that you maximise the amount of oxygen in your blood stream before things kick off and you go over the anaerobic threshold. The habit we have to achieve here is calm deep breathing during times of stress. We therefore have to practice drills that reinforce the habit of breathing calmly and deeply at times of stress. The drills should put us under immediate threat while we practice isolating the skill of breathing. There is a technique called autogenic breathing that will be familiar to most martial artists. There is a growing body of evidence in law-enforcement circles that shows that deep steady breathing under times of stress helps slow the heart rate and reduce the tendency for the forebrain to give up control to the midbrain.

The autogenic breathing technique can be summarised as: "breathe in, two, three, four, hold, two, three, four, breathe out, two, three, four, hold, two, three, four." Repeated about three times this can slow the heart rate. Practice under pressure to grow the habit.

Centre

Being centred is a much talked about concept in martial arts but it can be a difficult concept to define and explain. Often the concept will be shrouded in mystery with esoteric and spiritual meanings. These explanations will frequently be accompanied with demonstrations of "ki". There are few that cannot be readily duplicated by the keen observer, and given sufficient time and opportunity for close observation I am confident that all of these tricks can be duplicated without any mystical powers.

Being centred is simply a matter of correct alignment and control of the body. The difficult part is to have habitually correct alignment and control. To approach the building of the habit in a structured way we need to understand first what the correct body structure is for each situation and then we need to devise ways to ensure that we practice and drill these structures as part of each technique and movement we use.

The zone

A term that has come into regular use in athletics and sports psychology circles in recent times is "the zone" or a "flow state". This is a term to describe complete mental focus. It is the feeling of being entirely in the moment, with crystal clarity of thought and effortless action.

It seems apparent that this is a desirable state to be in during a conflict situation. The question then is "is it possible to enter this state at will?" If it is possible then how can this be achieved and how do we train to make it so?

These are certainly difficult questions. Firstly, entering the zone does not happen often to most people, but when it does happen it gives a fleeting view of what the mind can achieve. It is not possible at this stage to be convinced that it is possible to enter the zone at will, but what we can say is that we can train the mind to concentrate more deeply on certain tasks. So from a pragmatic view, we should be able to devise training methodologies that enable the karateka to learn how to focus more directly on the task at hand.

When training in kata we necessarily have to visualise our opponent. An interesting side effect of our visualisation process is to only focus on the opponent and not on extraneous details. By not constructing background settings for our visualisation, we are creating greater focus upon the opponent – a kind of tunnel vision on the opponent. This causes "zone" effects. By repeatedly practising this visualised encounter, we are practising to enter the zone and thereby increase our chances of this happening[1].

Speed

Most of us in the martial arts spend a great deal of time trying desperately hard to go faster, faster, faster in our techniques. Indeed, in many karate clubs around the world after shodan or nidan grades all there is to do is go faster and harder. Yet, in the long term this is an unsustainable quest. As age begins to make itself felt raw speed declines and if we have not

1 Page 88, NLP & Sports, Joseph O'Connor, Thorsons, ISBN 0-7225-3671-2

trained and drilled any other types of speed then we find the youngsters running rings around us in depressingly embarrassing ways.

When we talk about speed we often suffer from limited thinking. Speed is a deceptive thing and most of us define it as the time it takes to get from A to B. For example, we define speed as the time it takes to get our fist from a chambered position at the hip to the target. The faster it moves the greater our speed.

What we really mean by being fast is our ability to hit a target before our opponent can do anything about it. There are many ways to do this other than having raw speed (although of course raw speed does the job perfectly well if you have it).

Lack of superfluous movement is a key speed habit to acquire. Most of us make extra or superfluous movements when we perform any technique. At the initiation of the technique we often "wind-up" before we actually move. For example when punching we dip or pull the shoulder back before punching, when stepping we pull the front foot back first before moving forward. All of these extra movements really do nothing to add power to the technique but they do serve to "give the game away" and alert the opponent to what is coming. By removing these extra movements, we give no clue as to our intent and so when we do move we appear faster to the opponent. In other words, we look faster.

To build the non-superfluous movement habit, we really have a task of removing unwanted habits rather than building new habits. The best way to do this is to run a camcorder during a normal training session and review it afterwards with the specific task of identifying superfluous movements. It is best to have someone actually pointing the camera at you rather than standing it on a tripod. It is important that the camera be focussed on particular areas at various points in the session. For example concentrating on legs, head, arms etc. The person being videoed should not be aware of which bit is being watched. Ideally the filming should go on for long enough that the person being filmed forgets the camera is there. On reviewing the video footage use your observation skills to pick out what needs working on. Once the bad habits have been identified, create a structured programme of training and drilling to eliminate the bad habits.

Deception speed is where we use guile to fool the opponent into dropping his guard. In a self-defence situation, this is usually done by appropriate verbal means. Usually you will need to engage the brain of the attacker (sometimes difficult as they often don't have more than one or two cells) with a question. It needs to be a question which distracts him for long enough for you to strike without being seen. Your strike must be launched from a natural stance. Striking from a natural stance must be practised and again a camcorder on a tripod set up with the zoom adjusted appropriately behind a punch bag to give an opponent's eye view is a good drill to practice. Set the video recording and practice striking the bag using appropriate verbal distractions. Then watch the video back to ensure that the opponent would not be able to see the technique in time. Again, look for give-away superfluous movement.

Finally, look for "speed-matching". This is something that often gets built in with the various kumite, tegumi and flow drills that are common in karate. This partner work is a double-edged sword. On the plus side it gives benefits of actual contact with an opponent and teaches us to cope with a given level of variability. On the other hand the drills require a certain level of cooperation between the partners. Perhaps the most subliminal of the suite of cooperative requirements is speed matching. This is where each partner tailors his speed to that of his partner. It usually means the faster of the two slowing down to accommodate the slower of the two although it can swap and change as the flow of the drill takes one person from attacker to defender.

We all ought to be firm believers in the phrase "under pressure, you will do as you train to do." If you train to match your speed to that of your opponent then that is what you will do in combat. We need to ensure that our drills encourage us to be faster than our opponent. Rooting out this habit is not easy because it is hard to spot and it is also very difficult to create drills that discourage it from happening. Probably one of the best ways to tackle it is by using horizontal training and concentrating on this one habit throughout a training session, repeating on a regular basis.

Strength

Raw strength is clearly advantageous in any conflict. There is certain merit in being able simply to power through an opponent. However, correct and timely application of strength is the most important strength habit to cultivate.

The body is a wonderful collection of levers, hydraulic and pneumatic mechanical systems. Most of us fall into patterns of "use" (to borrow a term from the Alexander Technique) whereby those systems work against each other rather than in harmony. In our everyday movements we use far more energy that we need to because our posture forces muscles that should be used for movement, to work doing the job of postural muscles. At the same time, our postural muscles are not doing their job and so they atrophy.

The detrimental effects of these everyday usage patterns are nothing compared to the extra energy we all spend during times of high stress. We all have the tendency to tense when threatened. Some people have this tendency to an extreme, causing them to freeze totally. Most of us suffer from it to a reasonable degree, causing extra tension that means we are slower and cannot hit as hard as we would ordinarily be able to.

It is important to ensure that we practice working to release the additional tension that we feel at times of stress. The habit that we must develop is to use our strength appropriately and to be able to let tension go at the right time.

Posture

Posture and strength are closely related. If we can use our posture correctly, it allows the strength to flow to where it is needed or where we wish to apply it. The idea is closely linked to eastern descriptions of energy flow. This does not have to be some mystical force it is just the simple physics of alignment and levers.

As mentioned in the previous section about strength it is easy to fall into bad habits with our posture. In particular at times of stress the excess tension in our muscles causes imbalance and we lose our structure.

We need to cultivate the habit of creating beneficial structures which are inherently strong and which allow the strength to be used appropriately.

Mobility

In most of modern karate we actually train for poor mobility. It is built into just about every single training exercise that we do. We strive to freeze our stance between movements as if we are trying to pose for photographs in a book. Many instructors will disagree with this statement and claim that you have to master the stances first so that you can learn flow later. That would be fine as long as the people learning the staccato movements were told that they would have to drop that habit later. However, almost without fail it seems that this message never gets through, and when it does it is really very late to do much about it. The habit has been formed and is very hard to break. The result is that we are very stiff legged and find it hard to move our centre smoothly.

The staccato habit has to go and we have to learn to move naturally again. The first thing to do is to stop performing "book karate". The second thing is to stop worrying about getting into "perfect" stances. And finally, just start to move naturally to get your position and centre right. This is a hard habit to break because it strikes right to the heart of the way we practice karate. Our marching kihon, our kata to count, our one step kumite – static, immobile and locked we practice hard in a way that is counter-productive to creating flow.

Concentrate on the objective rather than the shape of the stance.

Mindset

Funakoshi wrote that "you must be deadly serious in training" and "your opponent must always be present in your mind"[2]. This is a clear statement about the mindset that we must habitually use. This means that we need to let the natural fighting instinct out each time we practice - that is we need to feel vicious and determined. We must cultivate the feeling of being indignant that anyone would have the audacity to pick on us. Maintain perception and concentration on the objective of winning.

In each and every technique we practice we must make sure we keep those feelings near the surface so that we can channel them, mixed with adrenaline at our opponent. The way to form the habit is to think it while drilling each technique.

Taking the balance

In each technique we use on an opponent, we must make sure that as far as possible it compromises his balance. If the opponent is even slightly off balance, it reduces his capability to damage you. It puts him on the defensive and thus gives you the advantage. Therefore, build the idea into each technique so that you take his balance without having to think about it.

2 Page 105, Karate-do My Way of Life, Gichin Funakoshi, Kodansha, ISBN 0-87011-463-8

Bipedal balance is a process of constantly correcting the tendency to fall. It is very similar to balancing a beanpole on one finger. In order to keep it balanced you have continually to adjust your finger to correct the beanpole as it starts to fall one way or another. For us, standing (static balance) is the same. Every moment we stand we continually make small adjustments of tension around our ankles to ensure that our centre of gravity stays directly over the centre of base that our feet create. Furthermore, dynamic balance (i.e. when we are moving) is even more complex. For example, walking is an exercise in controlled falling. In order to walk, we simply fall forwards and move our feet to catch ourselves on each step and to adjust and control the rate and direction in which we fall. Dynamic movement is more complex than walking but works on the same principle.

In order to disrupt someone's balance we need to change their motion before they can make an adjustment to correct it, or prevent them making an adjustment in time to correct their motion.

If we can take the opponent's balance their self-righting-reflex will take over before they can think about it and they will attempt to keep their balance by making an adjustment. While their mind is taken up with regaining balance we have opportunity to further disrupt their balance or inflict damage. The self-righting-reflex can be over-ridden with training, for example, people who practice grappling and throwing arts like judo and aikido will roll into a break-fall when their balance is taken rather than fighting against it.

Balance can be taken in many ways but essentially there is only one requirement, and that is that the centre of gravity falls outside the base and is prevented from being adjusted back in again.

Pre-emption and proactivity

There is an old saying "Action beats reaction". My father taught me this concept when he taught me to play chess in my youth. He said, "Sometimes the best form of defence is attack". Whether the strategy is for chess or combat makes little difference, it is a most effective strategy. It is important that once the attack is launched you keep the opponent thinking about defending. If you let up on your attack for even the slightest pause, the opponent will have time to counter attack and then you will be forced back into a reactive rather than proactive mode.

If we examine the history of karate, we can see that the strategy of pre-emption was clearly well known when the kata were originally created. It therefore makes sense that a number of techniques in each kata would be pre-emptive movements rather than the exclusively reactive techniques that we are used to seeing. Therefore in any set of techniques taken from kata we should see some which are pre-emptive.

Furthermore, all of the techniques should build in the idea of being proactive – taking the initiative - and we need to build the habit of moving forward and taking charge as soon as the action starts.

We must ask, is pre-emption really in kata? I present the following reasoning:

As mentioned elsewhere in this book, Patrick McCarthy has coined the phrase "habitual acts of physical violence": these are the acts that are played out time and time again in the arguments and ensuing physical confrontations that occur every day around the world. These acts are deeply ingrained in our physical and psychological makeup and change very little through the ages. Study of other primates such as the chimpanzee show striking similarities in the escalating stages of conflict. The evolutionary fact is that it is disadvantageous for any species to engage in intra-specific physical conflict and therefore strategies of show, intimidation and posturing have evolved over the millennia in order to resolve the inevitable squabbles that arise without resorting to physical violence and the injuries that inevitably result. It is reasonable, therefore, to make the assertion that physical conflict between humans has not changed appreciably in the last 1000 years (a blink of an eye compared to the long evolution of our species).

It is reasonable to assume that the people responsible for the creation of karate (and in particular the kata of karate) were wise to the fact of pre-emption (sen no sen). Given that they knew that, it would seem reasonable that they would include this concept in their kata. And, furthermore, it is therefore the case that the pre-emption that they put into the kata should still be valid now, as the nature of human inter personal conflict has not changed over the intervening period (as discussed above). Consequently, it is reasonable to assume that the kata has pre-emptive strategies that are still useful to us today.

There are a further two lines of thinking which I would like to bring to the reader's attention to support the postulation that kata contain pre-emptive techniques.

1. Contradiction
First, we look at a basic contradiction in our training (consider if you will a standard karate dojo for the purpose of this discussion. Most of us will know this point of reference - in particular, the majority of pre-arranged sparring is set up as one person attacking and the defender's response is to block and counter-attack). Nearly all of our training focuses on defensive work, by which I mean that there is nearly always an attack from our opponent which we identify (mostly in advance by arrangement), block and counter attack. Our main skill base that we develop is therefore one of REACTION to circumstances. Even when we are the attackers in kumite our mentality is often that of being there so that the defender can practice his defences rather than of honing our attacking skills.

So here is the basic contradiction: ACTION BEATS REACTION but we practice REACTION therefore we have given the advantage to our opponent. By definition he is the one that will be using action rather than reaction because we won't strike first. So you could say that we are training to lose, or at least acknowledge that we are giving the advantage to our opponent.

2. Probability Theory
Pre-emption is the natural outcome of Probability Theory. Go to the most probable end of the spectrum where there are techniques like grabs, pushes, pointing and gesturing etc. - many of these attacks are making the transition from verbal to physical assault. How can we best reduce the number of variables involved? - by being active rather than reactive. It is at this time that the pre-emptive movements can be used most effectively.

I believe that the Okinawans followed a similar line of thought to the Probability Theory. They knew the types of common attacks they would face and devised specific methods of defence (see the research by Patrick McCarthy). They used kata to act as a framework to help practice those techniques. They only needed one or two kata because it is essential to reduce the number of techniques to a handful in order to prevent undue hesitation when the technique is required (called "log jam" by Peter Consterdine). In light of this, it is my belief that kata contain techniques which may be used to pre-empt many of the habitual acts of violence.

Note 1: A note about the law: In English Law you may only use reasonable force to stop an attack upon yourself. Pre-emption must be used lawfully and it is the reader's responsibility to research the law, understand it and then only apply pre-emptive techniques in a lawful manner. Be warned that use of pre-emptive techniques could very easily put you on the wrong side of the law and you must be able to show after the event that you acted reasonably. For readers in other jurisdictions you should check your local laws.

Disorientation and distraction

If our opponent is disoriented or distracted, any attack he tries will have less chance of succeeding. Quite simply, we must ensure that we try to build in to all of our techniques some way to seduce the attackers mind away from the intent of attack.

Methods of distraction can range from verbal and gesturing through to striking. Disorientation usually means taking the opponent's balance but also incorporates kiai (shouting) and subtle forms of suggestion.

Redundancy

The concept of redundancy in techniques is quite simple. It means that the techniques utilised have built-in fail-safes, so that if one particular aspect of the technique does not work the other aspects still cause the opponent problems (pain, injury, distraction, unbalancing etc.).

Redundancy can be thought of as the combining of many other habits so that should any one of them be absent in a particular instantiation of a technique it does not compromise the overall effectiveness.

Building in redundancy is about ensuring that not only do we conform to the individual habits but we ensure that we do them all at the same time. This can be trained using the kata by practising and drilling each habit in isolation, then in pairs and then in multiples.

Strike vulnerable points

There are many areas around the body that are more vulnerable to attack than others and there are areas where the effect of an attack is far more marked than in other areas. The areas, which are more vulnerable to attack with good effect, are called vital points. See Vital Points on page 87 for details.

In order to make our karate more effective it makes good sense to strike the opponent in the areas that are worst for him. In order to do that we need to study which areas are the weakest around the body and know how to manipulate them for best effect. Once we have the knowledge, we need to build the habit of affecting those areas rather than the areas that are less effective.

Create links

It is essential to train the mind to be one move ahead of the body so that we can flow from one technique to the next without pausing. This is particularly important where we are attempting to be proactive. If we are to maintain the initiative, we have to keep flowing from one technique to the next. Much of traditional karate training builds in a "stopping mind". In most of the kumite practices we complete the technique and hold that position. This is good for the teacher because it helps him to check that everyone in the class has roughly the right position, but it is really bad for the students because it ingrains the habit of stopping without keeping the mind alive to the next possible movement.

The habit of creating links is to have the mind always thinking, "next move, then next move, and then next move". More than that, it is important to build the habit of actually moving into the next technique. I call this creating links. We need to have practised links so that when we finish one technique the next one appears spontaneously. Using kata to train this we have to understand that the whole sequence of the kata is merely for mnemonic purposes. All the techniques that are catalogued therein are supposed to be used in whatever order is appropriate in any given situation. Remember, "spontaneity doesn't just happen!"

Timing

Timing is a somewhat elusive art. There are two aspects to timing – the first of the two, most obviously, is about "the when". The second, less obvious quality is about "the where". Putting the two together shows us that timing alone is not enough, we must be "in the right *place* at the right *time*". So looking a little deeper we can see that just trying to work on our "timing" is not particularly helpful. What we really need to be working on is our *anticipation*.

Without exception the karateka who are most skilled in the art of timing are those who can read body language well. These karateka have the ability to buy the extra fractions of seconds necessary to arrive in the right place at the right time.

The real habit we are after acquiring then is anticipation which stems from having a proper feeling for reading subtle body language indicators and being able to react to them with unconscious competence.

Use heavy hands

Heavy hands are another expression of using strength appropriately. Heavy-handed striking can only be accomplished by proper relaxation of antagonistic muscle groups so that the full power of the active groups are transmitted to the target. People who prefer the ki paradigm will express this as letting the ki flow.

Use verbal commands

In the kata .of traditional karate (particularly the modern competition varieties) we have standardised on just two kiai in each kata and yet verbal commands are an excellent weapon that should be in our armoury. Like any of the techniques we use it needs to be drilled until it is our habit to use it. Simply shouting twice during a kata performance does nothing to encourage us to be vocal at times of stress.

It is essential that with each movement in the kata we practice appropriate vocalisations to enhance the effect on the opponent.

The use of verbal commands in modern kata training has been reduced to a couple of kiai at set points in the kata.

Remember that under adrenal dump conditions verbal skills are reduced significantly, so your practice should include only simple, to-the-point verbalisations.

Stimulus – response – OODA loop

It is one aim of our drilling techniques that when a particular stimulus occurs we act with an absolute minimum of thought. If we understand that a proactive methodology is an optimal strategy we therefore have to build a habit of taking any adverse stimulus, responding to it in a positive way to take the initiative and then pressing home the advantage proactively.

OODA stands for Observe – Orient – Decide – Act. Observe means take in all of what is happening around you. Orient means to process the observed scene to make proper sense of it and understand what options are available. Decide means make a decision on the optimal course of action. Act means carry out the action without hesitation. While the action is being carried out we start to observe again and so we continue around the loop until a satisfactory conclusion is reached.

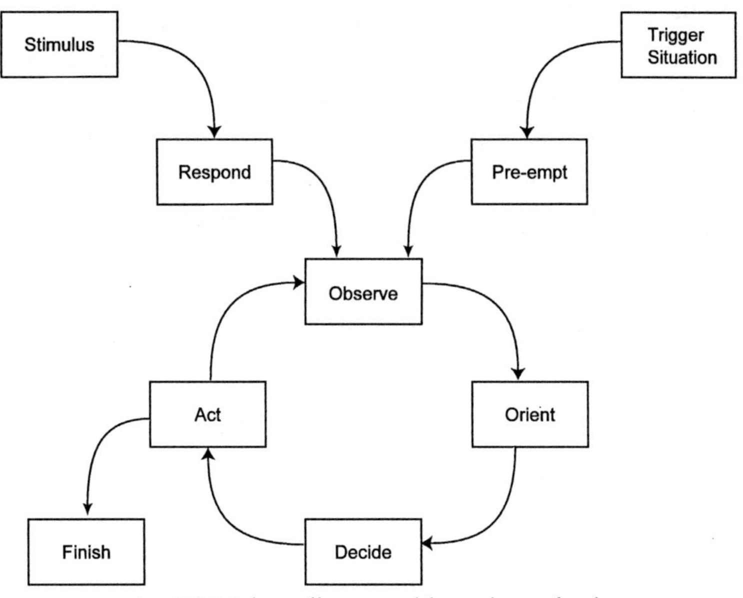

An OODA loop diagram with entries and exit.

The OODA loop is the glue that links our techniques together. As one technique ends we are observing what is happening, processing options, deciding what to do next and then flowing into the next technique.

The diagram above shows how we get into the loop. We either enter through the opponent providing a stimulus to which we respond, or some trigger conditions are met and we pre-empt and enter directly into the loop. Going into the loop via stimulus-response is inherently more risky than going in via the pre-emption route simply because there are fewer unknowns in the latter.

All of our techniques should have this concept built in so that we acquire the habit of entering quickly into the loop and exiting at the first opportunity.

Developing the habits through kata training

The question remains, then, as to how kata can be used as a training tool to instil these good habits. The answer, as with most habit training, is to work first on a conscious level and then at a conscious level under stress and then at a sub conscious level with no stress and then at a sub conscious level with stress.

The first work can be done without visualisation of the purpose of each movement. Work through the kata concentrating only on the desired habit for each movement. Remember, you should practice each movement in the kata until you feel you have it correct to a reasonable level or as time allows before moving on to the next technique. It is important that during your practice time you use the kata as a mnemonic for the material you need to do rather than just blasting through it.

Stress can be brought into the equation in varying degrees. The first addition of stress should be by visualisation of the opponent. Again, work each movement in the kata concentrating on the habit but with the opponent correctly visualised.

The next level of stress should be with bag work, and then bring in a partner, starting slowly and building up speed. Remember you are working on your conscious habit skills so that is what you should be concentrating on; if the technique stinks, so be it.

When trying to work your habit into your sub-conscious you need some form of external monitoring device. A video camera can be useful but an observant training partner is best.

Vital points

Introduction

The study of "pressure points" (more properly called vital points) has enjoyed considerable popularity over the last ten years (i.e. through the 1990s and into the 2000s). There are many different definitions of what vital points are and some of these are highly complex. There are three main schools of thought with regard to explaining how and why vital points work. The first paradigm is "modern western medicine" (MWM) where the vital point theory is explained in terms of western medical anatomy. The second is "traditional Chinese medicine" (TCM) where the vital point theory is explained in terms of the acupuncture meridians and "laws" of Chinese medicine.

Both schools of thought have some merit; however, it is yet to be conclusively shown that there is any predictive value in studying these disciplines. That is to say that the proponents of each view are of the opinion that understanding why the vital points are effective will result in the practitioner being able to predict other combinations of strikes that would also be effective. There is no compelling evidence from either camp to show that they have been successful *yet*, although that does not preclude the chance that they may some day achieve their goal. It must be noted that any empirically derived "science" cannot have true predictive qualities. Nevertheless, it is interesting to note that in certain cases we can observe commonalities between anatomical structures at various vital points.

The third paradigm, and the one I subscribe to, is the JHH method or to give it its full name "just hit here". JHH does what it says on the tin. There is no science to it. Quite simply it is about knowing the places where the human anatomy is weak and hitting (or manipulating) there. As Rick Clark says, "It doesn't matter why it works. It only matters that it works![1]" Note that I will often use the term "manipulating". This is an important distinction because not all vital points are attacked by striking. Some are hit but others are pressed, jabbed, poked, rubbed, or gouged.

The JHH method appears to have been the most widely used in martial arts through the centuries. Most schools of karate list between 15 and 40 vital points that they use.

In order to avoid confusion we need to work with a definition for what a vital point is:

"A vital point is a place on the body which when manipulated causes a higher-magnitude reaction when compared to other less sensitive areas."

Manipulation can be any type of strike, grab, press, rub or kick as long as that point on the target body is adversely affected.

Modern karate has (probably due to competition rules) reduced the number of vital points to three or four i.e. eyes, throat, solar plexus and groin. These are a good start, but the techniques

1 Pressure Point Fighting, Rick Clark, Tuttle, ISBN 0-8048-3217-X

within the kata contain manipulations of many other areas that give the karateka a better choice when the need arises.

Vital points used in Burgar Gojushiho

Most styles of karate list up to 40 vital points. I personally have about 20 that I use habitually and have described here. Of those 20, some comprise clusters of two or more points. I do not regard it as a useful exercise to distinguish between points that will be hit during a single impact. Rather, it is more useful to think of target zones.

Side of chin

Just back from the point of the chin on the lower jaw.

Point on the side of the chin

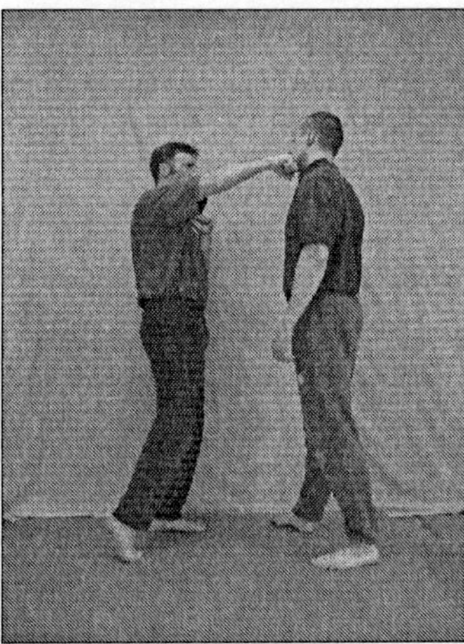

Punching the point

Palm heel to the point

From MWM we can see that at this point is at the site of the mental foramen. A foramen is a small hole in the bone; usually there will be a nerve bundle coming out through the bone at that point. Striking this point seems to have two effects: 1. The major effect is that the rotational acceleration that is imparted to the head when the point is struck at about a 45 degree angle is high, which has a considerably adverse effect on the brain. 2. The facial nerves that exit the foramen are compressed against the jaw bone so that there is a strong impulse sent along the nerves. Rattling the brain around in the skull is probably the largest of the two effects. It should be noted that rubbing this point hard with any bony part (e.g. Knuckles) will cause the opponent to move their head to the side.

In order to maximise the rotational impact of a punch it is necessary to ensure that the angle of attack is in at 45 degrees and slightly downward. Even if the exact spot is not hit you will still affect the head, or if you miss by more you still have a chance that you may hit the neck or elsewhere on the side of the head or on the face.

Rubbing the point with the knuckles

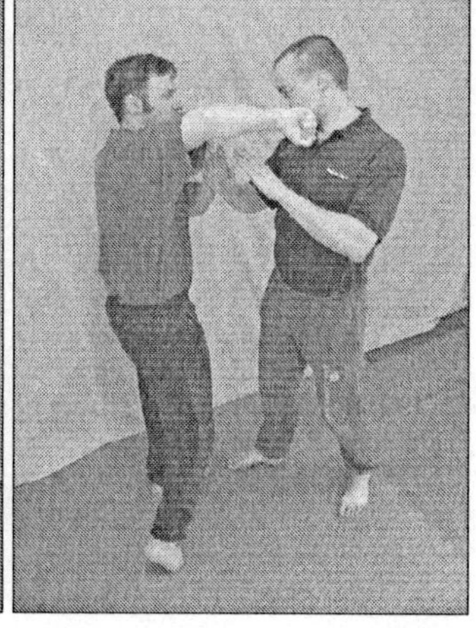

View of trajectory from above

Groin

This target hardly needs any explanation except to note that it is very well protected by a well tuned flinch reflex and the effects of hitting there can sometimes be delayed. Fast, upward movements are usually easiest to make work. Redundancy is built in because if the opponent flinches he will probably move his hips back and extend his head forward giving the opportunity for immediate follow up to open targets. If you are kicking and you miss there is a fair chance that you could hit his inner thigh, which would not be bad for you.

Eyes

Again there is no real need for an in-depth explanation of this target, except to note that most of us have an inbuilt horror of actually damaging eyes, and this should be taken into account. If you are relying on your ability to attack a target then when the time comes you had better be able to carry it through or you will hesitate which could be fatal. Flicking at or feigning to the eyes will often induce a reflex action of blink and turn which can be used to advantage.

The areas around the eye are quite interesting. The infra-orbital foramen under the centre of the eye is useful for pushing the head back in grappling. The supra orbital foramen when struck straight on at a slight upward angle has a disorienting effect and has plenty of redundancy built in. Again it is assumed that hitting the nerves and squashing them against the bone causes good effects.

Back of neck

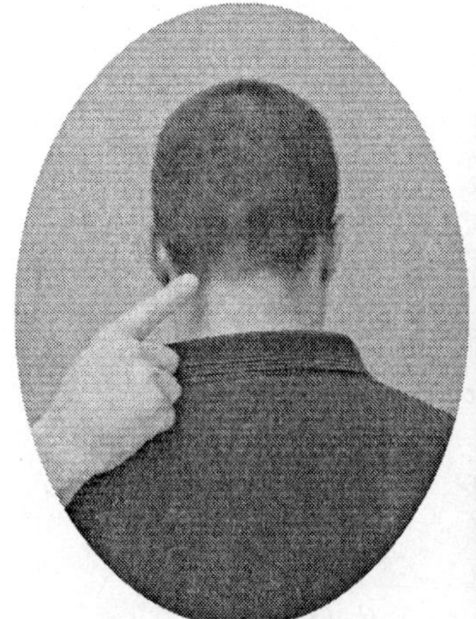

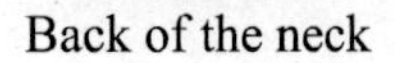
Back of the neck

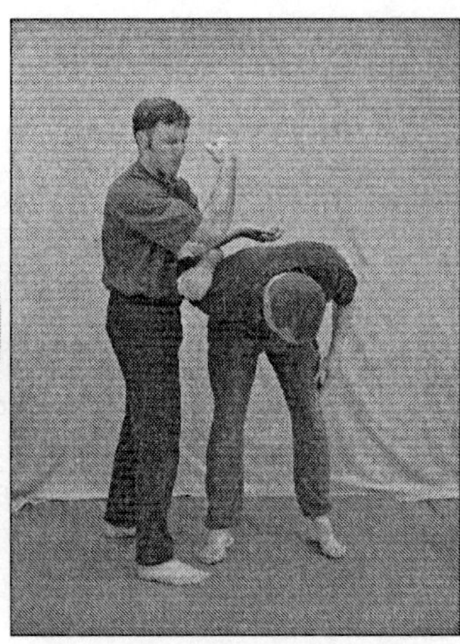

1. Attacked from behind

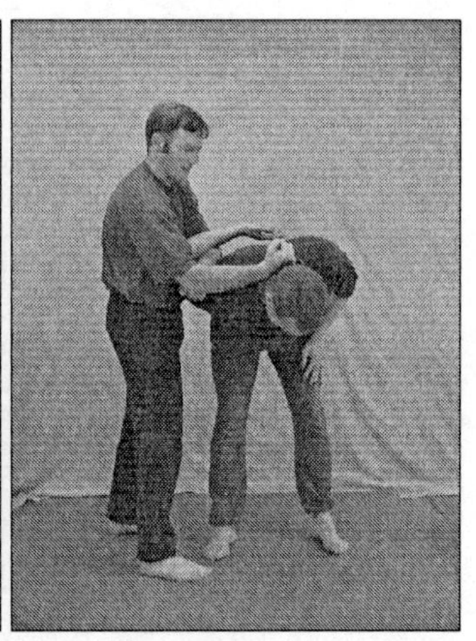

2. Attacked from behind

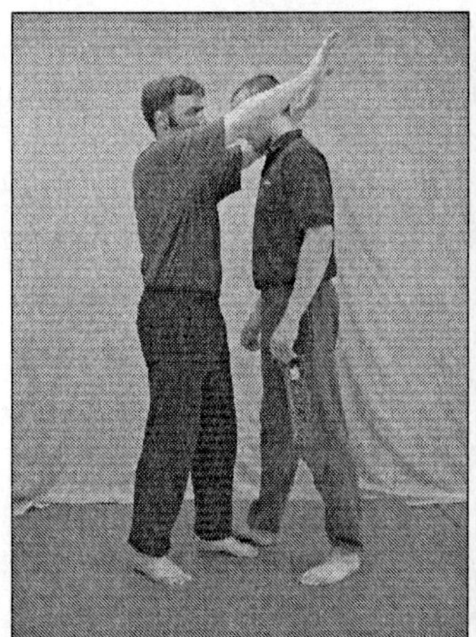

1. Attacking the points...

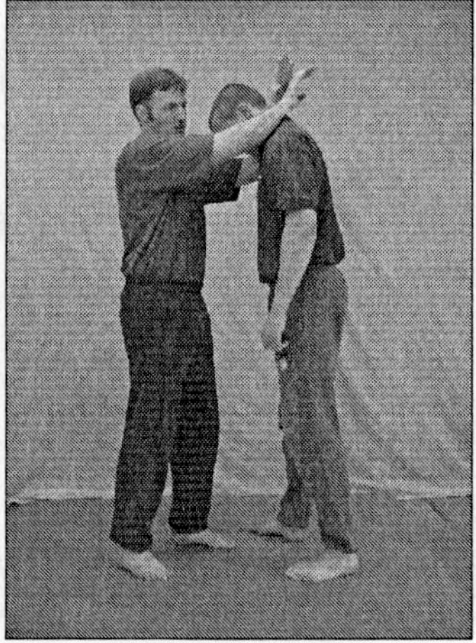

2. from...

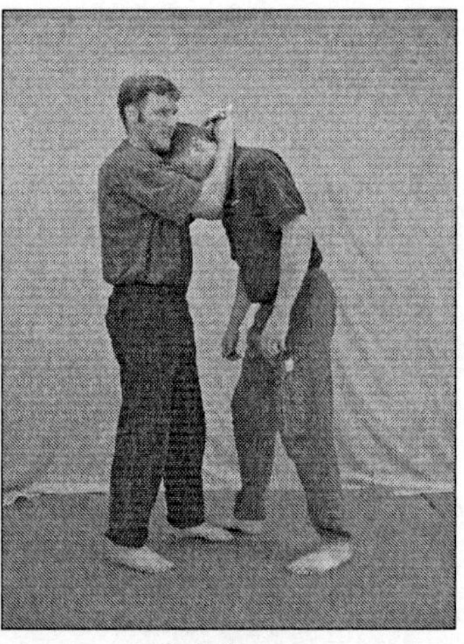

3. infront.

If you look at combat sports and ask which targets are forbidden then you can build a pretty comprehensive list of vital points. In boxing, for example, the back of the neck is a forbidden target.

This target is best attacked on a trajectory from the back of the neck up towards the centre of the forehead, which can be done from in front of the opponent by a withdrawing hand motion or from behind the opponent by an extension.

Inside of shin

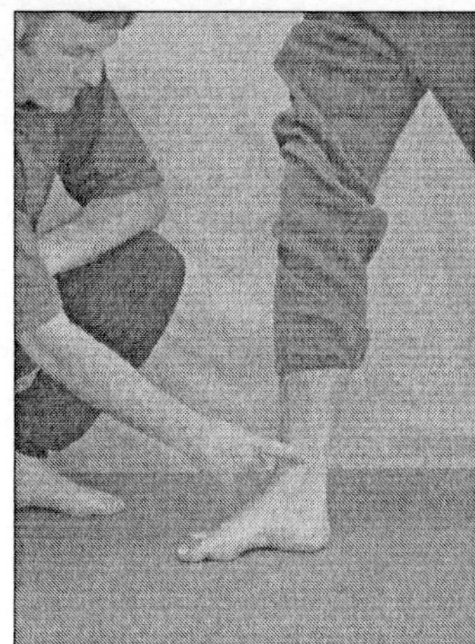

Inside of shin

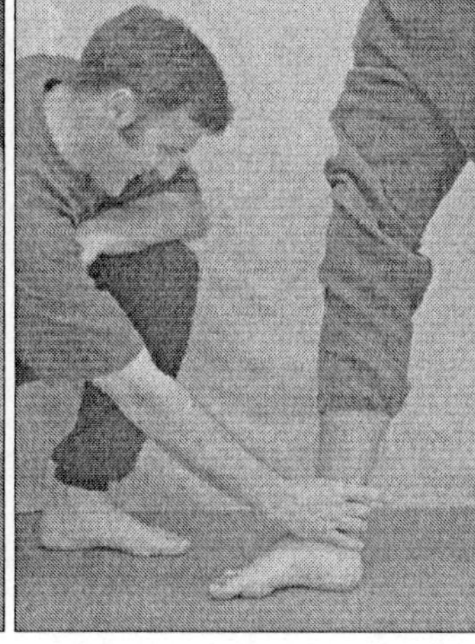

Practice pressing to locate the point

Kicking or sweeping the point

About four fingers up from the ankle bone on the inside of the leg is a sensitive spot. You can practice locating the point by grabbing so that the base of your hand is just above the ankle bone and then pressing the bony part at the base of your index finger into the point.

More usually in application we would be kicking the point, which has redundancy built in due to the unbalancing, sweeping effect or we would be mashing the point against the bone by standing on it or after grabbing the leg.

There are points on the outside of the shin but they are not so easy to attack.

Top of spine

Dropping weight into the top of the spine

Between the top on the shoulder blades in the centre of the spine.

Wrist

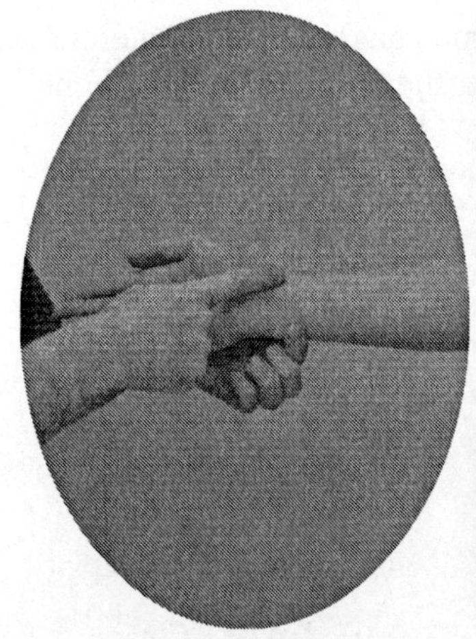

One of the tender points at the "corners" of the wrist.

Inside wrist points

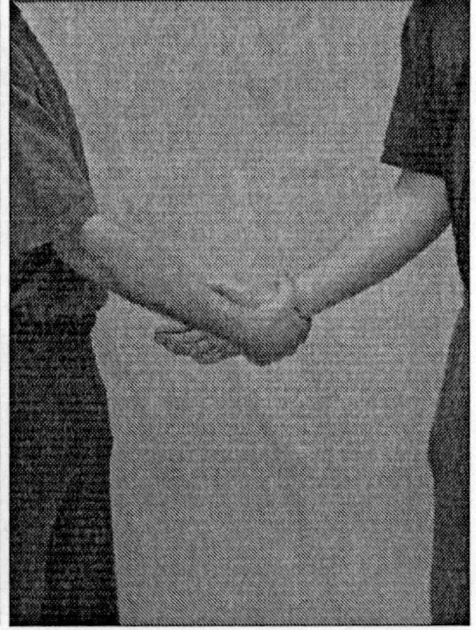

Grab and mash (note the exaggerated wrist bend is only for the photo - don't do this)

Similar to the points around the ankle there are six points around the head of the wrist (just above the knobbly part of the bone). These points are activated by pressing or striking the nerve against the bone. In seminar learning conditions each point will often be taught separately but the essential skill to pick up is grabbing, pulling and twisting (hikite action) so that as many of the points as you happen to grab are mashed against the bone at the same time.

Corner of forehead

If you imagine the head as a cube then striking the two front top corners in and downward at about a 45 degree angle has a disorienting effect on the person being struck.

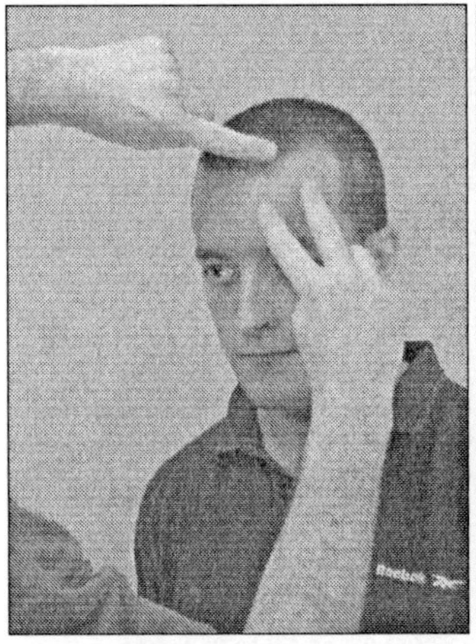

Cluster of three points on the "corner" of the head

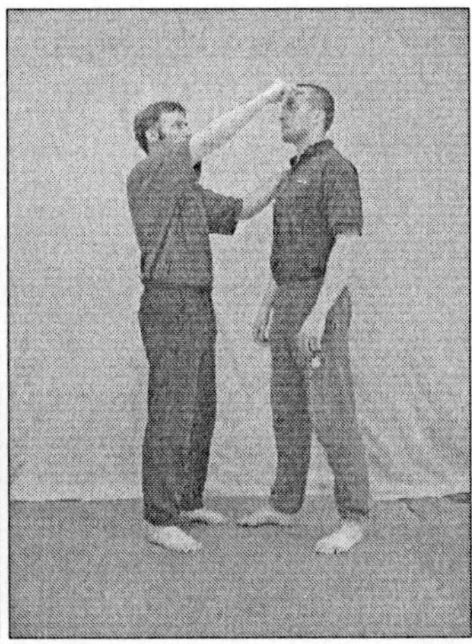

Three points on the forehead

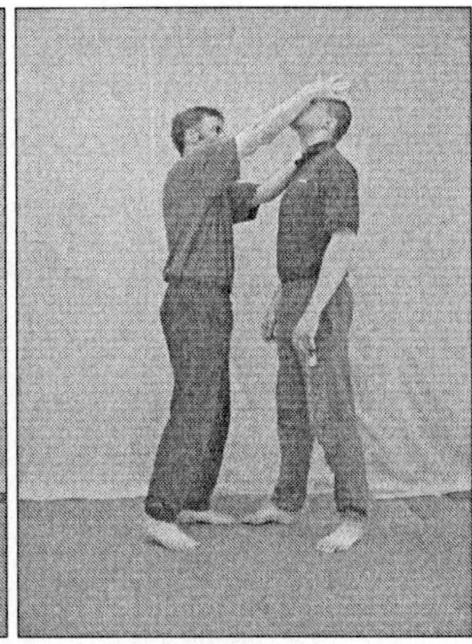

Striking the points

In TCM there are three points shown, GB13, GB14 and GB15. Strike with a slightly cupped open hand with a solid but rapid percussive motion.

Under earlobe

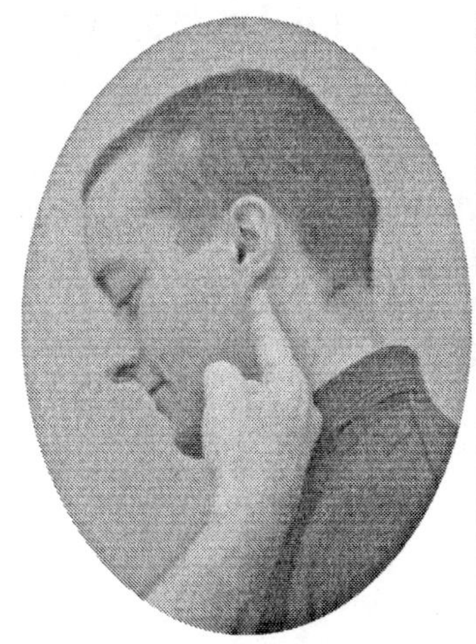

Go under the earlobe and then the direction is up towards the centre of the forehead

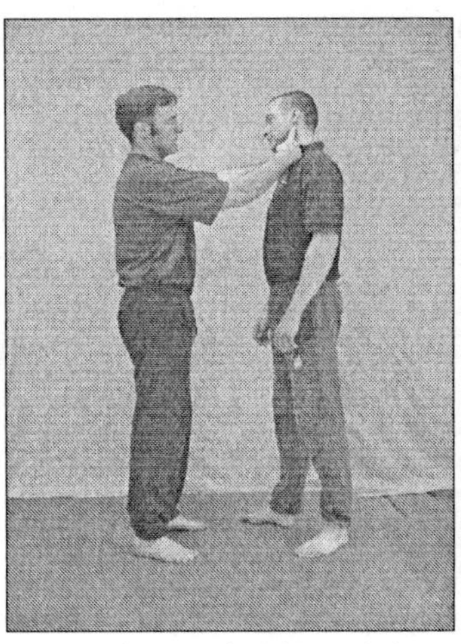

In and up under the earlobe

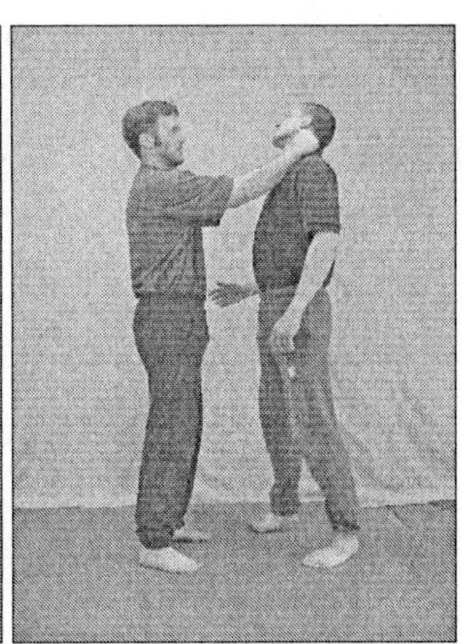

Press in with the thumb

There is a small dip just beneath the earlobe which is painful when gouged. The most effective direction is in and up towards the centre of the forehead - this is most easily done with the tip of the thumb.

Inside of thigh

Susceptible to heavy penetrating blows (kicks, knee kicks and elbow strikes); the inside of the thigh about one third up from the knee.

Inside of the thigh

Attack using the knee

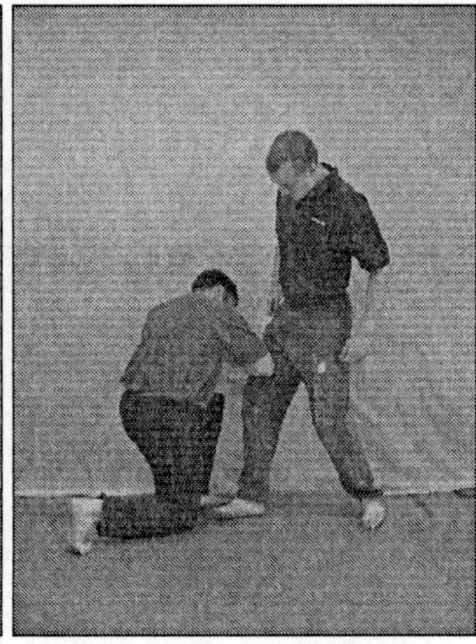

Attack using the elbow

Attacking the inside of the thigh has built in redundancy due to the mechanical effect on the leg which compromises balance.

Outside of thigh

If you stand upright with your arms down by your sides, hands open, the tips of your fingers will be in the right area for the vital point on the outside of the thigh - commonly known (to most school boys) as the dead leg point. A heavy and penetrating blow, usually from a round kick but under certain circumstances with arm techniques such as the elbow.

Outside of thigh

Strike with the knee

Elbow

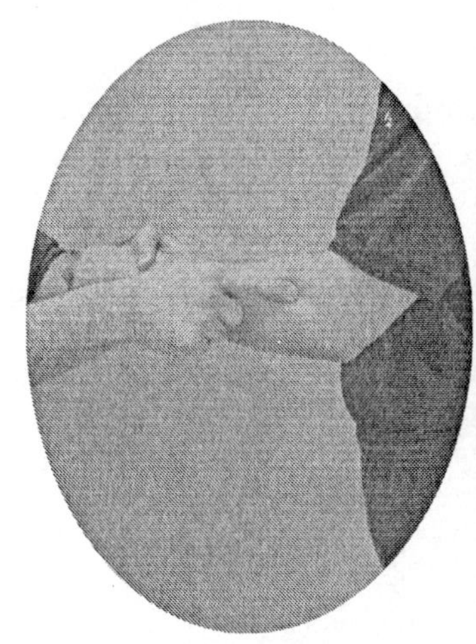

Point on the outside of the forearm, there is another on the other (top) side of the arm

Points near the elbow

Strike the points to get a redundant mechanical reflex response

There are several points located around the elbow. The most easily and reliably struck are those at the front top of the forearm on either side of the muscle. These are susceptible to gouging and striking. You can build in redundancy into striking these points by holding the opponent's wrist at the same time. By doing this the force of the blow can be directly transmitted to the head, causing a rotational acceleration which may account for the "arm point" knock-outs that are possible from striking at the elbow.

Side of neck

One of the most dangerous target areas. There are many anatomical structures in this region that are susceptible to damage and striking this area in practice should be strenuously avoided.

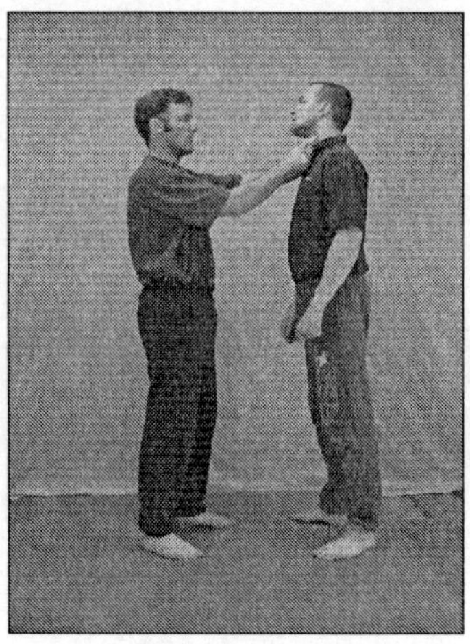

Side of the neck

This target area can be opened up by striking to the extremities first so consider hitting other vital points like the elbow points in combination with this one.

Solar plexus

The solar plexus is a major bundle of nerves near the surface of the body which are best struck up or down at an angle of 45 degrees.

Strike up

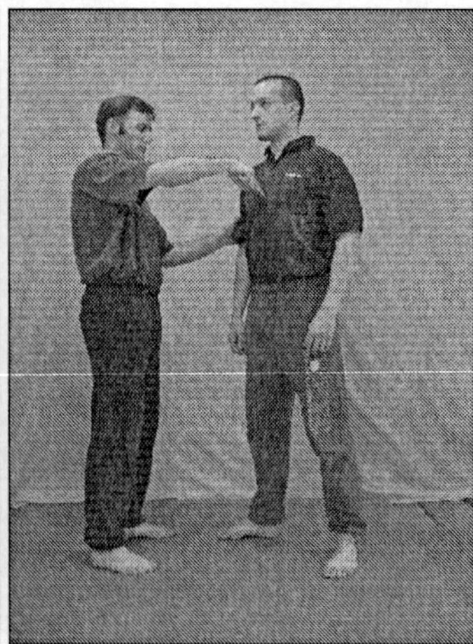

Strike down

Floating rib

Hit in and upwards towards the spine.

Floating rib

Bridge of nose

Not generally recognised as a fight stopper but does cause the eyes to water, which reduces vision, which clearly gives an advantage.

Collar bone

One-third along the collar bone from the neck; press in and down.

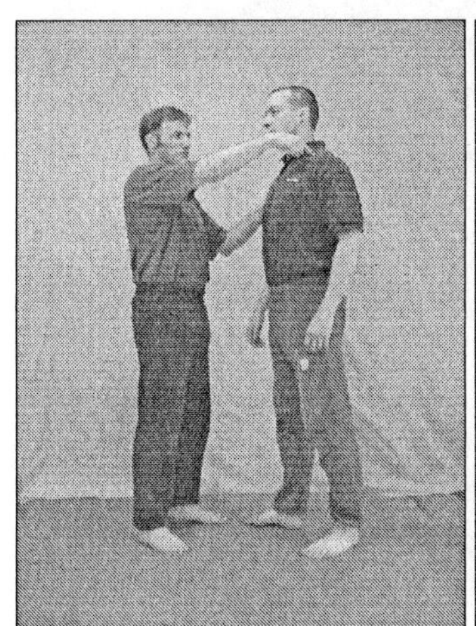

Collar bone

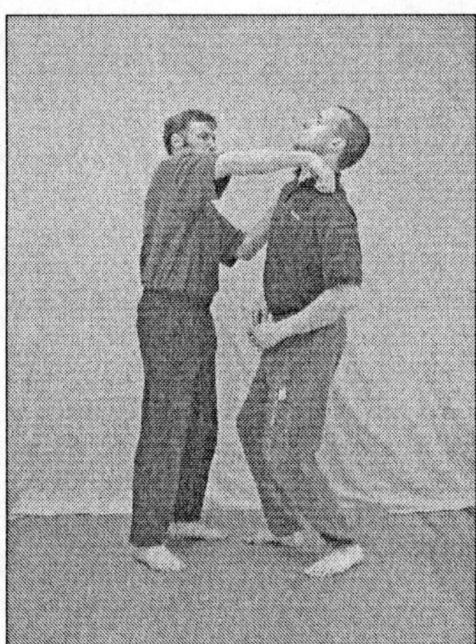

Press in and down

Grab from behind and drop into a strangle

Back of the hand

Strike the back of the hand to release the grip.

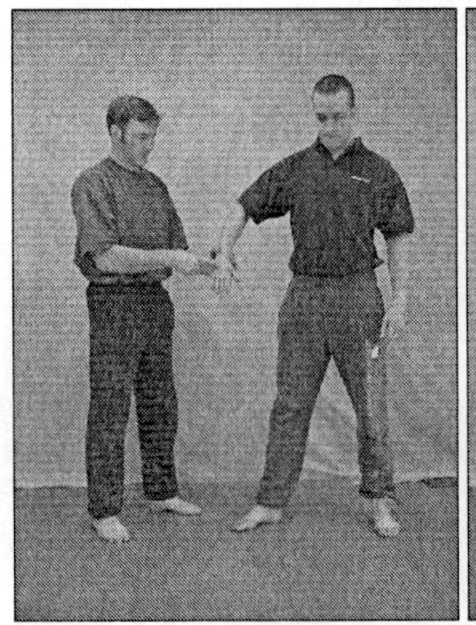
Strike the back of the hand

Strike...

back of the hand

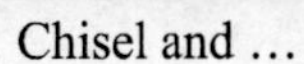
Chisel and …

hammer.

Back of the calf

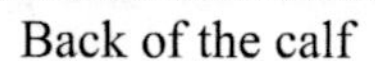
Back of the calf

Use the snap back of a front kick

To strike the point and sweep

Kick the back of the calf with the retraction of a front kick. This can cause loss of function in the leg and has built in redundancy in that it can sweep the opponent's leg out from under them and put them down.

The bunkai myth

Bunkai from 1900 to 1950

During the period 1900 to 1950, karate was introduced into Japan in the universities and education system. It was brought in to serve up to the military machine (along with many other martial arts activities) a body of fighting fit young men ready to die honourably for their country. When we read about improving character, we need to ask the question "improving to what end". It is documented[1] that one reason for having karate introduced to the school system was to create people with a militaristic mentality. The character improvement we read about in karate terms is really all about making the Japanese youth conform to what was expected of them.

In the West when we read the words *character improvement,* we automatically make the association with self-improvement and being a "nicer" person.

With this new era of using Karate for character improvement, the applications for civilian self-defence were no longer a requirement and they simply disappeared from use (with the exception of a number of dedicated Okinawans who continued to practice the kata with a view to self defence techniques).

Bearing in mind that for the most part people do not stay with their instructor over a very large number of years (especially in a university setting) it is easy to see that it would not take more than about 10 years for the concept of applications to be almost erased from practice. Funakoshi[2] himself says that the karate of today [1950s] is "not the same karate that was practised even as recently as ten years ago, and it is a long way indeed from the karate that I learned when I was a child in Okinawa."

So we can see that by the time karate was ready to start again after the war years there was little or no understanding of what the kata movements were, for except for a fairly silent minority. Add to that the utter devastation that the war caused among the Japanese and Okinawan population with karateka being equally affected we can see that very little in the way of deeper understanding of karate was preserved.

Bunkai from 1950 to 2000

Soon after the war, karate was being practised again and was being taught to American troops stationed on Okinawa. Between 1950 and about 1975, the "first wave" of karate books aimed at a non-Japanese audience was created. Over the following 20 or so years a whole library of books was published which used the first wave as *the* source of information to back up the instruction that the authors had received from the first wave authors.

1 Itosu Anko October 1908 "In this way karate could be disseminated throughout the entire nation and not only benefit people in general but also serve as an enormous asset to our military forces."

2 Page 36, Karate-do My Way of Life, Funakoshi, Kodansha, ISBN 0-87011-463-8

Very little overall space is given over to bunkai in any of the early books. We can trace a growing interest in the subject during the late 1980s and the 1990s. However, if we cast a critical eye back to the early books it seems incredible that we believed that the applications were in any way representative of real life fighting.

The bunkai we purchased – caveat emptor

The karate book-buying and later video-buying public purchased the contents of those books and in the majority of cases, we wanted to believe that the techniques would work for any number of reasons. I suspect that for the most part we wanted to believe that this mystical art was invincible. Whatever, there is a growing awareness that either we had been taken hook, line and sinker by the first wave authors or they just didn't really know what they were doing in terms of bunkai. Either way, the buyer became aware, and there are a growing number of people who are no longer satisfied to believe something just "because sensei said so" and who can look with a critical eye at what is being said.

If we are to study bunkai in any serious way, we must know what is good and what is bad in any of the techniques we are shown. We must not be afraid to question what someone has said, written or shown on video just because of who they are or because of the high dan grade certificate that they possess. Caveat Emptor – let the buyer beware.

Bad bunkai filter

There are categories of bunkai that we can identify that are open to criticism. We should apply these rules to all bunkai that we see from others or that we create ourselves to ensure that they measure up to a reasonable standard. We have all heard of BS filters, the following categories should form the basis of your "bad bunkai filter".

Techniques that defy probability theory

There are a good number of examples in books and videos of techniques that rely on a set sequence of attacking techniques, for example a sequence of two punches to the head (say right followed by left). A good example is the so-called arm bar at the start of Heian Nidan. The attacker punches jodan, which is blocked, now the attacker punches a second time to the face. The punch is blocked and the arm broken. The only way that we could even begin to rely on this technique (we can't, actually, but for the sake of the narrative stay with me) is if our response to the right-handed punch was always to be the first move of this kata. If that were the case then we could begin to make an argument for being able to make the second technique in the sequence work. The next attacking technique could be another punch to the head but it may also be an upper cut to the guts. Given that the second technique could be anything, we have to consider the position we are in after effecting the first block. By any sensible measure, we have to concede that we are not in an advantageous position; we have done nothing to become proactive in this engagement and have left ourselves badly exposed.

In a survey (that you can easily repeat for yourself) of 100 randomly-selected bunkai shown in standard Shotokan texts 38% of the bunkai relied on two or more specific techniques or actions of the attacker. The implications are important. If you agree with the proposition that this type of technique cannot work, then it discredits nearly four in every ten of the bunkai presented in standard karate texts.

Techniques that rely on a sixth sense

Many martial artists claim to have developed a sixth sense that enables them to detect when an attack is about to occur. In fact, through training, they have learned to see the minute body language signals that give away the intent of the attacker. This is easily put to the test by having the clamant close their eyes. If another sense other than vision were in use then they would still be able to know when the attack was about to start without looking. I have met nobody to date who can truly claim to possess a sixth sense.

Therefore, no bunkai should rely on any sense other than those that we naturally possess. Unfortunately, many bunkai shown in books do rely on being able to see the blind spot behind you to know that an attack is about to start and to know what sort of attack it is.

Simultaneously dealing with more than one attacker

Defences against more than one attacker cannot be addressed with specific techniques for specific circumstances. The probability of the correct combination of techniques being used against you, in the correct combination of timings is not sufficient to allow you practice time to become proficient at them all. Nor is it possible for the defender properly to determine the combination and timing of a simultaneous attack and select an appropriate response from the set of practised techniques.

The only meaningful way to deal with multiple attackers is sequentially and proactively, using sensible strategy and tactics.

Fighting range is unreal

Fact: nearly all fights take place at close or very close range. Once the talking is done, the combatants have to close the range to shorter than arm's length in order to damage the other. It is only our shiai experience (competition and free sparring) that falsely leads us to believe that fights happen at long range. If we were to fight another karateka, it may be the case that the fighting range would be long. However, this is not so likely. It is more likely that when we are attacked it will be at short range. We should therefore be suspicious of any long-range bunkai.

In a survey of 100 randomly-selected bunkai shown in standard texts 81% of techniques were performed at long or very long range. Only 5% were close range.

Continual blocking

Taking the initiative is an essential ingredient on the way to winning a confrontation. If techniques are practised that do not rapidly take the initiative then their effectiveness must be questioned.

Simplicity of skill acquisition

There are a number of bunkai shown in standard texts that come under the category of "would work given enough practice". It should not be necessary to have to practice for 20 years to make a technique work. It should be simple enough to work with minimal training and should be easier to apply with more training.

If we view a particular technique as a solution to a problem, we can apply Ockham's Razor that states that the simplest solution to a problem is usually correct. Whenever there is a complex technique to counter any other technique, we should always be able to substitute a more simple technique to solve the problem. The act of kata refinement then becomes an exercise in reduction to the simplest set of techniques possible; any complex techniques must be regarded with suspicion.

Defences against karate techniques

Many martial artists make the mistake of thinking that everyone will attack in the same way they would. This goes against the probability theory. It is much less likely that anyone would be attacked by a karate technique than a habitual act of violence. That is not to say that defence against karate-style attacks should not be practised, but the time currently spent in the average dojo is disproportionate to the threat posed. In a survey of 100 randomly-selected oyo shown in standard texts 73% were defences against karate-style attacks.

The future of bunkai

Now at the beginning of the new millennium, there is considerable and growing interest in rediscovering the lost bunkai. There are a great many karateka working diligently to reverse engineer the techniques from the kata. Having pursued this path for a great many years and specifically on one single kata for more than five years it is my opinion that reverse engineering is just a stage that the karateka may go through on the road to discovering a better way to do things.

Patrick McCarthy's work is important in this regard. His view is that kata are not the tools to teach technique but are created at the culmination of learning in order to act as a mnemonic. I absolutely concur with this line of thinking, and suggest that the future of bunkai will be in the practice of kata created by individuals for their own purposes rather than practising the old fossils that we play with today. See The Burgar Kata Hypothesis on page 317 for reasoning that is more detailed.

Reverse engineering kata

Introduction

"Reverse Engineering" is a term used to describe the act of figuring out what a product does by just looking at or taking the object apart. There are no instructions or a design specification to read in order to understand how the product works or was constructed. Reverse engineering requires different skills than the original engineering process and it is always easy to make the wrong assumptions about what something is for and go down a blind alley.

We no longer know what the techniques in kata really mean. The inventors (original engineers) of the kata are long dead and no accurate records (instructions and design specifications) exist for us to read. All we have is the product – the kata. Being curious, we naturally wonder what all of the movements represent and so begins the process of trying to work out what the techniques are for. This is bunkai: the analysis of kata movements.

As mentioned above this is an error-prone process and we can never be sure if we have found the use for a technique that was originally intended or whether we have made something completely different compared to the original. Whatever, we have to accept that we will never know. The only criteria we should be applying to the applications we discover is "does this meet my objectives?" If it does meet the objectives then it is a good analysis.

In carrying out the exercise of reverse engineering, we can come up with a considerable amount of rubbish (these are the blind alleys). We need to measure our discoveries continually and be prepared to throw them out and replace them with newer, better ideas.

Below are some guidelines and tips to follow to enhance your productivity in selecting appropriate applications. The following chapter suggests ways in which we can measure their effectiveness. One criticism levelled at many bunkai/oyo is that they are not practical or effective. It is essential to bring some objective measure to each application to ensure that we are not fooling ourselves into believing that cute applications are effective.

Working bunkai (analysis of kata) to discover the oyo (applications) can be an engaging, creative and stimulating exercise that many karateka enjoy.

It is important to not only examine each movement but also to create balance over the whole kata. That is, each kata was originally created to be a complete mnemonic for a fighting system. Sometimes the complete fighting system may be spread over a small handful of kata, but overall there must be a spread of techniques through the kata so that good ranges of situations are covered. It would not be useful to have a whole kata with say 40 different movements all used to defend against a round punch. That just builds in redundant techniques that would cause log-jam under adrenal conditions. There must be a mix of techniques that defend against starter HAOVs [1] and others that are used after things have kicked off. This stage

1 Much of the (progressive) bunkai analysis that has been done over the last 20 years has only looked at the individual technique level and has not examined the kata as a whole unit. By studying a single kata we are forced to consider the kata as a whole as well as its constituent parts.

of gaining balance can only really be done after the individual techniques have been put together. We then discard duplicates and replace them with techniques that defend against something not yet used by us in the kata.

Use lateral thinking

It is very important to be flexible in our thinking. Just because something looks like a block does not necessarily make it a block; it could be a strike, a hold, a lock or anything else our imaginations care to dream up.

Lateral thinking is a skill that needs to be developed. We do not expect beginners to do heavy sparring with dan grades. Instead, we start them on one-step sparring and build them up. So it is with lateral thinking. In order to develop the lateral thinking skill you can use some of the techniques below. The way they work is to list items to compare to a technique in a kata. By following this rote method, you will soon learn to home in on how a technique can be used without reference to the lists.

Reverse engineering by usage comparison

This is a fast and easy method to examine a particular technique in a kata. Quite simply take the technique you are interested in from a kata and for each item in the list below ask "Could I use this technique as on of those", e.g. "Could I use this technique as a punch?" "Could I use this technique as a Block?" You will find many techniques have multiple uses and that some techniques simply do not match most of the items in the list. But by the time you reach the end of the list you will certainly have at least one application for the technique and it may not necessarily be anything that was obvious before you applied the list.

Punch, Strike, Block, Parry, Trap, Hold, Lock, Takedown, Throw, Sweep, Pin, Choke, Strangle, Kick, Knee strike, Head butt, Bump, Push, Escape, Lock reversal, Unbalancing, Distracting.

Note that you can naturally use combinations of the above.

Reverse engineer by the HAOV method

Similar to the usage comparison method described above is the HAOV method. Instead of listing the various usages of the movement, we use a list of the habitual acts of violence to compare to the technique. For each HAOV on the list (see the list starting on page 52), simply ask the question "Could I use this technique in some way to defend myself against this HAOV?" If you can find a use for it then fine, otherwise just move onto the next HAOV. By the time you reach the end of the list you should have one or two workable techniques.

There is a good reason that this method works so well. If we look at the history of karate, we can see that it is mainly comprised of a civilian defence method. This means that each technique is designed to win in a civilian fight situation. Therefore, all we have to do is to compare the things that could happen in a civilian fight to the technique until we find the one that matches. Naturally, we must bear in mind that the kata movements of today are somewhat removed from their original so it is worth spending some time to look at how other styles do the movement or how the movements used to be performed.

Change the range

The next excellent method for discovering good applications is used in conjunction with the usage comparison and HAOV methods. Quite simply, change the range. Instead of being at long range step up close and personal and repeat the usage comparison and HAOV methods to see how the perspective is changed.

Take for example in Gojushiho kata where the hands are crossed in preparation for a tate-shuto (vertical hand) block.

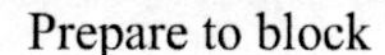

Prepare to block

Block (vertical knife hand block - tate shuto)

Notice how this assumes the attacker is a long distance away and in actual fact you are not in any real danger at that range. Now if we put the opponent right in front of us we can use the block preparation movement to take the opponent down.

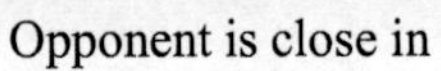

Opponent is close in

Use the preparatory movement to take him down

Or from later in the kata:

Arms circle

And block the long range punch

Or by changing the range and having the opponent do a double lapel grab:

This opponent is closer and grabs

Strike onto his elbows

To break his balance

Change the position of the assailant

This method is similar to changing the range. Simply apply the usage comparison and HAOV methods with the attacker in other relative start positions for example to the side or behind you.

Traditional texts have this movement turning 270 degrees to block to the side:

Turn

And block to the side

Now let's change the range and use a head twist take-down instead.

Head twist

To take him off balance...

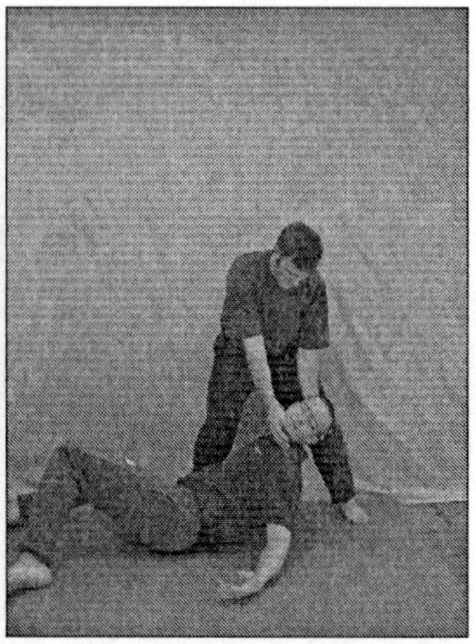
and down.

Be prepared to discard most ideas

Many of the application ideas you generate will not stand up to the measurement criteria (see Measurement of Oyo Effectiveness starting on page 119). You must be prepared to discard them if they do not pass the measurement tests. Be objective.

Do not be afraid to steal!

There have always been many books that present applications for kata techniques. This method is very simple and has three approaches.

Firstly, just go through books and videos and see what other people are doing. Apply the measurement criteria as if you had created the idea yourself. If the technique passes the measurement tests then you can set about making the technique your own.

Secondly, look at any martial art book or video (jujitsu is particularly useful) and think about where the technique they are showing appears in kata. Then apply the measurement criteria and if the technique passes you can set about making the technique your own.

Thirdly, find people who have good bunkai and go and learn them. Again, always apply the measurement tests to ensure that what you have learned is suitable for your purposes.

It is important to take ownership of what you have learned – make it your own.

The examples of techniques in my version of Gojushiho kata that I have permanently borrowed from various sources are too numerous to list.

Preparatory movements are blocks and strikes

Just about every block in traditional karate has a preparatory movement. These movements can be used as the actual block or entry into the opponent and what is traditionally regarded as the actual blocking movement is now used as a strike. You have already seen an example of this in the earlier section about changing the range but there are numerous other examples. Lets take a look at the "basic blocks" common to most styles of karate.

Down block

Preparatory movement

Down block

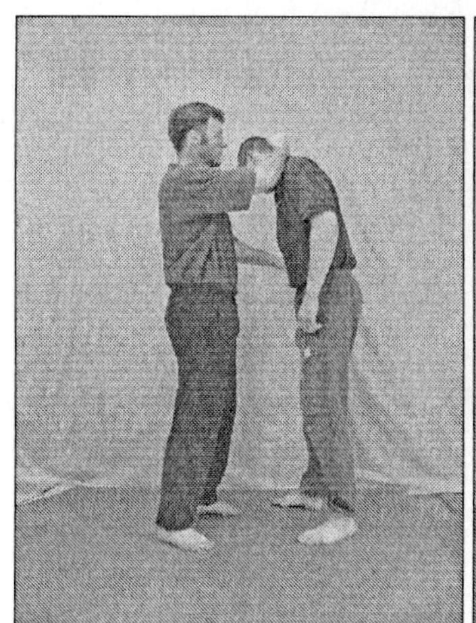

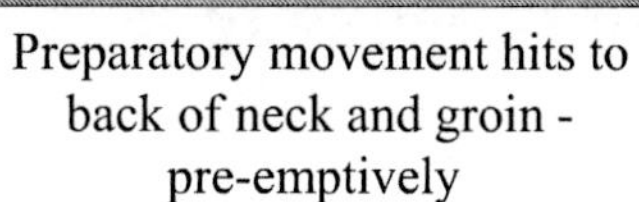

Preparatory movement hits to back of neck and groin - pre-emptively

Down block finishes the job

Upper block

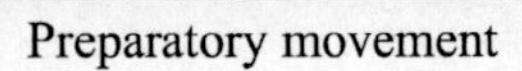

Preparatory movement

Upper block

Use the preparation to strike the elbow

Then strike under the chin with the "block"

Outside-in block

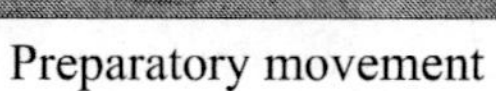

Preparatory movement

block

Block and strike with the preparatory movement

And strike hammer fist to the neck to finish with the "block"

Knife-hand block

Preparatory movement

Alternative preparatory movement (old style Shotokan)

Block

Block with the preparation

And strike

Block and strike with the alternative preparatory movement

And check and strike with the "block"

A block is a strike

This is essentially a combination of the ides of change the range and using the preparatory movements of blocks to parry. What we are looking at here is to take a movement which is generally thought of as a block and use it to strike a vital point on the opponent. There were some good examples of this in the previous section.

Using a "block" as a strike - shuto uke

Using a "block" as a strike - age uke

"Blocks" can also be used to strike the opponent's arm when he has grabbed. So for example if he has grabbed you by the lapel, you can use an outside-in (soto uke) blocking movement to strike the opponent's arm and bring him in line for a follow-up strike.

From a lapel grab

Hit the arm with soto uke as you step back

And hit where you have created an opening.

Both hands are always in use

Hikite, the chambering of the fist at the hip, is a seemingly redundant movement: how can we make sense of this hand position? First, we should note that both hands should always be "live". Its rare that one hand is inactive for any long period in our everyday lives. Just try going for a day only using one hand and you will soon see just how much we use both hands in a complementary fashion (see predominant side on page 70). It is important to make sure that both hands work together in combat and that we are not withdrawing a weapon and not using it.

The hikite can be used to grab the opponent and pull. This should be just about the only reason for pulling this fist back to our hip.

Drop in stance implies controlling

Considerable force can be generated by dropping your weight. Dropping in stances (particularly kiba dachi and kosa dachi) implies that you are using your weight to aid what you are doing to your opponent. For example if you have your opponent in a lock, rather than just using your arms to control him you can drop your weight to add a great deal of force to your technique.

For example, when applying an arm bar we can make it effective by angling our body (using our shoulders) to get force into the opponent's elbow.

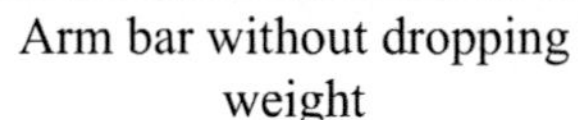

Arm bar without dropping weight

Arm bar with dropping weight

Or we can drop our weight, which applies much greater force to the elbow with much less effort on our part.

Use different parts of your body other than the obvious

In Gojushiho kata there is a repeated movement of a triple spear hand (nukite). Most people looking at a nukite strike would imagine that you are striking with the tips of the fingers and are then ready to believe that the practitioner would have spent considerable time strengthening his fingers for the purpose. However, just because it looks like a finger-tip strike does not necessarily make it so (it doesn't preclude it either). If you place your hand alongside the target rather than pointing at it it is clear that you can actually be striking with the palm at the base of the thumb.

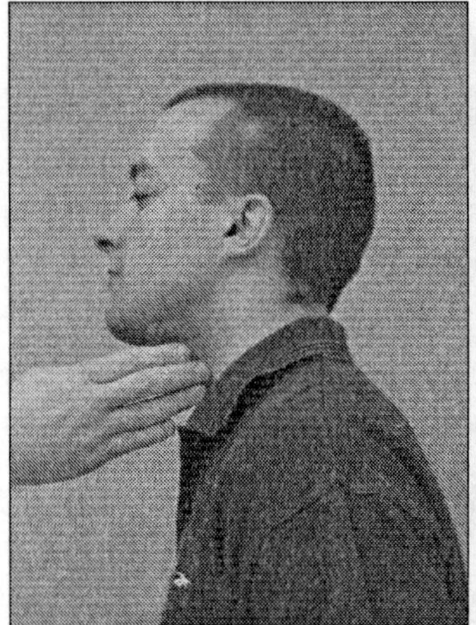

Striking with the finger tips or...

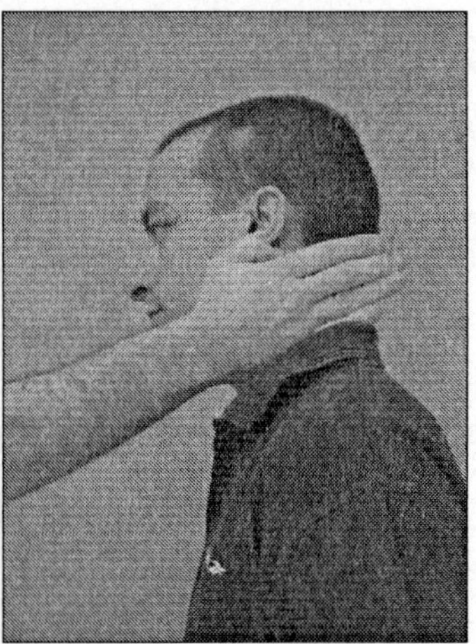

Striking with the palm at the base of the thumb.

Is it a pre-emption?

There are many possibilities for pre-emptive techniques in any karate kata. See page 81.

Measurement of oyo effectiveness

Introduction

When engaged in bunkai (analysis), creating oyo (applications) we can sometimes get sidetracked by applications that are complicated and are just a bit too clever. It is essential that we maintain some objectivity. It is therefore a sensible step to apply some measurement criteria for each technique. If it scores well against the criteria then we have a good application. For techniques that do not score well we should consider dropping them from our repertoire. We can also apply these measurement criteria against other applications that we see in books, on video or which are taught in person.

Measurement criteria

Below are some suggested measurement criteria listed in no particular order. I have not suggested an actual scoring system - although it is possible to devise such a tool I do not believe that it is of practical use. The reason for using this tool is to gain a rough feel as to how useful the application is and not to rank applications against each other. Having said that, should you need to compare two applications against each other in order to choose which one to use, you could use these criteria to make the comparison.

Remember, when measuring a technique it cannot be taken in isolation. We have to bear in mind the before and the after. After each technique, we have to assume that we are flowing into another appropriate technique. Of course, we always have to be selecting the next technique to use (see OODA Loop on page 85). In making this selection, there is often a thinking gap required to choose. A part of each measurement criteria is to consider how it will leave us to flow into the next technique.

Proactive

The proactivity scale ranges from pre-emption through to total reaction. The further we are to the pre-emption end of the scale the more we increase our chances of keeping control in the confrontation. At any point in a technique where we are nearer to reactive working, we must look to see if the technique puts us in a position to work proactively. The lower on the proactivity scale the whole technique is the less effective it will be.

By way of example we can look at three techniques, one pre-emptive, one 50%-50%, and one which is totally reactive.

Pre-emptive kick

Strike to the head

Pull into shoulder

Turn takedown

In the pre-emptive technique, we can see that the aggressor is hit unawares and the advantage is pressed home. This technique scores well on the proactivity scale.

Right hand shove Turned aside check

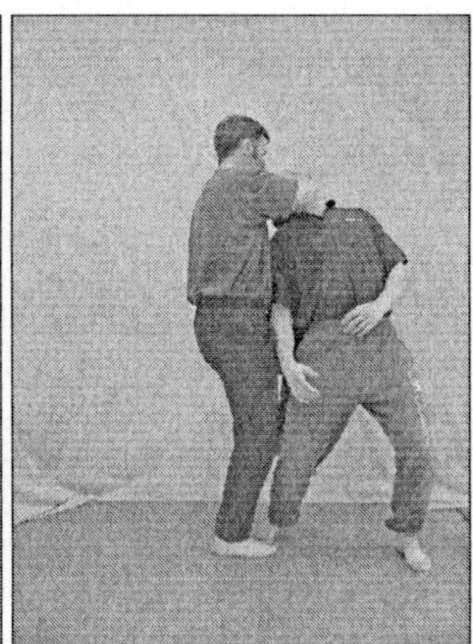

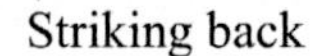

Striking back Taking down

In the 50% reaction / 50% proaction technique we start in a totally reactive mode. From a fence position, we quickly parry the shove, brush, and grab. Notice how initially we are reactive but we are now looking immediately to move to proaction. The initial movement has put us in a good position to go on the offensive and finish by making sure he goes to the ground.

Incoming punch

Block

And wait for next technique

Here we see that we are totally reactive. We have managed to block the first attack but have only moved back and left ourselves with no option but to be reactive again. Although it is undeniable that the technique worked (i.e. we didn't get hit), it does not score well on the proactivity scale because it has left you in a poor position to seek to attack.

Keeps initiative

Once the initiative is ours, we must ensure that the technique does not let our opponent assert any control. This goes hand in hand with proactivity, but it is a measure applied at the end of the technique to see how easy it is to flow into another proactive technique. If the oyo leaves you off-balance and poorly positioned to continue being proactive then it scores badly. If you are left in a position of superiority and are primed to continue attacking then it scores highly.

Maximizes safety

There is no safe place in a fight but there are safer and less safe places to be. For example, being out of range is safe, moving to the outside is safe, off-balancing the opponent is safe.

The other side of the maximising safety coin is that we must ensure we are damaging the opponent. In order to do this some risk is required. We need to balance maximum safety with sufficient risk.

Maximises redundancy

Building redundancy into techniques was discussed previously (see page 83). The more redundancy a technique has built in the better. Therefore, when we measure a technique we should look at the level of redundancy it has built in – high redundancy equates to a good technique.

Workable under influence of adrenaline

When adrenaline starts to flow there are many effects on the body and the mind. Depending on how extreme the circumstances you may experience any or all of tunnel vision, auditory exclusion, the loss of complex motor skills, lack of ability to think clearly, muscle spasm (the shakes), instability in the lower limb and so on. All of these effects appear to be negative. However, they are simply preparing the body for action. The thing that we have to ensure is that when we train we do not do things that will fly in the face of these expected natural reactions. Therefore, any techniques that work with nature and do not go against the expected effects should be scored highly on this measure. Any techniques that go against the effects should be scored lower. For example, any technique that relies on hearing or seeing anything to the side or behind should score lower, any technique that relies on fine motor skills should score lower and so on.

Works with instinct

Similar to working under the influence of adrenaline is the measure of working with instinct. When you get onto autopilot, you tend to do what comes naturally rather than what you have trained for. If instinct and technique are similar then you have a better chance of performing the technique as you have trained it. Remember you will do as you train – as long as the drilling of the technique is sufficient to overcome nature's barriers. Where the barriers are low it is easier to drill a technique into your subconscious. Where the barriers are high it is much harder, and more prone to failure when you need the technique most.

Maximises predictable response

In this measure we are looking at how the technique elicits a predictable response. For example, kicking someone in the groin will tend to make them move their head forwards and their pelvis back, or holding someone's wrist and striking at the bend of the elbow will cause their knees to buckle and to turn their chin away from you exposing targets of opportunity. The more reliable a predictable response a technique elicits the higher the score on this measure.

Opponent bends forward because he flinched...or

He bends forward because he was hit.

Strike crook of the elbow - bends forward and turns chin away, arm flies back

Unbalances the opponent

Unbalancing the opponent sets us up to keep the initiative using a suite of proactive techniques. A technique will score highly on this measure if the opponent is forced off balance and becomes preoccupied trying to regain balance. Conversely, a technique will score badly if it leaves the opponent perfectly balanced.

Leads the mind of the opponent

Any technique which forces the opponent to think about something other than attacking scores higher on this measure than a technique which allows his concentration to remain on the attack.

Low maintenance

Low maintenance techniques are those that require little ongoing practice to keep at a workable level. These are usually the simple, brutal techniques that are most in harmony with the natural defensive system and are easily visualised. On the other hand, techniques that are complex are harder to maintain and therefore consume more practice time than they are worth, and consequently score badly on this measure.

Range

Does the technique being measured work at a realistic range and deal with a probable habitual act of violence? The better the acknowledgement of range the better the technique scores.

Simple

Keep It Simple: everyone agrees that in order to be effective our techniques should be simple. But what do we really mean by simplicity? How do we apply some objective measure to our techniques to ensure that they are indeed simple? All too often, when we create applications for kata techniques we leave simplicity behind, and find ourselves practising complex actions that require fine motor skills that are absent under adrenal dump conditions.

Here are some beginning criteria for measuring simplicity:

Simplicity Measure	Qualities that maximise simplicity measure	Qualities that minimise simplicity measure
Simple to perform under stress.	Macro movements, direct movements, easy-to-hit large target areas, target directly in front, hit using hands on targeting	Small fine motor skill movements, hard-to-hit small target areas, target in peripheral vision
Simple to learn	Natural movements, easy actions to perform, easy to visualise	Unnatural movements with complex actions, difficult to visualise
Simple to maintain	Easy to remember, natural movement, easy to practice repeatedly in a short space of time, easy to practice alone (using impact equipment)	Complex to remember, needs a large number of repetitions on a regular basis to keep competence level, needs lots of time to keep decent level of skill.
Simple to perform under difficult conditions (poor light, uneven or slippery surface, cramped space)	Does not require conscious thought, natural movement, not overly reliant on any single sense.	Relies on fast mental processing, unnatural complex movement, relies on only one sense.

Transferrable skills

Does the technique use skills that are readily transferrable to other tasks? If it does then whilst practising one skill you are automatically practising another. The more cross-over there is between techniques the better, provided there is limited scope for confusion between them. So, for example, skills that rely on simple punches score well on the transferrable skill test.

Overall balance of the kata

In nearly all modern analysis of kata each application is considered in isolation from the rest of the kata. This gives an uneven distribution of defensive techniques. For example, there may be a preponderance of lapel grabs or an excess of round punch defences. This may give reasonable applications for each movement, however, as an entity the kata is not a sensible system of defence. It is deficient in the habitual acts that are left out and will produce log-jam in the techniques which have many defence instantiations. The kata should have a good spread of defences to the most probable acts of violence and should not have duplication of responses, in order to reduce log-jam effects. This final measure should be taken by viewing the applications of the kata as a whole.

Section 2 - The Example of Gojushiho

This section puts the theory from section 1 into practice using the singular five year study of Gojushiho as an example.

Note:
If you have been tempted to skip directly to this section merely to find out what the bunkai of Gojushiho are then, although you probably will not be entirely disappointed, you will have missed the point.

Within this section you will find for each movement or set of movements:

- The "standard" Shotokan (Shoto-ryu) Gojushiho movement for reference purposes,
- The Burgar Gojushiho movement, which has some deviations from the standard Shotokan but not so much that any Shotokan (or similar) karateka cannot practice it without confusion from their version,
- The Burgar Gojushiho oyo which shows details of how the movement can be used to deal with the habitual acts,
- A what-if analysis for each oyo showing the common variations (henka) that may be forced upon the defender by circumstances,
- Using the criteria set forth in section one the applications are measured objectively, and areas for improvement are shown.

Gojushiho bunkai - introduction

A major point to note about the presentation of "Burgar ha Gojushiho" is that the directions and the turns are not too important, nor is the sequence - but the key feature that I would like the reader to notice is the rich interconnectedness of the whole. Notice also the powerful mnemonic characteristics of the kata, the way it pulls together the techniques to deal with HAOV and confrontation, the underlying skills training and the background theory necessary to produce an effective mix.

The sequence and directions of the kata are not explicitly shown[1]. It is important to note that performing the sequence of techniques from start to finish is not the goal. The sequence **only** acts as a mnemonic to facilitate the practice of the whole system. Each movement is practised from a flexible start position, which once again emphasises the fact that the sequence of movements is only a mnemonic and not necessarily a flow of technique to be used in a confrontation in a particular order. The Links and Flow sections show how each movement can flow into other movements in the kata but which are non-sequential.

Remember that in moving from one technique to the next we do not have to move from static position to the next static position. Remember, as discussed previously (Mobility - page 80) we are trying to quash the habit of staccato movement. Pause between each technique and properly prepare the scenario for the next in your mind. Rushing from one movement to the next simply eradicates much of the benefit of kata practice, reducing it to simple dance movements rather than a serious mental rehearsal tool.

A word about how I have presented the numbering: when thinking about the techniques during practice or mental rehearsal time I never gave labels to the techniques. However, as soon as we need to communicate regarding the techniques we need to give them names or labels so that we all have a common point of reference. After discarding many ideas I finally came down to the presentation you see in the following pages. I have numbered each technique Mnemonic 1 though to 29. Each has one or more oyo (applications). You must understand that this is simply for convenience and ease of reference in a book. Under no circumstances should you be learning the techniques by these numbers - that makes no sense.

1 If you already know the kata then you will know the directions. If you are learning the kata from the book it won't matter which way you go as long as it is easily memorable.

Mnemonic 1

Traditional kata begin and end in a ritualised movement of bowing and preparation. Some of the kata that are considered more advanced have their own unique preparation movement. A number of people argue that rather than being a preparation ritual these first movements are techniques designed for a specific purpose; others maintain that they are simply ritual. It is certainly true that getting into the correct frame of mind for practising is really important and so either method could easily be the original intention. Personally I do not use a preparation movement or ritual.

Shotokan movement - preparation

1. Bow 2. Circle the arms 3. Assume the "ready" position

Burgar movement - none

Due to the fact that I have moved out of the mainstream dojo karate training system and train at home alone and with selected training partners the need for formality has entirely disappeared from my training regime. I therefore no longer need to adhere to the ritual that surrounds formal dojo practice, hence no movement for the equivalent Shotokan bow and ready position.

Mnemonic 2

One of the signature
movements
of the kata

There are two movements in this kata that are strongly identified with it; this one and the triple nukite (spear hand strikes). This movement appears twice in the kata.

Shotokan movement - augmented back-fist

1. Start to step and circle the right arm

2. Continue the step and circle

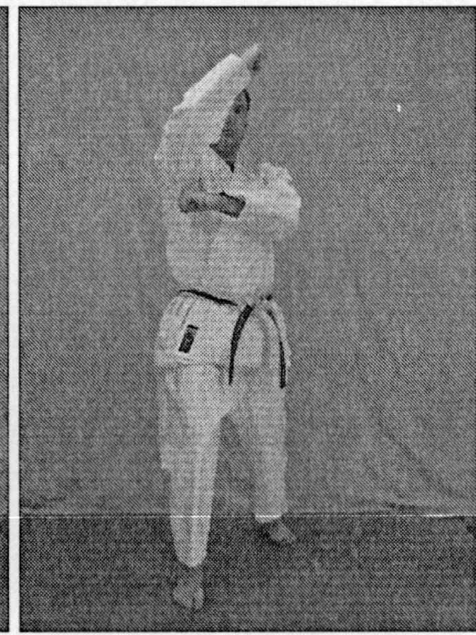

3. Right arm goes above the head

4. Bring the left arm down horizontal and right arm in a vertical backfist

4a. Finish with the elbow resting on the fist

Step forwards with the right foot into right front stance. Concurrent with the step, circle the right fist past the left side and drop it down in a vertical backfist strike. Concurrent with the right hand circling motion, move the left hand in a small forward moving arc down in front.

Burgar movement

There are several minor differences in movement compared to the Shotokan version. The reasons why will also be clear from the description of the oyo (application) below.

1. Kamae (standard fence position)

2. Don't withdraw the right hand prior to punching

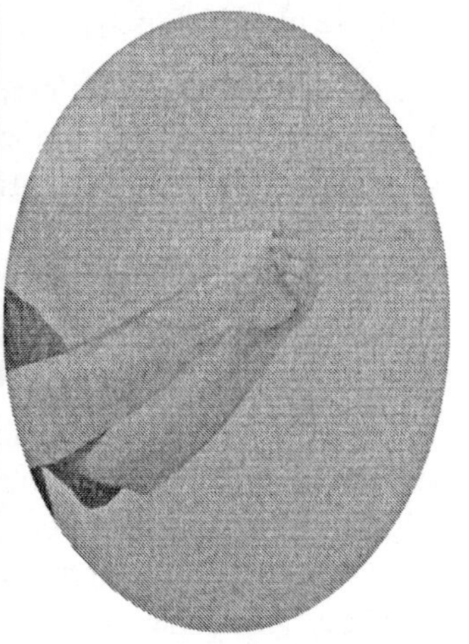

2a. Punch into the hand as a target marker

3. Use the step forward higher than normal

4. Force the left hand down- hand open

5. Elbow down

Key points are you feel your weight through your centre into your back leg on the first part of the technique. This uses the mechanical strut principle as if you are leaning against a wall. The first punch must be fast with no extra movement to signal its start and should strike into the left hand. The step forward should be exaggerated with the feeling of kicking the opponent's leg out from under him. The left hand should have a feeling of pressure in the fingertips as you pull it down and the right elbow should come down just in front of the left hand. Do not freeze at the end of the movement - keep moving (see section on links and flow). Refer to the oyo section below for further details of the feel of the technique. Remember the solo practice should use identical imagery to the partnered practice.

There are several minor differences between the Shotokan movement and my movement. The technique evolved through about half a dozen HAOV before settling on this one. For each HAOV there were slight variations on the movement. This movement is different only in that the left hand stays out at the start of the movement, the right hand strikes into it and the right leg is raised in stepping forward.

Oyo - Defence against space invasion

This movement of the kata gives us a mnemonic to a situation where the aggressor is pushing closer, invading our space. Our fence is keeping him at bay but we are feeling very threatened and he has repeatedly ignored our verbal efforts to persuade him to stop; we have been driven to the point where we have no choice but to be proactive. The decision-making process of knowing exactly when it is time to be proactive is very difficult and depends on many factors of the particular scenario you find yourself in, your role, how many other people are involved and their apparent and actual objectives. Some roles lend themselves to making more decisions in advance and thus narrowing the range of decision making. It is important to consider different roles and scenarios that you may find yourself in and work out as much of the decision-making process as you can in advance. Then, if you find yourself in such a scenario you have a better chance of a reduced decision tree.

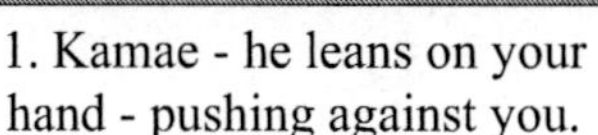

1. Kamae - he leans on your hand - pushing against you.

2. Move your hand to his neck - he stumbles forward.

3. Punch - use your left hand to guide the punch to target.

From the fence or kamae position push against him so that he pushes forwards more strongly. Suddenly release the pressure so that he starts to fall forwards. Before he can catch himself slip your hand around the back of his neck and then punch into your own hand. Your right hand must only move forward, not back. You should find that this targets the vital point on the side of the chin. (Photos 1 to 4).

Then while still punching sweep strongly to the inside of his right leg with your right leg, targeting the vital point on the inside of his shin but in any case ensuring that you sweep the leg out from under him. (Photos 4 and 5). This should make him bend forward or fall on his face.

Keep pressure on the back of his neck with your left hand so that it stays glued to his neck then bring down your elbow just in front of your hand. For the second time in this sequence you are using "proprioceptive targeting"[1] i.e. you have one hand on your opponent's body and are using the feel of its position to land a strike on target. (Photos 6 and 7).

1 Term coined by Steven Webster.

4. Punch - follow through keeping your body weight moving forward and leg sweep

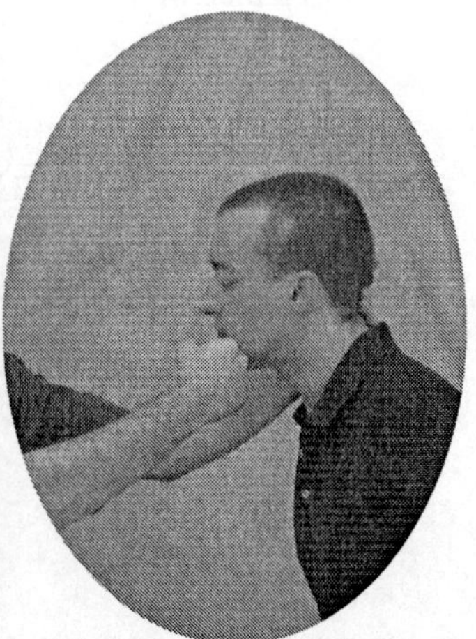

4a. Hit the side of the chin

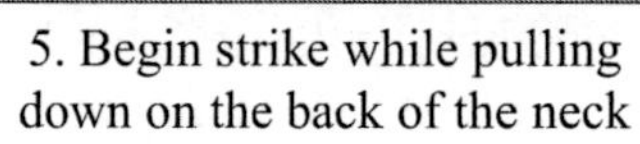

5. Begin strike while pulling down on the back of the neck

6. Elbow strike

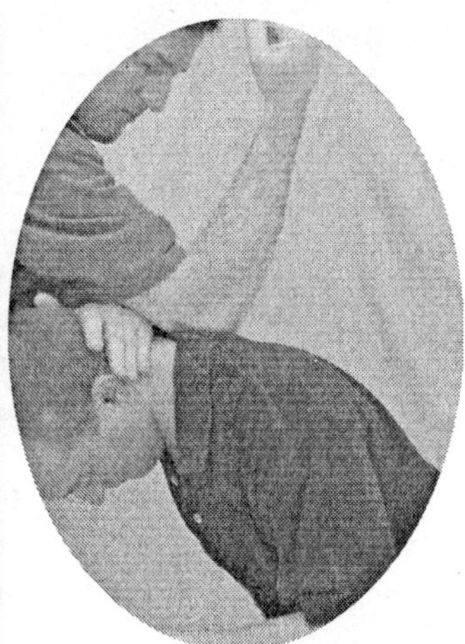

6a. Use your left hand as a marker

Measured

Measure	Comments
Proactive	Top end of the proactive scale (i.e. pre-emption)
Keeps initiative	By attacking first high and then immediately low and then moving to a third target area this technique scores well on this measure.
Maximises safety	Not a top score. You are forced to keep the opponent at bay by placing your lead hand on his chest which ties it up somewhat. Also, in order for you to be in range to strike him he is also in range to strike you. You can maximise safety by ensuring that you are the first to strike.
Maximises redundancy	The technique can suffer multiple misses and still succeed therefore it scores well on this measure.

Measure	Comments
Workable under influence of adrenaline	The first target is well within the tunnel vision area which is good. The technique does require you to lift your foot which is a negative point (sometimes getting your feet to move under adrenal dump conditions is difficult). However, due to redundancy the footwork can be lost and the technique still succeed. The technique uses gross motor skill movements which are retained better under adrenaline-filled conditions.
Works with instinct	Instinct is to punch to the head which is where this technique starts. Once you get into the technique then training tends to take over. So this technique scores well on this measure.
Maximises predictable response	Hitting the chin with your other hand behind the neck tends to send the opponent to the back on your left. Sweeping the leg tends to drop the opponent forward. So this technique scores well on this measure.
Unbalances the opponent	Kicking one leg away certainly compromises the balance - so good score on this measure.
Leads the mind of the opponent	As you have first strike you have the element of surprise, therefore the opponent suffers from momentary confusion. Secondly, his angle of orientation changes suddenly (from vertical to horizontal) when his leg is swept out from under him.
Low maintenance	Punching and sweeping are fundamental skills to a karateka and comprise natural movements which require little practice to keep them functional.
Range realistic	This is mid-range where the opponent is just on the edge of the right distance to be punched with a pre-emptive strike. The use of the hand on the chest being suddenly removed and causing him to move into range and onto the punch means that the technique scores well on this measure.
Simple	There are no complex movements and a minimum number of things that can go wrong.
Transferable skill	Punching and sweeping skills are readily transferrable to other techniques and so are reinforced during drilling of other techniques.

Measure	Comments
Overall balance of kata	This is the only technique in this kata that deals with this type of space invasion. Therefore log-jam is minimised.

Henka 1

We now need to consider and practice the variations that we expect could happen in this type of scenario. The first thing that springs to mind is that if you place your hand on the aggressor's chest his most likely reaction is "get your f*****g hands off!" accompanied by forced removal of your hand. That could be a slapping away of your arm or grabbing the arm and pulling or pushing you in any direction. If you see any of these about to happen or happening hit him on the chin and sweep him anyway. After all, predominantly that is where your mindset will be just prior to a pre-emption technique. The result is that you may be punching from a less balanced position than you would like, he may be more balanced than you would like and you don't have the same level of hands-on targeting that you would like to have.

1. The arm is pushed away

2. Strike anyway

3. And continue with the sweep

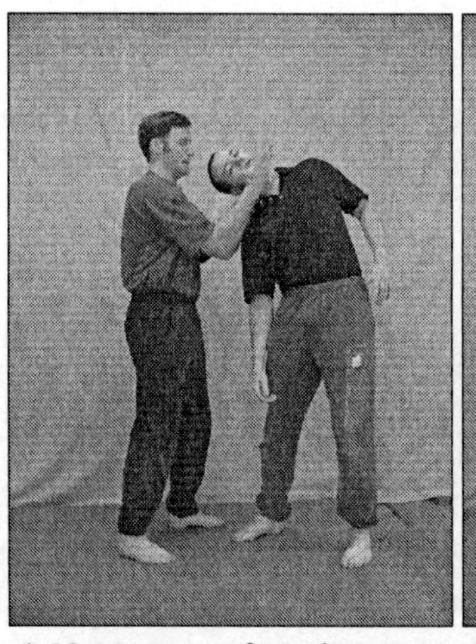

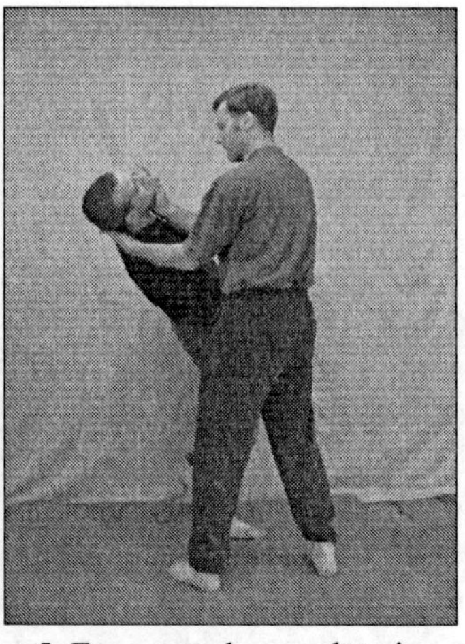

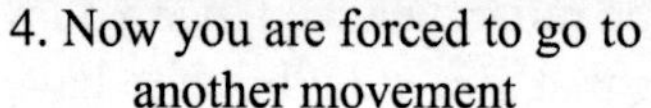

4. Now you are forced to go to another movement

5. For example a neck twist take down (see Mnemonic 13)

If the moment passes for the pre-emption then you will find yourself in a new position which will be that you are being grabbed or pushed. That is when you need to switch to another technique. See the Links and flow section below for example links.

Henka 2

He may grab your arm, most likely at the elbow, to try to control you. This then is an elbow grab and you could go immediately into Mnemonic 18. Please note that although I write "go immediately into Mnemonic 18" that is merely a description for you to follow. The sub-conscious thought process in action is only "he's grabbed my elbow and I react with this technique". There is no translation in thought to numbers, the kata or any other intermediate thought. It is simply a reaction to his action to make sure he cannot do anything else. After mnemonic 18 which includes a slap you might move into mnemonic 13

1. Holding back

2. He grabs the elbow

3. Switch to attack his wrist (mnemonic 18)

Of course, after grabbing your elbow here he may punch with his left too... (See mnemonic 18 for other what-ifs).

4. Turn it quickly over (mnemonic 18)

5. You could press the elbow or put pressure on the wrist

6. Now start striking again

Henka 3

He may try to do a round punch over the top of your left arm with his right arm or punch with the left arm. Go straight into the defence for a round punch (mnemonic 3) or the equivalent to defend his left punch or a cover (mnemonic 18) depending on the circumstances.

1. Punch initiation (feel him twitch before the movement really starts)

2. Defence with mnemonic 3

3. Get on the offensive quickly

Links and flow

1. Missed the sweep

2. Flow to mnemonic 6

Some example links and flow have been shown in the previous henka sections which show some "what if" scenarios. We need to be comfortable enough with our techniques that we can flow from one to another as circumstances dictate. Below are some examples of links and flow for this technique.

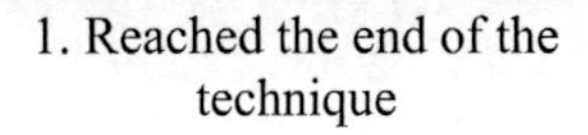

1. Reached the end of the technique

2. Spin into mnemonic 23

2. Or if he tries to stand up go into mnemonic 25 (close-in work)

Practice

This technique can be practised alone with visualisation, on the tall bag or with a partner. It is important to practice the verbal tactics along with the physical. As with all verbal practice you need to build in appropriate trigger points to help you be pre-emptive when needed (Neuro-linguistic Programming -NLP- verbal cue). One of the problems with pre-emption is that you have to overcome the barrier that you face - even when you know you have absolutely no choice but to pre-empt there is still an enormous mental barrier. Practising the verbal along with the physical helps put you on home turf in a confrontation, which allows you to get into a flow state (the zone) more easily. Simply put, any practised skill will be easier to perform at times of stress.

So for example, in this technique you may practice giving the verbal command "BACK OFF". You are then in an OODA loop, you assess the reaction of the opponent by feel: are they pressing forward or did they back off slightly? Command again, "BACK OFF". If he is still pressing forward hit him as you shout "F*** OFF". Using assertive, expletive language is a tool to help bring out your natural aggression which you need at this time in order to carry out the technique with sufficient conviction to ensure its success..

When practising with a partner take care to avoid injury. I recommend keeping things slow. Your practice partner should give you continual feedback as to your performance. Did you punch without warning? Was the punch accurate? Did you take verbal command of the situation? How much adrenaline release did you induce in him due to the way you acted? And so on.

Mnemonic 3

Shotokan movement - wedge block to the left

1. Step out with the left leg, cross arms

2. Step out uncrossing arms...

3. And complete the "wedge block"

Step out with the left leg. The Shotokan movement uses back stance.

Burgar movement - blocking movement to the left

1. Kamae

2. Direct to "wedge block" in a sloping forward stance

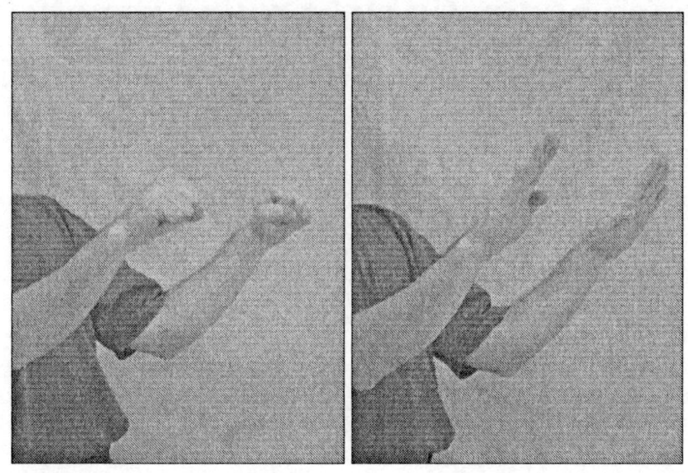

Hands can be closed or... Open

Step forwards and keep the hands high in a wedge. Compare this movement to the one from the Shotokan version and to the that presented by Shoshin Nagamine[2]. Note, that Funakoshi[3] states under the comments for this same movement in Jion kata, "...the hands may be formed either into fists or into the sword hand...". Also, note that in my version the stance is more forward and there is a lean forward with the torso. The reason for this difference is that the way I practise has to match the application so that I am practising exactly what I will do, rather than a stylised version.

2 Page 207, The Essence of Okinawan Karate-Do, Shoshin Nagamine, Tuttle, ISBN 0-8048 1163-6

3 Page 190, Karate-do Kyohan, Gichin Funakoshi, Kodansha, 1976, ISBN 0 7063 1996 6

Oyo - defence against a right round punch

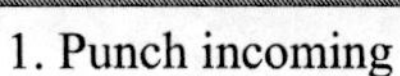

1. Punch incoming

2. Strike

3. No pause!
Open hand strike

From your kamae position move inside the punch and strike his arm and shoulder (wedge block position) and then flow instantly into attack. 2 and 3 are done with no pause in-between. The defence can also be done with open hands. The right arm should attack aggressively either to the side of the neck or using the forearm or elbow more into the chest. The left arm follow-up can be used to either strike the side of the chin or to check the opponent's left arm. Immediately after striking with the left, flow into a barrage of head strikes mixed with low kicks.

Or 3. Checking the arm

4. And then moving into barrage mode

Having the block demolished but...

e.g. flow into a push to the chin

Throw.

Make sure that on the initial block you throw your weight into the action, so that if possible you bump him backwards a bit and stop his forward momentum. This means he will be off-balance to the back and will have to adjust to get moving forward again.

Measured

Measure	Comments
Proactive	Although this technique starts from behind a fence it is reactive to start with so scores lower on the proactivity scale. However, it quickly turns that around by using a simultaneous counter-attack and thus a good attempt is made to get onto the attack straight away. So although appearing reactive, this technique is redeemed by the immediate subsequent use of proaction.
Keeps initiative	The initiative is initially lost but quickly regained by going on the offensive immediately things have kicked off.
Maximises safety	Both hands are up in the kamae and remain up during the technique protecting the head.
Maximises redundancy	If either hand is not sufficiently active the blocking technique can still work and any number of natural follow-up techniques are possible. On the counter-strike across the chin this can be used redundantly to check the opposite arm if necessary.

Measure	Comments
Workable under influence of adrenaline	Much of the action happens in the tunnel vision zone and no complex motor skills are used.
Works with instinct	The flinch response to a head strike is to raise both hands. This technique is in direct accordance with the flinch response. Immediately following the flinch we can move into proaction.
Maximises predictable response	Given that we block the attack and bump the person back a bit the predictable response is him attempting recovery, which gives us a time frame to get on the offensive. Without a successful bump their most likely next move is punching with the left hand which can be readily checked.
Unbalances the opponent	The bump to their centre compromises their balance.
Leads the mind of the opponent	The bump which causes loss of balance shifts their mind to preservation of balance. The strikes to the head shift their mind to defence.
Low maintenance	Since this is built upon a natural flinch response it does not require much practice. Stepping forward into the centre zone does take some practice.
Range realistic	This works inside the range of a round punch.
Simple	There are no complex movements. The whole technique is simple and fast.
Transferable skill	The blocking skill and open-hand striking skills are simple and transferrable.
Overall balance of kata	This is the only technique in the kata that reacts to a right round punch.

Henka

Things that could go wrong here include not seeing the punch in time and getting hit or grazed, making a partial block so that you are too off-balance to make the counter, being knocked backwards by the punch, or he follows with a second punch from his other arm immediately after the first. Once action has gone beyond push and shove to the ballistic stage you have to be proactive and use appropriate tools to stop him quickly. Appropriate tools would be a mixture of multiple impact and unbalancing. So for example we might move to mnemonics 5, 6, 7, 8, 13, 18, 25 and any other appropriate technique according to the circumstances. Notice how in the kata bunkai there is a proper mix throughout the whole kata of techniques that deal with initial HAOV, and techniques that are “in the thick of it”, and others that are take downs and throws.

Links and flow

On success of the block it is important to move directly into striking. My personal favourite is to move to the triple spear-hand technique (which is a signature movement of the kata). Note that with the spear hand I actually strike with the palm heel, which is good for impacting bony areas whilst minimising risk of injury to me.

Mnemonic 4

Shotokan movement - wedge block to the right

1. Step across and cross arms 2. Step out with right leg and uncross arms 3. "Wedge block"

Burgar movement - blocking movement to the right

1. Step at an angle to the right 2. And raise the arms to block

This movement is almost identical to that in mnemonic 3 but is executed to the right.

Oyo - defence against a left round punch

This technique is identical to the one shown in mnemonic 3 but is against a left round punch. Make sure that you angle your body in and immediately go into proactive mode with multiple strikes.

Mnemonic 5

Shotokan movement - prepare for tate shuto to left

Step up and "prepare to block"

Step up and look to the left whilst preparing the hands to "block".

Burgar movement - step up left arm low, right arm high

Step up raising the left foot slightly - hands ready

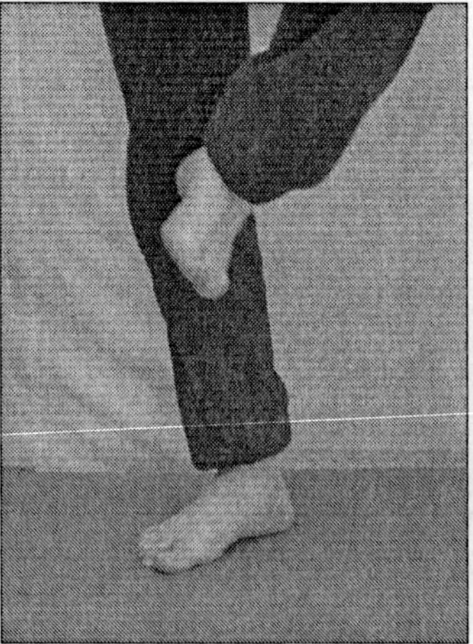

Foot position

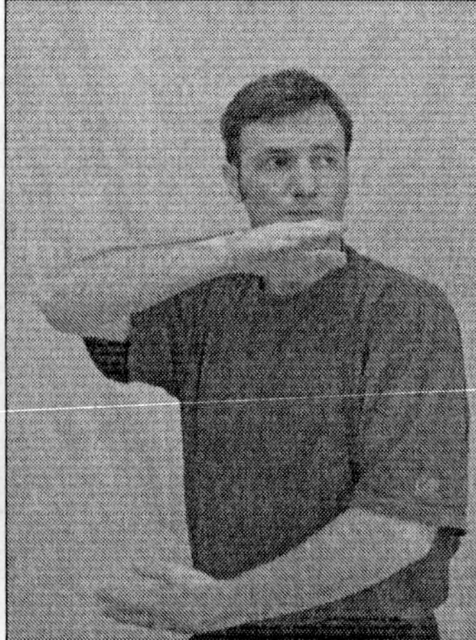

Final hand position

Bring the left leg up and cross the hands. The left hand should be held at about waist height and the right should be at head height and they should follow through in a scissor movement with the left remaining at about hip height but the right coming down somewhat.

This Shotokan movement varies from association to association. In some the left hand starts the movement above the shoulder and in others it starts under the right arm. My movement is slightly different in that the forearms are held reasonably horizontal.

Oyo - close-in takedown

In situations where you have got in close and along-side your attacker you can take his balance by placing one hand in the small of his back and the other on his forehead and scissoring them. It can help to put your foot in the back of his knee but this is not essential.

Its important to make a scissoring action with your hands to tip his head back and his hips/ small of his back forward. Do this with the feeling of pushing his head to his heels in a semi-circle.

As you make contact with his head do it forcefully to disorient him but make sure that it is more of a heavy push than a strike.

Be careful in practice to do this slowly and gently because your partner may go down very fast and may also sustain a neck injury.

Practice in situations where you turn aside the close arm as in the example below or try ducking under the arm and coming in close, or from pointing or grabbing situations.

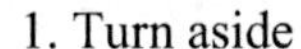

1. Turn aside

2. Start of take down

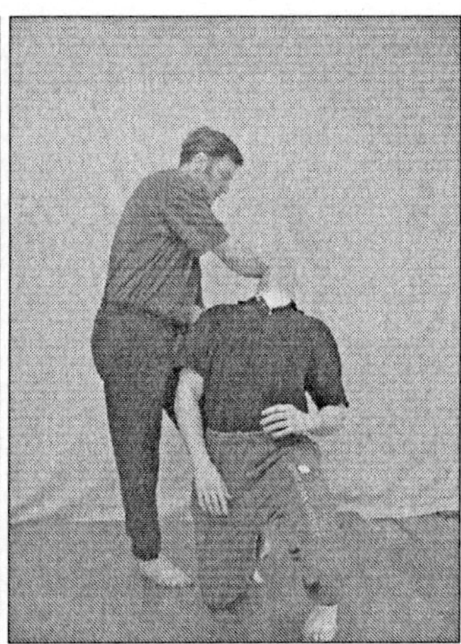

3. Take down

This take down should be practised on both sides. See corresponding movement in kata a few moves on from here (Mnemonic 7).

Henka

There are several things that can change the outcome of this technique. First of all it is important to do this move quickly so that you have the element of surprise. If you don't then the opponent will set against you by tensing his neck and it will be hard to move him. In this case you will need to flow to another technique, for example an assisted head butt, followed by pulling him down and getting your knees working (see flow section below).

Second, he may roll out by turning away from you, when this happens you need to flow into grabbing, punching and kicking him.

Third, he may bend backwards but manage to step back with one leg and then set against you. Again you need to flow into another technique as soon as you feel the tension in his body.

Measured

Measure	Comments
Proactive	This leads the opponent.
Keeps initiative	The fact that it unbalances the opponent either totally or partially means that the initiative is kept.
Maximises safety	Not a perfect score on this count because both of his arms are free and able to strike you. However, even by partially unbalancing the opponent it makes the close quarters environment slightly safer. Standing on one leg this close is risky and often you will feel that it is just not safe to do it - the foot kicking out the knee is not essential to the technique (see Maximises redundancy below) so safety can be improved as the situation dictates by omitting the foot technique.
Maximises redundancy	If the hands don't find their targets the foot technique could still put the opponent on his knees. If the foot technique is not used the hands can work successfully. If only one hand works you can still succeed in striking his head or pushing his hips which may unbalance him. If it all goes to hell you still end up in a clinch where you have your arms over his and the opportunity to work your head butt and knees.
Workable under influence of adrenaline	The foot lift is harder under the influence of adrenaline. One target (the head) is in the tunnel vision area and no complex motor skills are required.
Works with instinct	The scissoring action of the hands is a natural "hugging" motion and pushing someone's face away is also an instinctive action. Based on simple pushing and pulling actions.

Measure	Comments
Maximises predictable response	When the technique works, it works well and the response is that the opponent drops at your feet. Where the technique is only partially applied the responses are reasonably predictable usually resulting in the person bending back and moving his head and torso away from you.
Unbalances the opponent	When fully applied the opponent is on the floor. When partially applied the opponent is off-balance.
Leads the mind of the opponent	Due to the fact that the opponent's orientation (from vertical to horizontal looking upwards) is suddenly changed it is very disorienting and so the opponent's mind is taken.
Low maintenance	This large macro movement takes very little practice.
Range realistic	Close quarters.
Simple	A simple, easy to remember and easy to apply movement.
Transferable skill	The foot in the back of the knee is a common motion.
Overall balance of kata	No other techniques for close-in situations where you are to one side or another of the opponent.

Links and flow

1. He resists going down

2. Turn the elbow in and...

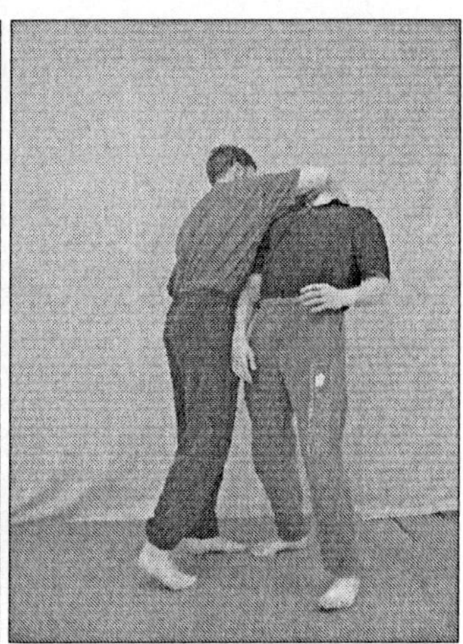
3. Strike with the elbow

1. He rolls out before the technique is finished

2. Flow to mnemonic 6, grabbing, punching

3. And kicking.

1. Maybe he grabs you to prevent himself from falling

2. E.g. He grabs you around the neck

3. Use mnemonic 27.

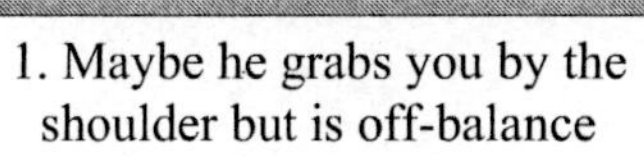
1. Maybe he grabs you by the shoulder but is off-balance

2. Flow to mnemonic 9

3. Mnemonic 9

Mnemonic 6

Shotokan movement - tate shuto, punching, kicking to left

1. Tate shuto

2. Gyaku-zuki

3. Jun-zuki

4. Mae geri - stepping forwards.

4a. Mae geri

5. Oi zuki

Burgar movement - grabbing, punching and kicking

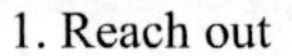

1. Reach out

2. Punch above and to the right of the left fist

3. Push the left hand up and high chamber the right

4. Kick low

5. Punch above and to the right of the left fist.

Some key differences to note between the Shotokan version and mine is that I keep my hands up and the kick is low. In particular the left hand hardly moves throughout the technique. Movements 2 and 3 above happen almost simultaneously.

The Shotokan movement and my movement are only different in terms of stance length and target areas. My kicks are usually aimed at low targets and punches to the head.

Oyo - grabbing, punching and kicking

Get some body momentum moving forward and simultaneously punch with the right fist, followed by the left (a short push), then a right low kick followed by a right punch.

1. Grab

2. Hit just above where your other hand is

3. Push with the grabbing hand

4. Always kick low

5. Keep hitting to finish

The feeling here is of unloading a flurry of aggressive strikes to a variety of high and low targets. The sequence and number of punches performed in any instantiation of the kata is not important – only the feeling. You will find that uttering an expletive or two and summoning up feelings of anger and indignance will help to achieve the correct mindset for the technique.

When a fight has kicked off there is no time to think. It is important that when the distance is mid-range you have effective punching and kicking skills. Punches are prone to miss the target, things are often moving too fast for you to land any telling blows. One tactic in these scenarios is to grab hold of the opponent to a) stop them moving about so much and b) give you a tactile sense of where to hit; this is sometimes called proprioceptive targeting.

Oyo - grabbing, punching and sweeping

A variation on the punching and kicking technique.

1. Grab the sleeve or arm

2. Punch

3. Pull to unbalance

4. Lift the leg behind the opponent

5. Sweep and strike

Measured

Measure	Comments
Proactive	This technique is all-out attack - highly proactive.
Keeps initiative	The idea is to barrage the enemy with strikes so that his mindset is forced to the defensive.
Maximises safety	There is no particular thought of defence so there is the chance that the opponent could get strikes in. However the tactic is to overwhelm the opponent so that he cannot make an effective counter-attack.
Maximises redundancy	There are multiple techniques so if anyone should miss then there are others that should not miss. By grabbing hold of the opponent you increase your chances of hitting a target.
Workable under influence of adrenaline	Punching and kicking are two of the most natural weapons and as such are good techniques to use under the influence of adrenaline.
Works with instinct	Grabbing, punching and kicking are natural techniques.
Maximises predictable response	Provided some of the punches and kicks land we could hope that the predictable response would be that the fight is finished quickly in our favour - however, in actual fact it is hard to predict an outcome for this technique.
Unbalances the opponent	Punching high and kicking low have an unbalancing effect.
Leads the mind of the opponent	An aggressive attacking flurry should put the opponent's mind on the defensive. It is important to maintain the initiative once it has been gained.
Low maintenance	Grabbing, punching and kicking are simple, natural skills and as such do not take much work to maintain at a reasonably destructive level.
Range realistic	Grabbing, punching and short-range low kicking is a realistic range.
Simple	You can't get much more simple than this one.
Transferable skill	Common skill with all other impact techniques.

Measure	Comments
Overall balance of kata	Only place in the kata where we grab with the left hand and attack with the right. There are two places in the kata where we unleash a barrage of punches and kicks. They are very similar the only difference being the side of the body. In this type of technique it is important to be capable on both sides of your body.

Henka

1. Punch

2. Charge and knee

3. Take a target of opportunity

Links and flow

After the initial barrage of techniques it is important to flow into something that puts your opponent on the ground either through further impact or a sweep or takedown. As such you could go to any of mnemonics 5, 7, 13, 23 or similar.

Mnemonic 7

Shotokan movement - prepare for tate shuto to right

Pull front foot back and cross arms

Burgar movement - step up, right arm low, left arm high

Cross arms and raise knee

Oyo - close in takedown

Same as in Mnemonic 5 but on the other side. It is important to be able to do this technique on both sides.

Mnemonic 8

Shotokan movement - tate shuto, punching and kicking to right

1. Move to the tate shuto open hand block

2. Complete the right hand tate shuto

3. Gyaku zuki

4. Jun zuki

5. Mae geri - step forwards

6. Oi zuki

Burgar movement - grabbing, punching and kicking

Identical to mnemonic 6 but on the other side.

1. Reach out with the right hand

2. Punch

3. Push or jab with the right

4. Kick

5. Punch

Oyo - grabbing, punching and kicking or sweeping

Same as shown in mnemonic 6.

Mnemonic 9

Shotokan movement - rising elbow, turn, push back

1. Step back with left leg

2. Rising elbow strike

2a.Rising elbow strike

3. Turn to rear, bringing the right leg up (position after the turn)

4. Step back with right leg and push arms back...

5. "Block" to the side

Burgar movement - rising elbow, turn, push back

1. Step back swinging around the front 'pivot' foot raising the elbow.

2. Turn 180 degrees away dropping the right elbow

3. Step back with the right leg and push the right elbow back.

The Shotokan movement and my movement are only different in that my stance is shorter and in the final movement my elbow is more prominent to the back.

Oyo - defence against a left-hand lapel grab

1. The grab

2. Hit the elbow

3. Turn and drop your weight

Okay, so you messed up! He should not have been allowed to grab you but it happens. Grab his grabbing hand and simultaneously turn your body and hit his elbow with your rising elbow. Roll over the top of his forearm on the vital points there, simultaneously turning and dropping your weight into the elbow. It is important to bend your knees so that your weight bears down on his forearm near the elbow. Also keep your shoulders down so that your weight is transferred efficiently.

4. Elbow smash

5. Follow through to knock him down.

Then as soon as his head becomes a target, hit it with your elbow (ensuring that you turn your hips). If you get the chance follow through to unbalance him and possibly throw him down, by getting your upper arm / elbow under his chin and taking his centre of gravity past his heels with his legs sufficiently bent that he cannot step back.

Measured

Measure	**Comments**
Proactive	This technique scores quite well in terms of proactivity. Once you have decided to act you do take charge of the situation and control the opponent's balance. The technique can be executed quickly and ends with a heavy impact with the elbow.
Keeps initiative	Good score on this count because as soon as you have started the opponent is pushed off-balance and then pulled and pushed in various directions which change rapidly, giving him no time to adjust and compensate.

Measure	Comments
Maximises safety	The most likely follow-up is that he is going to hit you with his right hand i.e. grab with the left, punch with the right. By whacking his elbow across you force his chest forward and make it very difficult if not impossible for him to punch with his right hand. After that he is quickly pulled off-balance which makes it hard for him to get any significant impact on you.
Maximises redundancy	Occasionally your first elbow against his may slip over the top but the turning of your body still forces his chest out to some degree making it difficult for him to hit you. You can then move on in the technique without pause.
Workable under influence of adrenaline	Most of the action takes place in the tunnel vision zone or is tactile so it's pretty good under these circumstances. Uses only gross motor movements.
Works with instinct	Not the most instinctive technique but when you reduce it to its basic elements - which are pulling on his arm and smashing him with your elbow - it's not too far from instinctive.
Maximises predictable response	Scores well on this measure. Hitting the elbow across gives a good predictable response of preventing him from hitting you. Putting your weight onto his arm has the effect of pulling him forward which is reasonably predictable.
Unbalances the opponent	Scores well on this technique due to pulling and pushing him in multiple directions and using his arm to influence his balance.
Leads the mind of the opponent	Yes but only providing that the first movement succeeds. The problem with this technique is that it attacks where he is strong and is applying his strength i.e. in his grabbing arm. In order to enhance the effectiveness of this technique you must use a distraction like a shout, spit or light kick to his shin.
Low maintenance	It's not hugely difficult to maintain, but the opponent can occasionally slip away as shown in the henka section below.
Range realistic	Grabbing and hitting range is realistic.
Simple	This uses gross motor movements and is simple to do.
Transferable skill	Not particularly transferrable.

Measure	Comments
Overall balance of kata	This is the only movement in the kata that addresses a left-hand lapel grab.

Henka

What if you are too slow to get the technique off in time or the opponent's arm is just too fixed to move, and despite you putting your hip into the technique it just doesn't move? In this case you can slip your elbow over the top to go to the cover position shown in mnemonic 18 and then blast through his left arm to your left. Remember, under the influence of adrenaline decision-making is impaired and it is difficult to let go of a technique once you have started, so it is often best to plan on that basis rather than hoping that you will be able to control the effects of adrenaline - remember chemicals control your base instincts and erase higher cerebral function.

1. He hasn't been moved by your raised elbow.

2. Cover and try to slip inside the inevitable punch

3. Push is chin with your right hand and spin him to throw.

1. You get him moving but he tightens his upper torso but his leg keeps coming forward

2. Sweep his front leg

3. Finish of your choice.

Links and flow

After the elbow you can easily flow into mnemonic 18 (slaps and covers) or into mnemonic 8.

1. Last movement but he hasn't gone down

2. Go on the offensive with a slap.

Mnemonic 10

This movement is the second “signature” movement of the kata.

Shotokan movement - block to front and side, triple spear hand

1. Cross the arms

2. “Block” to front and side

3a. Step forwards

3b. Step forwards nukite

4. On the spot nukite

5. On the spot third nukite

Burgar movement - parry, cover, control, attack

Almost identical to the Shotokan movement

1. Parry across with the left hand

2. Cover with the right and...

3. push out and down with the left

4. Step forward striking out with the hand held vertically.

5. Second vertical hand thrust, other hand comes back to level with elbow

6. Third vertical hand thrust.

The Shotokan movement and my movement are almost identical but the emphasis is different due to the application in mind.

Oyo - turn aside and attack

This technique is common to many karate styles.

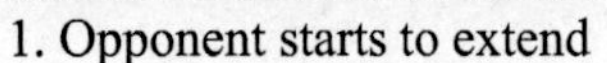

1. Opponent starts to extend   2. Redirect the push   3. Cover and continue the arm

4. Redirect and unbalance   5. Strike the side of the chin   6.&7. Use two open hand strikes to the head

Once the attack is turned aside it is important to press the arm to unbalance the attacker and prevent his other arm doing anything immediately. The strike to the chin must follow rapidly from the first part of the technique. The hand position of the strike is that of nukite but you strike the chin with the palm heel. You can then follow up with other similar strikes or do the in close takedown described earlier (mnemonic 5).

Henka

The most obvious thing that can go wrong is that you don't parry the push in the first place and his hand gets stuck on your chest. At this point flow directly into mnemonic 18 and attack his elbow.

1. Push gets stuck on your chest

2. Drop your elbow over the top and...

3. Press his elbow down and then step forward to strike him

Another possibility could be that before you have a chance to turn him he has launched a punch with his left hand. Your right arm is coming up anyway and can smoothly go into the cover of mnemonic 18.

1. Too late, a punch is incoming

2. Cover inside and...

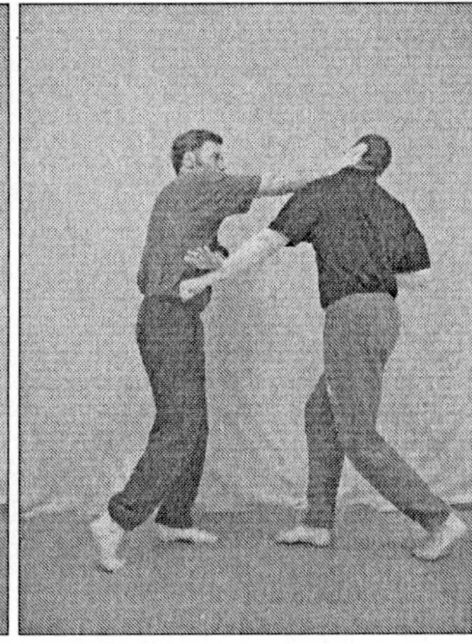

3. Continue with the strike you had planned.

Measured

Measure	Comments
Proactive	In the first instance the technique is entirely reactive, but it quickly reverses that trend by unbalancing the opponent and then going on the offensive.
Keeps initiative	Provided the first parry goes well you have the initiative. However, if the first parry is missed you may be defending once more before getting a strike off. However, any extra defence you have to make does put you in a position inside his defences which should allow you to get and keep the initiative.
Maximises safety	When you get the parry it takes you to his outside which is a safer place to be. If you miss it your next defence will put you inside and close to him for you to work your strikes. So scores well with a good parry, less good otherwise.
Maximises redundancy	In this technique we are making multiple parrying and covering movements with multiple attacking strikes, so it scores well on redundancy.
Workable under influence of adrenaline	Simple, macro, natural swatting movements and striking in the tunnel vision zone make this a workable technique under adrenal dump.
Works with instinct	The parrying movements are natural swatting flinch movements. The strikes to the head are instinctive.
Maximises predictable response	Turning the arm away and pushing it down should expose the chin to a strike.
Unbalances the opponent	Pushing and turning the arm can take the balance of the opponent.
Leads the mind of the opponent	The opponent's balance is compromised early in the technique. A barrage of strikes to the head shortly after, should shift his mindset to defence.
Low maintenance	Simple, macro, natural movements require little practice.
Range realistic	Pushing range is where fights often start.
Simple	Only the cover can be slightly complex. Most of the movement is simple and macro.

Measure	Comments
Transferable skill	Parrying, pushing and striking are all generic skills. An almost identical technique is used for pushes from the left hand and from both hands simultaneously, so the skills are directly transferrable to other related techniques.
Overall balance of kata	This is the only technique for dealing with a push from the right hand.

Links and flow

At the end of this technique you could flow into mnemonics 5, 19, or 25 depending on how he is placed.

Mnemonic 11

Shotokan movement - turn to front, block to front and side

1. Turn to front bring up right leg

2. Push back to side with right leg stepping back

3. Cross hands

4. "Block" to front and side

Burgar movement - turn to front, circle arms

1. Move forwards

2. Step back

3a. Start to circle hands

3b. Continue circling hands

3c. Finish circling

The Shotokan movement and my movement are very similar. In this instance (the movement appears several times in the kata) my movement is more circular.

Oyo - defence against an uppercut

If he starts punching you have to assume that he will continue punching and in rapid succession. You have to interrupt that flow by being proactive. That means stopping his attack and controlling him.

1. Jam and strike combination

2. Encircle the head

3. Control with a head lock

1. Jam the punch and hit the neck to stun

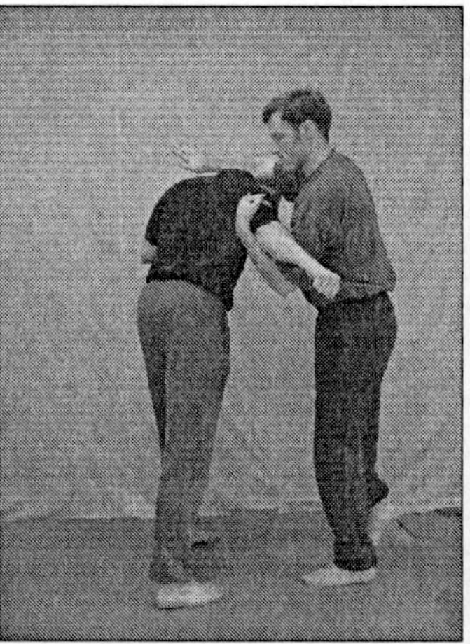
2. Quickly pull down and encircle the head

3. Head lock (or drive him into the ground)

1. He punches with his left hand. Use exactly the same movement

2. Circle

3. To the rear. The movement is the same.

Henka

You have to assume that he is going to punch with his other hand and to a great degree it depends on how hard you have managed to hit him. If he does punch you can cover (mnemonic 18) either low or high and flow into another technique. If you have hit him hard enough to gain a moment then immediately circle his head. He may also try to grab you with just about any hold available at that range.

1. Stop the first punch

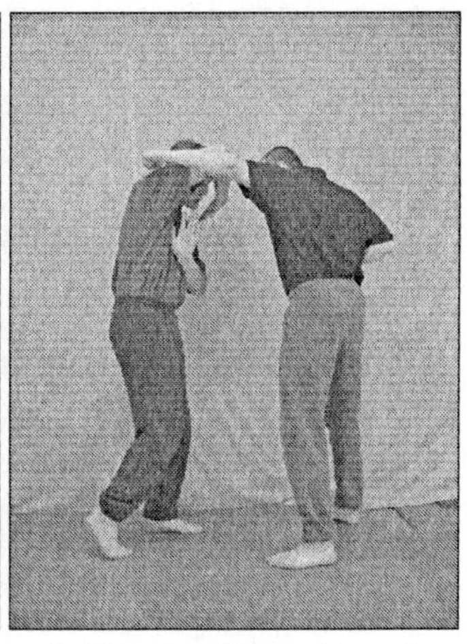

2. Stopping the next punch (low)

Measured

Measure	Comments
Proactive	Scores well with respect to the fact that the block and strike are simultaneous, and provided you have hit hard enough the following action is proactive too. If your strike is not hard enough then you may need to be reactive once more before getting the chance to go on the attack.
Keeps initiative	Similar to the proactive measure it scores well if you have hit hard enough to start with.
Maximises safety	Assuming that the block worked it leaves you the chance to be proactive but also leaves you in a position to cover rapidly.
Maximises redundancy	If the strike does not work it still leaves opportunity to work inside or push the opponent back.
Workable under influence of adrenaline	Large, macro and simple movements. Main target is in the tunnel vision area and wrapping the neck and pulling down is instinctive.
Works with instinct	The block is a natural flinch movement against a low punch and the strike out is part of the flinch movement. Also it is instinctive to grab around the neck.
Maximises predictable response	The block is structurally strong which leaves two most likely outcomes a) a pause in which to grab or b) another inbound punch from his other arm.
Unbalances the opponent	Grabbing and pulling his head down is an unbalancing movement.
Leads the mind of the opponent	The simultaneous block/strike means that the opponent can be stunned for a moment which gives you time to grab and pull him forward.
Low maintenance	Large, macro and simple movements are easy skills to maintain.
Range realistic	Medium / close range.
Simple	Easy macro movement based on a flinch response.

Measure	Comments
Transferable skill	Simple blocks, strikes and strangles are transferrable. Also it is used to deal with an uppercut from either side.
Overall balance of kata	Only technique in the kata to deal with uppercuts.

Links and flow

Once you have him bent over you can flow into mnemonics 23, 25 or 26 or if he cannot be bent forwards flow into mnemonics 8 or 18 or if he grabs you will need to deal appropriately with that.

Mnemonic 12

Shotokan movement - step forwards triple spear hand

1. Step forwards nukite

2. On the spot nukite

3. On the spot third nukite

Burgar movement - step forwards, triple spear hand

1. Step forwards (right foot at knee height) and strike with a right vertical hand.

2. On the spot push out the left hand across and down

3. Strike out with the right vertical hand.

On stepping make sure that the right foot is kicked out at knee height and that the left hand is held next to the right elbow. On the second move make sure that your left hand is pushed out by your body and not just under the power of the arm.

The Shotokan movement and my movement are different only in that I step higher on the forward movement and my arm placement is "off line" due to the application targets.

Oyo - defence against a right lapel grab

1. Grabbed by the left lapel

2. Kick the leg and smack the chin or check the shoulder

3. Force the elbow down and across

4. Palm heel the side of the chin

Photo 2 shows a strike to the chin; however, you may check the shoulder to pre-emptively stop the punch. Also at this point you start to push his right elbow across.

Henka

A likely scenario here is that he is angled away from you so that checking his left shoulder would not achieve anything. When this is the case his chin is usually a better target so just hit that first.

The other thing that can happen is that he tightens his arm and his grip is near the centre of your chest rather than on the outside. When this happens and his arms are longer than yours it can stop you reaching with your checking right arm. Usually, your leg will reach his due to the reasonably close range. If your kick does connect then you should normally be able to turn him and get in a good strike. However, if your kick misses you have to move to another technique quickly. Due to the fact that his arm is tight and straight a good one is mnemonic 23.

Other likely next moves on the part of the opponent are a head butt or a knee to the groin. The check to the shoulder and the kick to the knee have a good chance of preventing both of these - but you have to act immediately and proactively.

Measured

Measure	Comments
Proactive	Apart from the fact that you have an initial reaction to a grab the technique is proactive from there on.
Keeps initiative	The technique keeps the initiative throughout, except under the circumstances where there is complete failure due to the opponent straightening his arm and the kick missing.
Maximises safety	Given that the most likely next move on the part of the opponent is a left round punch the technique is tightly focussed on taking that away by kicking away the leg, checking the shoulder and pushing the elbow across. Other second techniques could be a head butt or knee, both of which this technique can deal with. Also the head is struck with the palm heel, which is safer than striking with the fist.
Maximises redundancy	There are three factors involved in the initial part of the technique so there is plenty of redundancy to ensure that it should work.

Measure	Comments
Workable under influence of adrenaline	Most of the technique takes place in the tunnel vision zone and the movements are direct and instinctive. The only part of the technique which can present difficulty is lifting the leg.
Works with instinct	The techniques are simple and direct and the primary target (the head) is an instinctive target.
Maximises predictable response	Kicking the leg away, checking the shoulder and pushing the elbow across all have a good predicable result which makes the chin an available target.
Unbalances the opponent	All three of the first movements (the kick, the check and the elbow push) all have a good unbalancing effect.
Leads the mind of the opponent	Taking the balance is good for leading the opponent's mind. Also he is being pushed and pulled in a couple of different directions in rapid succession and then receiving impact to the head.
Low maintenance	The movements are all pretty easy. The only part that needs a little more maintenance is the push on the elbow which can be missed if not practised properly.
Range realistic	Grabbing range.
Simple	All the movements are simple, macro movements.
Transferable skill	Pushing, striking and kicking are all transferrable.
Overall balance of kata	This is the only technique that defends against a right-hand lapel grab.

Links and flow

On successful completion of the technique natural flows into mnemonics 5 and 25 are available and upon failure into mnemonic 23.

Mnemonic 13

Shotokan movement - turn, double block to side

1. Reach up to front

2. Spin anti-clockwise on the right foot

3. Turn through 270 degrees bringing hands down

4. "Block" to the side

Burgar movement - turn, hands down

1. Reach up (left hand higher and right wrist bent back)

2. Extend the right hand up and pull the left down

3. Turn as in the Shotokan movement.

4. After starting the turn let the right hand lag behind

5. Then bring it down fast to catch up with the left.

The Shotokan movement and my movement are different only in that I let my right arm lag slightly behind the movement.

Oyo - head twist takedown

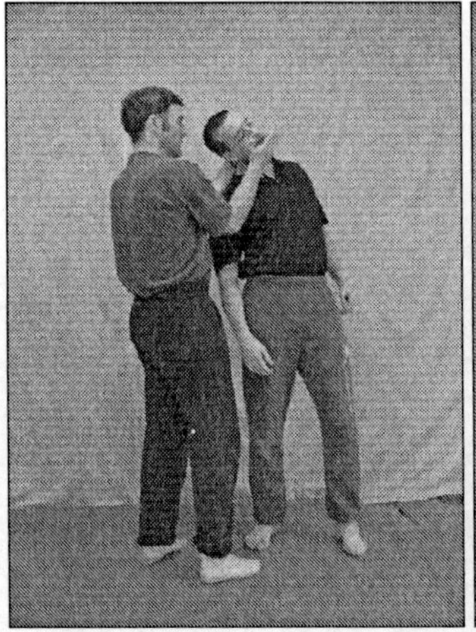

1. Grab the back of the head and the chin

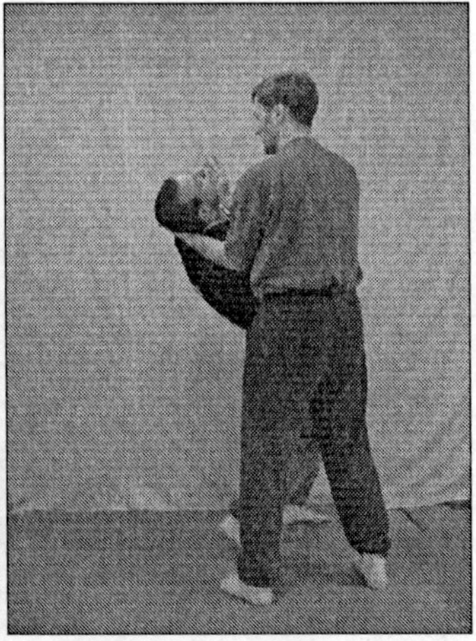

2. Progressively twist the head by pushing the chin and pulling the back of the head

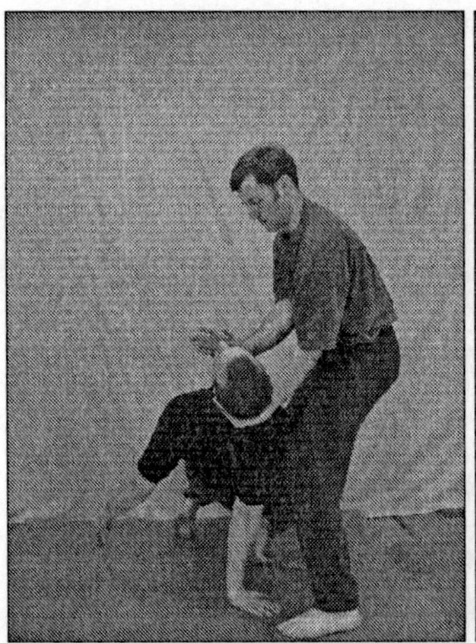

4. Hit his chin with your right hand

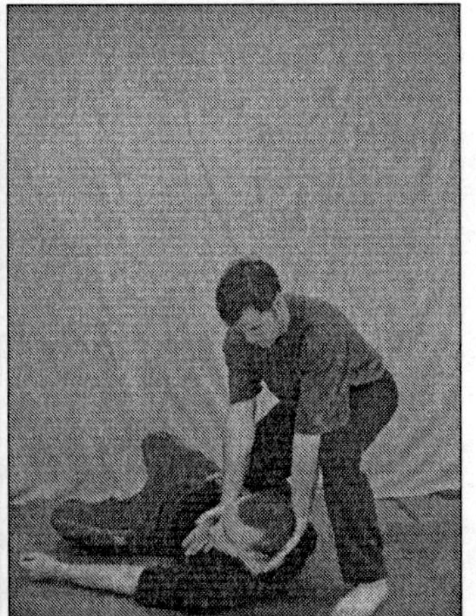

5. And push him down to the ground.

This is not intended to be a neck-breaking technique. There is little or no call for lethal techniques in today's society. This technique is purely designed to take the opponent down and so the neck twist is done progressively rather than as a sharp twist. If in doubt - **don't do it.**

Henka

To help the technique it is sometimes useful to use your left foot to press against the side of his right knee. This can also act as a distraction to stop him from tightening his neck so much that you can't make it work.

Measured

Measure	Comments
Proactive	The technique is used mostly when things have kicked off and you are close in and need to take him down. It is proactive in that it is an attacking movement.
Keeps initiative	Once you have his head moving his body will follow and he has little chance to counter-attack.
Maximises safety	The gap between grabbing his head and twisting it is the most dangerous because he does have a chance to counter-attack.
Maximises redundancy	This technique does not score particularly highly on this measure. If the head twist does not work then you must move to something else immediately.
Workable under influence of adrenaline	Very simple natural technique. The grab is in the tunnel vision zone.
Works with instinct	Grabbing the opponent's head is an instinctive movement.
Maximises predictable response	If the head goes the body will follow.
Unbalances the opponent	Takes him from vertical to horizontal.
Leads the mind of the opponent	One moment he is upright, the next he is looking up at the sky and being hit on the chin or neck. So yes, it does lead his mind.
Low maintenance	The technique is not difficult to apply with minimal training.
Range realistic	For use at close range.
Simple	Easy to do macro movements.
Transferable skill	Not a particularly transferable skill. The turning away is in common with other techniques.
Overall balance of kata	This is the only takedown technique for close in work where you are directly in front of the opponent.

Links and flow

Once the opponent is on the ground you can flow into other techniques that are appropriate - a quick exit would be best in most cases but in some circumstances pinning the opponent down or moving to the next may be appropriate.

Mnemonic 14

Shotokan movement - knee raise hands out and back

1. Step across with right leg

2. Raise knee and reach up with both hands

3. Land and pull back hands to left hip

4. "Block" to right with both hands

Burgar movement - rising kick, two-handed strike and pull back

1. Kamae

2. Rising kick

3. Strike with both hands

4. Pull hands back to the left shoulder

5. Throw both hands down to the right

This movement differs from the Shotokan movement in a couple of ways first instead of the knee raise I use a light flicking kick. Second, my hand pull-back is chambered higher than the Shotokan version.

Oyo - mid range pre-emption

1. Distract with a question

2. Quick kick to the groin

3. Strike the head and neck

First of all distract the opponent verbally and disguise the fact that you have transferred your weight to your right leg. Use your unweighted left leg to do a quick flick-kick to the opponent's groin. The kick will either land in which case he will probably move his hips back, or it may miss but he will probably flinch away from the kick to avoid it. Either way his hips will probably be back and his head will probably be forward. This gives you your next target which is to strike to his forehead and neck with both hands.

4. Pull in and strike with left shoulder

5. Twist head to take him down

The two-handed strike is fast by virtue of the fact that your hands were already out and primed. As you hit him, keep your hands on his head and, dropping your weight, forcefully pull his face onto your shoulder. Then with your left hand on his chin and right hand on the back of his head, progressively twist his head to throw him down. The aim here is not to break his neck (although that may have been the use in karate history). The aim nowadays is to throw him down. These days there are only very rare circumstances where lethal force is justified morally or legally. Twisting someone's head is dangerous and should be done with great caution. If it is done progressively rather than jerkily so that the opponent's body has time to follow the head then danger is minimised but the effect of throwing the opponent down is maintained.

Henka

There are several probable outcomes from the kick. First of all because this is a pre-emptive technique and you have time to unload the left leg before kicking, it can be very fast in terms of lack of telegraphing the movement so it has a pretty good chance of landing. The most natural reaction upon being hit in the groin is to move the hips back rapidly with both hands going to the site of the pain and for the person to double over forwards. If this reaction happens then the head is a good target to hit. If the opponent manages to flinch prior to the kick landing then you will see a similar movement, and once again the head is a good target and the technique can progress.

Occasionally however, if your kick is not well disguised he will move back out of range and you will have lost the chance to take the initiative. However, looking at the psychology of the situation, you have forced him to retreat and have shown that you will defend yourself if you need to. At that point it really comes down to how much he wants to fight. If you can get him to talk at that range then you may avoid trouble, however, if he is now determined to fight because he would lose face if he didn't then you can expect him to close the range quickly.

After the head strike, sometimes instead of grabbing the head he may fly backwards away from you under the impact of the blow. This tends to happen most when your arms go direct to the target rather than making an inward slapping motion. If he does move back then you need to move in quickly before he can recover his balance so you can be in a position to ensure that the fight is over.

When lining up the kick avoid glancing at the target which gives the game away. You need to practice looking at someone's chest which gives you a perfect understanding of where their groin is. Use the neck as a marker, kick to about 2 feet below that and you won't go far wrong.

Finally, if you are too close to kick you can make the pre-emptive strike with the hands only.

Measured

Measure	Comments
Proactive	Pre-emption is the most proactive you can get so this technique gets the highest possible score on this measure.

Measure	Comments
Keeps initiative	Yes, throughout the technique the opponent has little room for manouevre.
Maximises safety	Attack is the best form of defence. Also, the hands are kept high in a good fence position and are always in a good defensible position throughout.
Maximises redundancy	If the kick misses the technique can still work. If the person moves back under the force of the head strike so that you cannot get to grips with him then the technique will still have worked.
Workable under influence of adrenaline	Pre-emption with a kick can be difficult if you feel that you have very heavy legs. However, at this mid to longer range the legs are the best tools to bridge the gap - if necessary you can talk your way in, omit the kick and use the hands to do the pre-emptive strike. The head strike is in the tunnel vision zone.
Works with instinct	Kicking low and hitting the head and then grabbing are natural skills.
Maximises predictable response	Kicking the groin gives a good predictable response, as does twisting the neck.
Unbalances the opponent	Each component of this technique serves to unbalance the opponent.
Leads the mind of the opponent	You are proactive from the start and the opponent is always playing catch-up.
Low maintenance	Mostly an easy technique to maintain. The grab and pull to the shoulder and then twisting the neck is more complex and needs some practice to maintain. It is worth practising several exits to other techniques so that if the twist isn't going on easily enough you can move easily to another technique.
Range realistic	Pretty normal pre-fight verbal range. If you are sure that he is going to start fighting then this pre-emption may be your only chance.
Simple	Mostly simple but as mentioned in the maintenance section the pull into the shoulder and the neck twist can sometimes be a bit too tricky to work in a hurry.

Measure	Comments
Transferable skill	Kicking and striking are easily transferrable.
Overall balance of kata	This is the only mid-range pre-emption.

Links and flow

If the technique goes right though so that the opponent is on the ground no link or flow is needed. However, if he flies back from the kick or the strike to the head you would have to go to mnemonics 6 or 8. If the head twist won't go on easily mnemonic 25 would be a good choice, followed by a neck twist the other way from mnemonic 13.

Mnemonic 15

Shotokan movement - knee raise, two hands out and pull back

1. Step across with left leg

2. Raise right leg, reach up with both hands

3. Put down the right foot and simultaneously pull back both hands

4. Move hands forward and bring right leg to left

5. Push back to side

Burgar movement - sweep, two-handed strike and pull back

1.Reach out with both hands and sweep out with the right leg

2. Pull back with foot and hands (high)

3. Fold left hand to inside of right elbow

4. Pull back to the side

Oyo - close pre-emption

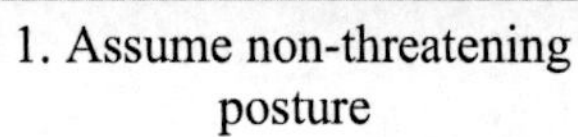
1. Assume non-threatening posture

2. Pre-empt to face/head

3. Pull him onto your shoulder

Try to talk the situation down but if it really isn't going to happen a pre-emption may be the only option available. Depending on the severity of the situation you can vary the hand strike to either hit the neck or the jaw. The more you can sweep the leg the better as it brings his head forward into your strike and also off-balances him significantly. After striking, the opportunity is there grab his head and pull forcefully onto your shoulder.

4. Head lock (Use your body to apply more pressure if necessary)

4a. Or off to the side if he starts to twist away.

This front neck lock puts very painful pressure on the neck. The advantage to it is that if you keep the same pressure on and he struggles it hurts him more so there is incentive not to struggle. If you turn your body away to the right it increases the pressure significantly.

Henka

The first variation is where after being struck he moves back away from your grip; in this case you have to switch to another technique.

If he has his hands up to the front you have to judge if you can get to the target quickly enough before he obscures the path with his hands. Kicking his leg first can bring his hands down (in a low flinch) to allow your attack to his head. However, there are other pre-emptive techniques that check the hands that would work better (see Mnemonics 20 and 21).

Measured

Measure	Comments
Proactive	Pre-emption is the king of proactivity.
Keeps initiative	This scores well for most of the technique however there can be a "dead spot" between striking him and generating sufficient force to pull him to your shoulder. You need to ensure that you drop your centre with your arms straight to get him moving before you pull with your arms.
Maximises safety	He is already well inside the range where you can be comfortable that you are safe, so striking first may be the only way to ensure you remain safe. You must be fully justified, using a pre-emptive technique.
Maximises redundancy	Medium score. The initial strike has several points of contact.
Workable under influence of adrenaline	The hand strike is in the tunnel vision area. However, the kick can be hampered by the effects of adrenaline. Simple movements.
Works with instinct	Striking the head and grabbing it are natural techniques.
Maximises predictable response	Kicking the leg out will cause him to bend forward.
Unbalances the opponent	Kicking the leg takes his balance and the neck lock forces him to bend his knees.
Leads the mind of the opponent	Because it is pre-emptive and unbalancing he is taken to a defensive mind immediately.

Measure	Comments
Low maintenance	The movements are simple and natural and therefore easy to maintain.
Range realistic	This is "heated argument" range just before things kick off.
Simple	The movements are easy to learn and carry out.
Transferable skill	The techniques are in common with many (striking to the head and kicking to the legs).
Overall balance of kata	Only

Links and flow

At the end of the technique you are in a position of superiority but your balance is not the very best. You can make an easy transition into mnemonics 13 or 25.

Mnemonic 16

Shotokan movement - block to front and side, triple spear hand

1. "Block" to front and side

2. Step forwards nukite

3. On the spot nukite

4. On the spot third nukite

Burgar movement - parry, check, multiple attack

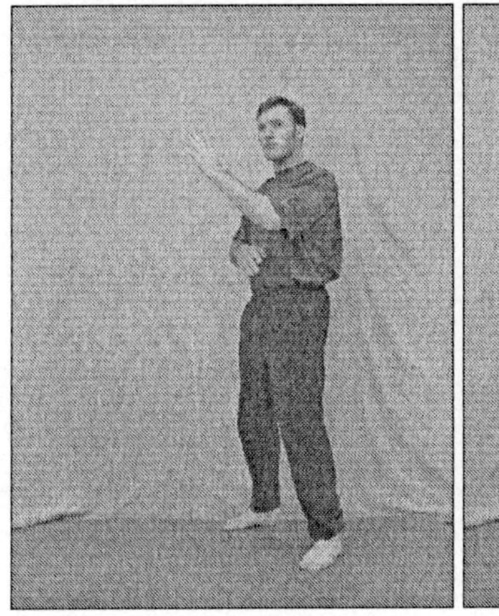

1. Left-hand cross parry

2. Left-hand check while right hand continues cover

This movement is similar to mawashi uke.

3. Step forwards right hand vertical

4. On the spot left hand vertical

5. On the spot right hand vertical

The triple nukite is a characteristic movement in Gojushiho.

My movement is almost identical to the Shotokan movement; the main difference being in the focus on the different part of the hand as the striking area. The Shotokan version tends to focus on the finger-tips whereas I focus on the palm.

Oyo - defence against left arm push

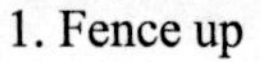

1. Fence up

2. Cross parry the push

3. Cover with the right hand and check the shoulder to prevent a punch

The cross parry is just a flinch. Immediately cover the pushing hand and strike his right shoulder, or if he is already punching hit inside his elbow.

4. Strike his shoulder or face

5. Strike the shoulder or crook of elbow

6. Finish

When you step forward you can strike his head or shoulders.

Henka

This push is almost certainly going to be followed by a punch with his right fist. The most immediate concern, then, is to check his right shoulder or elbow so that it stops the punch before it has built any momentum. In this technique we do the shoulder/elbow check as part of the technique regardless of what he does; this means that we don't have to think about whether he is or isn't going to punch, we just proactively do it anyway and get onto the attack.

1. Parry the left hand

2. The punch is coming already, check/block the elbow

Pushes are very hard to avoid because when the opponent goes to push you his objective is not to strike you hard but he wants to let you feel his strength and to force you to move, both of which give him a psychological advantage. If you are too late to check the push you can try to flinch your right shoulder out of the way by rotating your body around away from the push and reaching out your left hand to check his punch.

1. Push lands before you can react so give at the shoulder

2. And simultaneously check his right shoulder or elbow.

Measured

Measure	Comments
Proactive	Reactive at first but quickly getting into proactivity by checking any further attack and going on the offensive.
Keeps initiative	Provided you pick up the push early enough and are not taken off-balance by it.
Maximises safety	Makes a big assumption that the next technique will be a right punch. In most cases it will be and so safety is maximised but it may not be a safe assumption so you need to be aware of other possibilities.
Maximises redundancy	The mawashi uke type of block is a good cover and then the offense uses multiple strikes so if some miss, the technique would still be valid.
Workable under influence of adrenaline	For the most part this is an aggressively forward moving technique which has targets in the tunnel vision zone.
Works with instinct	The main target is the head area and the parrying is a natural movement.
Maximises predictable response	Checking the shoulders and / or elbows gives a fairly predictable response.

Measure	Comments
Unbalances the opponent	Provided you go forward assertively it can unbalance him. However there is no specific unbalancing technique here.
Leads the mind of the opponent	This technique is a little short on this measure and can benefit from an extra distraction technique as you get moving.
Low maintenance	Not a difficult technique to maintain, but detecting a push in time to do something with it can be difficult.
Range realistic	Yes, this is at medium range.
Simple	The technique can be learned and implemented quickly and relies on simple movements.
Transferable skill	The parry-cover-check (mawashi uke style) block is used in other situations in the kata as are the triple nukite strikes so this scores well on this measure. The right-hand and two-hand pushes are dealt with using the same technique so this helps with transfer training.
Overall balance of kata	This is the only technique that deals with a left hand push.

Links and flow

You can flow to mnemonics 5 and 25.

Mnemonic 17

Shotokan movement - turn right-hand shuto uchi

1. Turn to front

2. Right-hand shuto uchi

3. Step forwards and prepare for the next movement

Burgar movement - turn right-hand slap

1. Turn towards about through your left side

2. Slap

3. Elbow

Again the differences between my movement and the Shotokan movement are very minor, and are due entirely to the visualised application.

Oyo - defence against rear grabs at shoulders

1. Grabbed from behind

2. Turn with the hand held high

3. Evaluate the threat

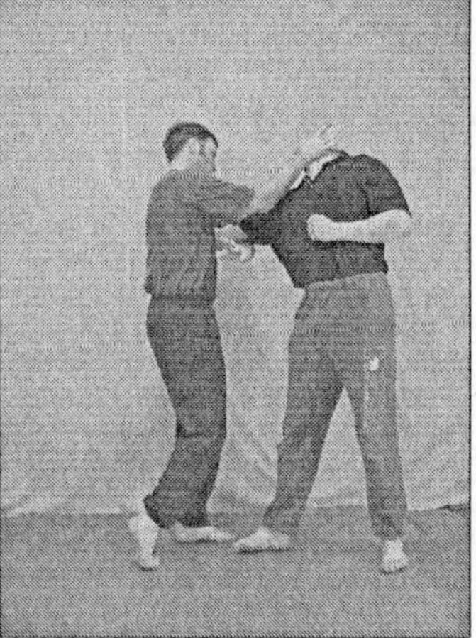

4. If necessary: slap

5. And then strike with the elbow.

When turning to the rear you don't know what you are going to find until you take a look. If things have really kicked off in a multiple attacker scenario you would not be unreasonable in assuming that you won't like what you find, and you should therefore be striking as you turn. However, in other scenarios where you have few clues prior to the grab you will have to evaluate before striking in order to stay within the law. In order to help with the evaluation turn with the left hand held high enough to protect the head and low enough to create some control over the grabbing arm to allow you to become proactive at the earliest opportunity.

Henka

There are many variations in this technique: the aggressor can grab you with either hand and on either shoulder or by the collar at the back of the neck or by the elbows. This turn takes account of those.

1. Grabbed by the right shoulder by his right hand

2. Turn, evaluate

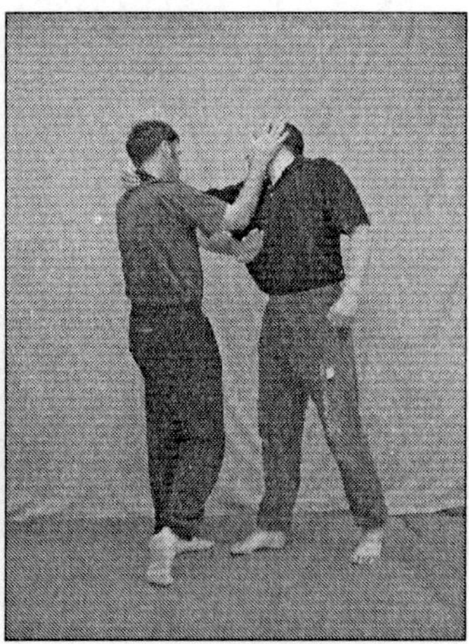

3. Strike if necessary.

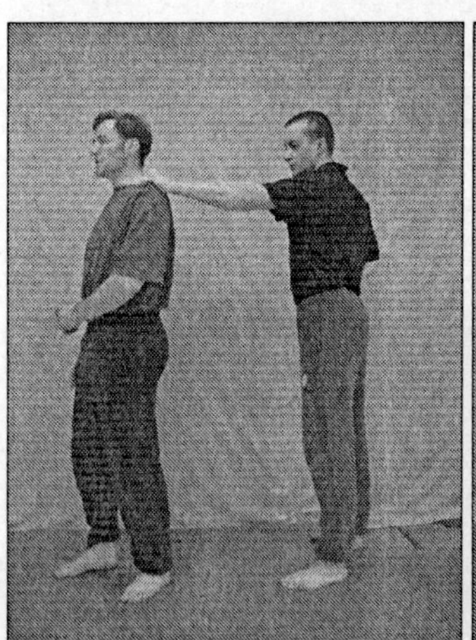

1. Grabbed by the left hand on the right shoulder

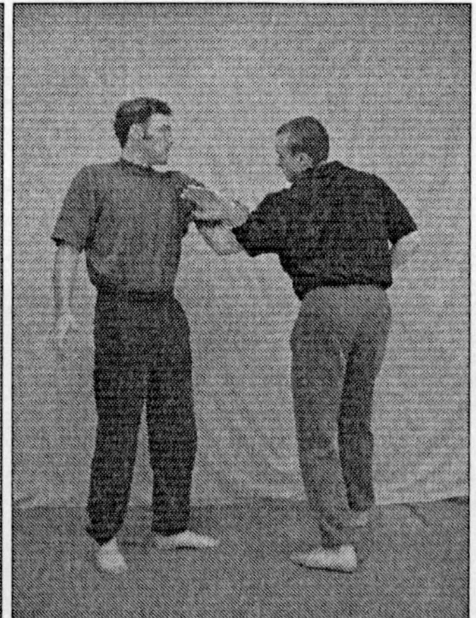

2. Turn, jolt the elbow and evaluate (Oops you made me jump - sorry or Oh no, trouble)

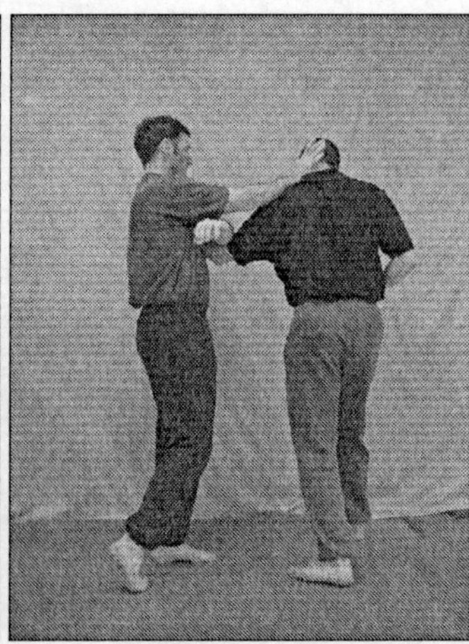

3. Strike if necessary

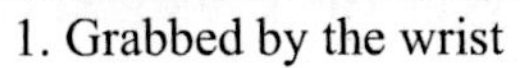
1. Grabbed by the wrist

2. Turn it over

3. Pull down and slap.

1. Grabbed by the elbow

2. Turn and evaluate

3. Slap if necessary

Measured

Measure	Comments
Proactive	In order to keep your actions reasonable you may have to turn to evaluate the threat before any kind of counter-attack. So this is necessarily a low score on the proactivity scale. However, if you do know in advance that you need to strike then this is almost pre-emptive.
Keeps initiative	Once you have struck you can flow to other slaps and strikes that are elsewhere in the kata.
Maximises safety	Given that there will normally have to be time for a reaction the best that you can do is bring your hands into play in a defensive role as you turn and start to evaluate, so that if necessary they have less distance to move in an flinch defence that occurs.
Maximises redundancy	You have a tactile sense on the arm of the attacker which can be used to advantage. Also even if the slap misses you may be able to influence your attacker through the control of his arm.
Workable under influence of adrenaline	Turn and slap is a simple movement. The slap is aimed at the primary target that you will naturally attack.
Works with instinct	The natural instinctive movement is to turn to face the danger and to strike to the head.
Maximises predictable response	There are a couple of outcomes: either you will knock him off-balance or down with the slap, or he won't move much in which case you are already deploying follow-up weapons.
Unbalances the opponent	Trapping the arm and slapping can unbalance the opponent but this is not guaranteed. So this is just a moderate score for this technique.
Leads the mind of the opponent	Once you decide to attack then you will be in a position to take charge. However, this technique does not score highly on this measure.
Low maintenance	This is an easy technique to maintain.
Range realistic	Grabbing range.
Simple	Large macro simple natural movements

Measure	Comments
Transferable skill	Slaps are used elsewhere in the kata and simple slapping techniques are readily applicable in many situations.
Overall balance of kata	Only technique that deals with grabs from behind.

Links and flow

At the end of the slap you can move into elbowing techniques that follow in mnemonics 17 and 18 or you could go into mnemonics 13 or 23 or any of the other close-in action techniques.

Mnemonic 18

There are many uses to this sequence of movements. The Oyo are presented and measured separately.

Shotokan movement - multiple stepping shuto uchi

1. Step forward

2. Shuto uchi

3. Prepare gyaku shuto uchi on the spot

4. Gyaku shuto uchi on the spot

5. Step forwards

6. Shuto uchi

Burgar movement - slaps and covers

1. Step forwards, bring elbow round

2. Reverse open-hand strike

3. Round slap

When bringing the elbow round make sure you cover low with the other hand. I have changed from the Shotokan knife-hand strike to the palm strike because I found that striking bags and straw bales was jarring my elbow and not transmitting sufficient power to the target. The palm strikes work better for me. This is a matter of personal preference.

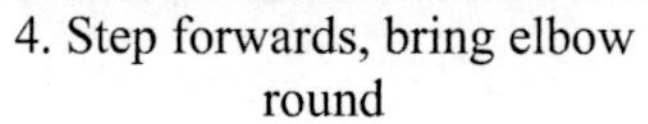

4. Step forwards, bring elbow round

5. Reverse open-hand strike

The difference between my movement and the Shotokan is that mine is more circular and flowing, but the movement is almost identical.

Oyo - attacking slaps

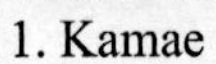

1. Kamae

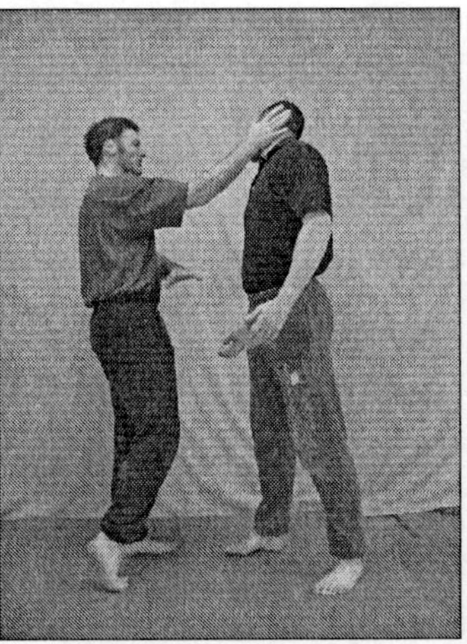

2. Strike using a slap

3. Use an elbow strike or go to a cover

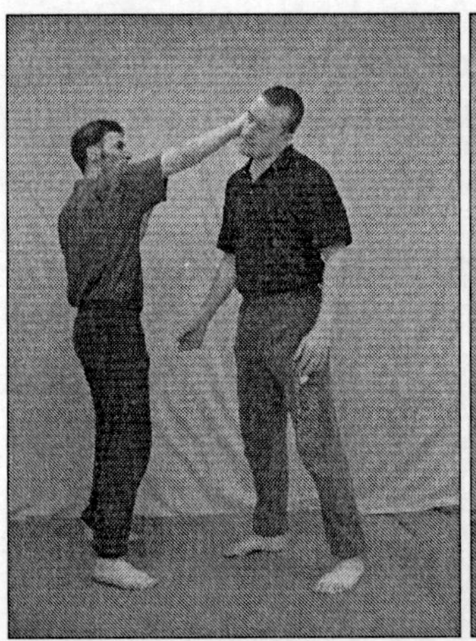

4. Round back-hand strike with the palm

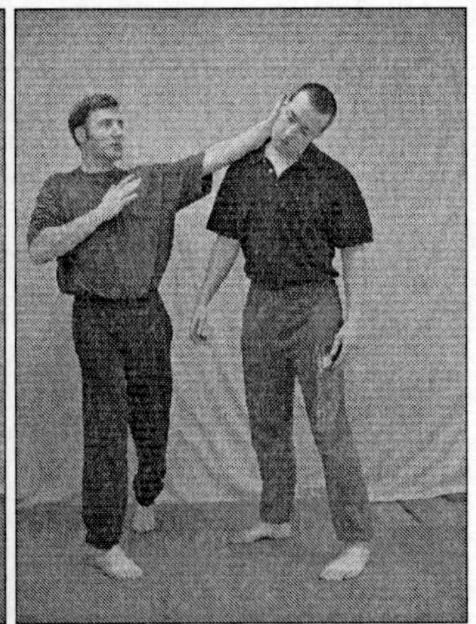

5. Another slap

Henka

You can mix the slaps and covers. Read more about covers in the following sections.

1. Slap

2. Cover to compose and defend and...

3. Come out with more slaps

Measured

Measure	Comments
Proactive	Slaps can be used offensively or defensively. For the most part they should be used offensively to force the opponent into defence. As such they are proactive and it is important to keep up a barrage of heavy hand slaps.
Keeps initiative	Provided you keep up a barrage of slaps you can keep the initiative. Combined with elbow covers you can deal with defensive issues while maintaining the momentum in your attack.
Maximises safety	It is easy to combine round slaps with defensive covers. Also, they can be used to force the opponent into defence and so your safety is maximised as much as possible under the circumstances.
Maximises redundancy	Using a barrage of slaps means that if any one in particular misses it does not compromise the whole series.
Workable under influence of adrenaline	Round slapping to the opponent's head is inside the tunnel vision area and is a simple and natural technique that even when the brain is diminished in processing power can be used effectively.
Works with instinct	This is a natural technique to the most natural target - the head.
Maximises predictable response	This should force the opponent back and or he will cover his head with his arms opening other targets of opportunity; low round kicks can be used to great advantage here.
Unbalances the opponent	He is forced back and may be off-balance to the back. However, this technique has no specific off-balancing use.
Leads the mind of the opponent	This forces him onto the defensive so his mind is occupied with that.
Low maintenance	Slaps are easy to maintain. A few minutes on the bag is all that is required to keep them with a heavy yet fast feel.
Range realistic	Striking range.
Simple	Easy to do. You should ensure that the arc is not allowed too wide; keep it narrow and continually accelerating to its target.

Measure	Comments
Transferable skill	All round techniques that use the hip.
Overall balance of kata	Only round, attacking movements. Complemented by the direct attacks of mnemonics 6 and 8.

Links and flow

You should be able to flow between slaps and elbow covers.

Oyo - defence against same-side wrist grabs

This oyo uses the movement shown below which is the step forward "preparing" for the shuto uchi (knife-hand strike.)

Shotokan step forward and prepare for shuto uchi

Burgar step forward leading with the elbow. Cover with other hand.

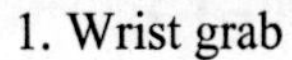

1. Wrist grab

2. Secure his fingers onto your wrist as you push your elbow forward

3. Continue to push your elbow forward to damage his wrist and put on the arm bar.

This technique needs to go on fast but steady at first and then with a sharp movement of the elbow forward to stress his wrist severely.

NOTE: Wrist grabs in books are shown in this sterile format to convey what is happening; see the henka section below for an example of how it may be used.

4.Drop your weight to get the arm bar on

5. If reasonably necessary then follow up with a back-hand slap

Henka

1. Gone to a clinch and you are hitting

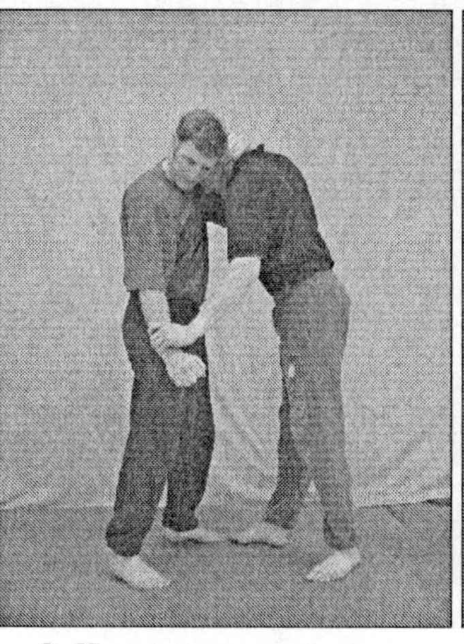

2. He attempts to stop you hitting by grabbing your wrist and forcing it down

3.Break away

4. Clamp his fingers on, turn his wrist and force him down

5. Start striking.

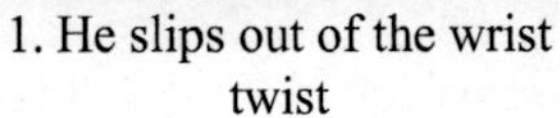

1. He slips out of the wrist twist

2. Move in fast with slaps or as shown here by going into mnemonic 19

When the wrist lock or arm bar fails as they will often do in the heat of the moment, or if he struggles violently as he will almost certainly do, you must abandon the technique and start striking again. Remember, the strategy of karate is to put yourself in a position to carry on striking. Therefore this technique should be viewed as a way to free yourself from a grab, damaging him in the process, and start striking again.

Measured

Measure	Comments
Proactive	Initial reaction to a grab but is proactive after that.
Keeps initiative	Enables you to free your hand so that you can start striking again. Its a good way to gain the initiative and damage him in the process.
Maximises safety	This technique, by turning to his outside, means that his other hand, which is a potentially live weapon, is momentarily controlled away from you.
Maximises redundancy	By bringing the elbow up you can use it as an elbow cover even if you have not removed his grip.

Measure	Comments
Workable under influence of adrenaline	This is not a particularly simple movement. However it is certainly not complex either. Keeping the wrist lock on is not easy to do, however the objective of the movement is to free yourself so you can continue to strike and also as a secondary objective to damage the wrist if that can be done. Pushing the elbow is pretty much all that is required which is achievable under the effects of adrenaline.
Works with instinct	This is probably a lower score than most techniques as it is not particularly natural and so requires more training to ingrain than some others (particularly the striking techniques).
Maximises predictable response	The response is pretty predictable. When it goes on it will cause the opponent to buckle at the knees, with a cross extensor reflex taking away his other arm.
Unbalances the opponent	The buckling of the knees tends to put the opponent on his toes which compromises his balance.
Leads the mind of the opponent	Puts him on the defensive.
Low maintenance	This does not score so well on this measure. This needs a reasonable amount of practice to maintain. Not so much in terms of the technique itself but in terms of getting the trigger scenarios.
Range realistic	Grappling range.
Simple	Only a medium score.
Transferable skill	Transferrable to all wrist twisting and grip escapes.
Overall balance of kata	Only technique for same-side wrist grab.

Links and flow

Flow to slaps or mnemonics 5, 19 or 25.

Oyo - defence against cross-side wrist grabs

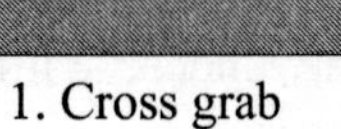

1. Cross grab

2. Turn the wist by going to the outside

3. Elbow over an put pressure downwards

4. By dropping your centre and making his knees buckle

5. Strike

Henka

Similar to the previous section, the technique will probably not be entered from the sanitised form shown above. Let us suppose that you have grabbed and are punching his head as per mnemonic 6. He will instinctively try to get his hands in the way to stop you.

1. Grabbed him and punching to the head

2. He gets his arms in the way and manages to grab your wrist or forearm

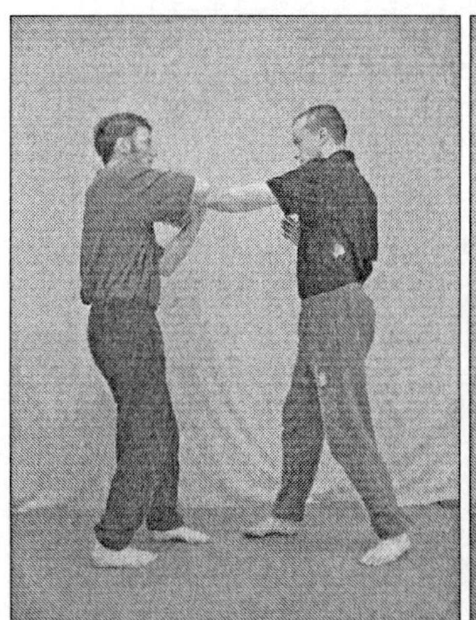

3. Go around the hand

4. Pull down and get your elbow over the top

Measured

The measurements are the same as for the previous oyo.

Links and flow

The links and flow are the same as for the previous oyo.

Oyo - defence against arm grabs

The stepping forward and chambering the shuto uchi movement can be used to defend against all manner of arm grabs anywhere from the wrist (as described in the previous section) all the way up to the shoulder.

Same-side arm grab

Cross-side arm grab

Same-side shoulder grab

Use this stepping forward and bending the elbow motion to defend. The rule is that you use the elbow on the same side as the hand that he has grabbed with regardless of which of your arms he has grabbed and where on the arm he has grabbed.

1. Start to bend the elbow and move the leg forward

2a. Turn the arm to put pressure on the wrist or...

2b. Or pressure on the elbow

3. Once the pressure has gone onto the wrist or elbow immediately go back to...

4. Striking

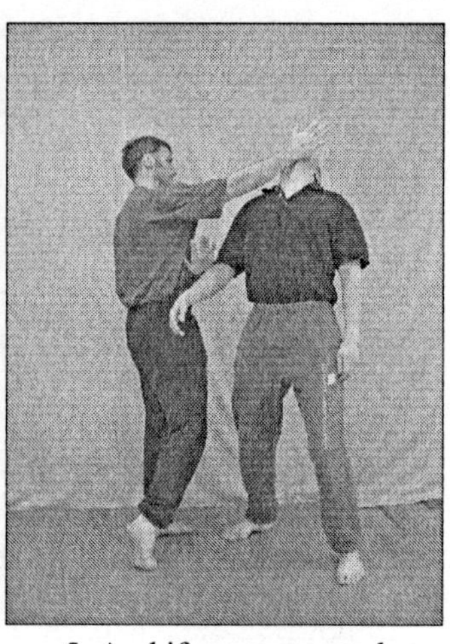

5. And if necessary and reasonable - again.

Henka

The main variation to this technique apart from the position of the grab and which hand he uses is that he may grab your clothing rather than your flesh. Generally the same technique will work depending on what clothing you have on. The important thing here is to limit his range of freedom so that any pressure you put on his joints is maximised. Remember you only need to twist his joints momentarily to off-balance him and loosen his grip.

Measured

Measure	Comments
Proactive	Initially you are reacting to having been grabbed but from then on it is entirely proactive.
Keeps initiative	Once he has grabbed you and you start to apply the technique you should be able to maintain the initiative.
Maximises safety	We always move to his outside and so we are moving to a position of maximum safety. When we get pressure on his wrist or elbow it takes his other weapons away.
Maximises redundancy	If the joints do not get any pressure on them the arm is still moved to a position where it is possible to escape the grip and go back to striking.

Measure	Comments
Workable under influence of adrenaline	These are fairly simple movements to make but do need some practice to be able to see when to use them. Under the influence of adrenaline it is easy to get stuck in a wrestling match rather than switching out to another technique.
Works with instinct	Not really. Instinctively when someone grabs us we tend to try to pull away. This technique requires us to move forward. Therefore a higher level of training is required for it. However this would be the case for most escape techniques.
Maximises predictable response	If the wrist or the elbow joints are twisted correctly then there is a predictable response.
Unbalances the opponent	If the wrist or the elbow joints are twisted correctly then the opponent will be put off-balance.
Leads the mind of the opponent	To a degree. First of all he is grabbing you and then (ideally) suddenly he has his wrist or elbow jarred. He should then be on the defensive.
Low maintenance	As mentioned above this set of techniques is not well aligned with instinct and so they require more practice to keep them functional.
Range realistic	Grabbing and grappling range
Simple	These are elementary grappling escaping techniques and as such are about as simple as they can be.
Transferable skill	They all work on the same principle of twisting the wrist or shoulder so when practising one you are getting some cross over training on the others.
Overall balance of kata	These are the only techniques for releasing from arm grabs.

Links and flow

Once the grabs have been released then you can go back to any of the striking or other suitable techniques.

Oyo - defence against pulled-in lapel grabs

There are essentially two types of lapel grab - the extended grab and the pulled-in grab. The extended grab is likely to be followed by a punch. The psychology behind it is one of holding you away (possibly because there is some fear that you may hit him) and being teed up ready for a punch. The pulled-in version is most likely to be followed by a head butt or a knee to the groin.

Held out lapel grab

Pulled close lapel grab.

We have dealt with the held-out lapel grab elsewhere (mnemonics 9 and 12).

As you are pulled in bring one leg across to cover the groin and bring your elbow round to cover your face.

There are several scenarios. The most usual is that as you bring your elbow round you smash the side of his face with it. The second is that it is in place just before he head butts in which case he will butt your elbow with his face. The third is that you stare at each other across your elbow which will be a short distance from his face - that's probably a good time to pre-empt with a reverse hand slap followed by others.

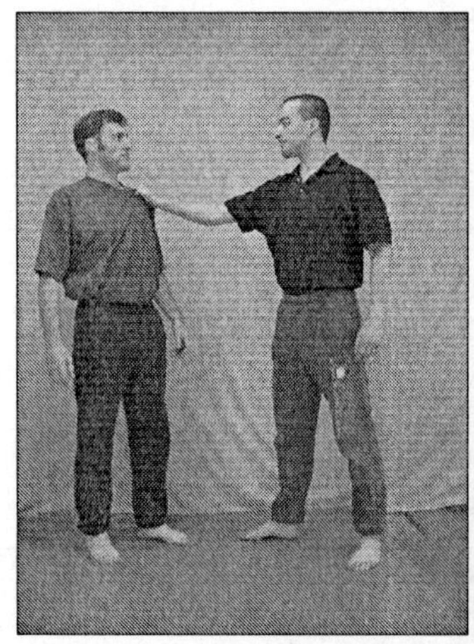

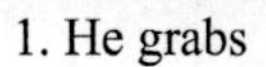

1. He grabs

2. You feel him pulling you in

3. Don’t resist, swing your elbow round and if necessary cover you groin with your leg.

Henka

A. You hit the side of his head

B. He head butts your elbow

C. You stare at each other over your elbow.

Measured

Measure	Comments
Proactive	It's a reaction to circumstances, but as soon as you have done it it puts you in a proactive position which you can maintain.
Keeps initiative	Provided you immediately follow up with other techniques then you will keep the initiative.
Maximises safety	You cover the most obvious targets. Your cover may also work offensively so safety is maximised.
Maximises redundancy	The major outcomes from the techniques are all satisfactory so if any particular part goes badly you still have your cover which you can fight out of.
Workable under influence of adrenaline	This is almost a flinch response and so even under adrenaline influence it is still workable. Your primary focus is to his head which is in the tunnel vision zone.
Works with instinct	This is almost a flinch response so is reasonably instinctive.
Maximises predictable response	The three major outcomes are listed above.
Unbalances the opponent	This does not directly unbalance the opponent although clearly getting hit by the elbow may have that effect.
Leads the mind of the opponent	Only leads the mind of the opponent if he is hit by the elbow strike.
Low maintenance	Reasonably low maintenance.
Range realistic	Close range.
Simple	Lifting the elbow and knee are simple skills.
Transferable skill	The elbow movement is the same as the arm escapes.
Overall balance of kata	Only technique to combat pulled-in lapel grab.

Links and flow

Once the first part is done you can flow into slaps as per mnemonic 18 or possibly (depending on distance) go for the head lock shown in mnemonic 15.

Oyo - cover

Yet another use for the lifting of the elbow on the preparatory movement of the shuto uchi is to cover to defend multiple punches.

Shuto uchi preparatory movement - used as a cover

Then strike with shuto uchi

Defending the punch

Strike

Get proactive asap

Measured

Measure	Comments
Proactive	Reactive but gives good opportunity to get proactive quickly.
Keeps initiative	Only if you go proactive quickly.
Maximises safety	You will probably get hit but the cover minimises damage to you. If you can catch him inside his arm with your elbow then you will damage him, but that is really down to the dynamics of the moment.
Maximises redundancy	No, but desperate times call for desperate measures. You are covering as best you can; if you miss your block you will get hit.
Workable under influence of adrenaline	It's a good flinch response to train in and is workable under the influence of adrenaline.
Works with instinct	Covering up in this way is a very natural thing to do.
Maximises predictable response	He is attacking so you could probably expect him to continue to do so. However this technique does not give any particular predictability.

Measure	Comments
Unbalances the opponent	Not explicitly.
Leads the mind of the opponent	No, although if your block is successful and he didn't expect it it may cause a hiccup in his motion.
Low maintenance	This is an easy skill to maintain.
Range realistic	Close/medium range.
Simple	This is a simple technique to learn and use.
Transferable skill	There are not many elements of this technique in common with others.
Overall balance of kata	This is the only "desperate" covering technique.

Note that given the above measures the technique does not fare too well. However, given the context that it is used in it is a good technique. Things have kicked off and you need to get proactive quickly. This is one of the few techniques that might just allow you to do that.

Links and flow

Explode out of the cover with punches, kicks and slaps.

Mnemonic 19

Shotokan movement - uchi uke, kick, drop, reverse gedan barai

1. Prepare gyaku uchi uke (inside forearm block)

2. Gyaku uchi uke

3. Mae geri (front kick)

4. Drop, "prepare" for gedan barai / left downward punch

4a. Reverse gedan barai

Burgar movement - twist right arm forward then up, left arm down

1. prepare

2a. Circle left forearm anticlockwise and right arm clockwise

2b. To an inside forearm "block"

3. Kick low

4. Push down with left hand, pull up with right and drop weight

5.Pull back with clasped hands

The main difference here is in the last movement, which I have changed to be both hands pulling up in a naked-strangle hold rather than a "downward block to the rear". It's a natural follow-up to the previous movement - so I changed the movement.

Oyo - defence against double upper limb grabs

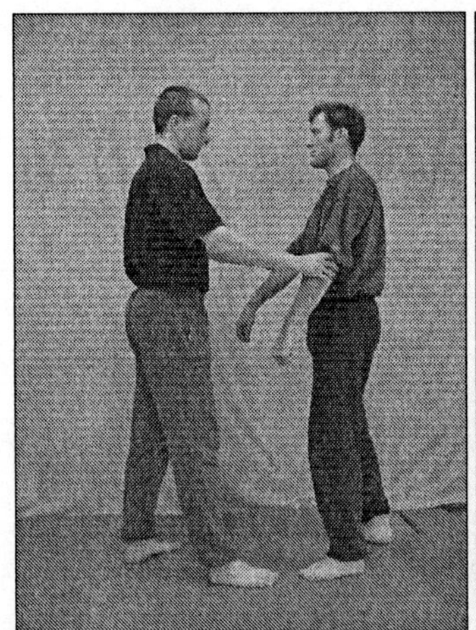

1. Grabbed by the elbows

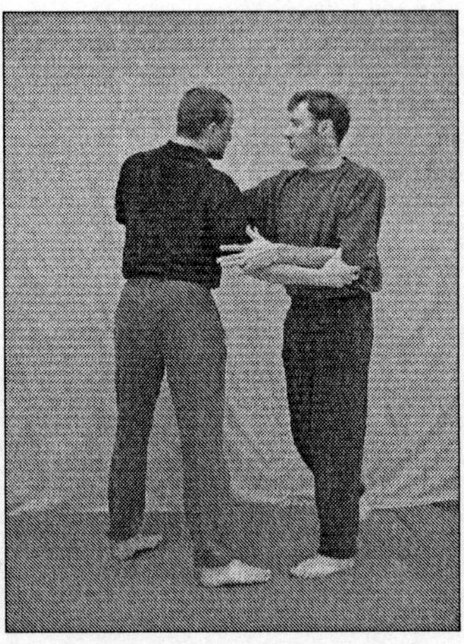

2. Turn your hands to escape his grip and force your hips through to twist him

3. Kick his leg to keep him turning and off-balance him

4. Encircle his neck and push his hips forward

5. Pull him back in a neck restraint

Henka

Things that could vary this technique are that you may not release your arms on the first movement, the kick may miss his leg or you may not spin him adequately. In each case there is sufficient redundancy and there are enough exit points that you can go to another technique if necessary.

He may not be just controlling your arms but also pushing you back.

1. Running you back

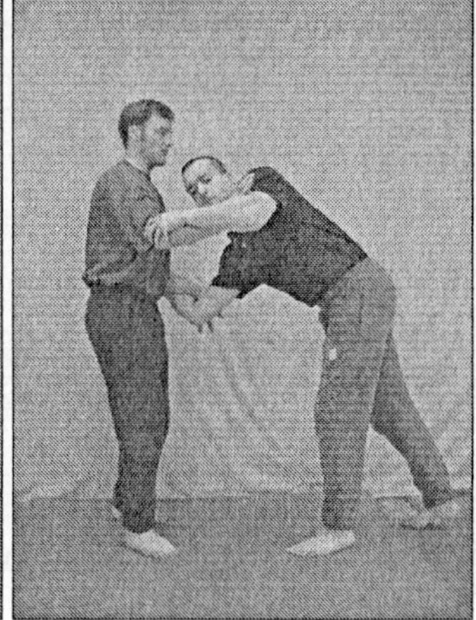

2. Reverse his grip

3. Redirect him

Measured

Measure	Comments
Proactive	Initially a reaction to having your arms controlled, this technique goes into proactive mode immediately.
Keeps initiative	Once you start the technique you keep the initiative.
Maximises safety	By turning him away from you you move out of the direct line of his weapons.
Maximises redundancy	There are several components of this technique that could fail but not compromise the success of the overall technique.
Workable under influence of adrenaline	This is a technique which uses large movements but none-the-less still requires some co-ordination. However, it is a simple escape compared to other techniques.
Works with instinct	This technique is not directly aligned with instinct and therefore requires more practice.
Maximises predictable response	The initial part of the technique should make the opponent spin. Pushing the hips forward while pulling the head back will unbalance him.

Measure	Comments
Unbalances the opponent	The spin, the leg kick and the pushing his hip and pulling his head all serve to unbalance the opponent.
Leads the mind of the opponent	Spinning an opponent is a very good way to disorient him. There is a sudden reversal of his expectation and so this technique does lead his mind.
Low maintenance	This needs more maintenance than simple gross motor movement techniques. Medium maintenance.
Range realistic	Grabbing range.
Simple	Moderately simple but does need some maintenance.
Transferable skill	Components of the technique are in common with others.
Overall balance of kata	This is the only technique for being grabbed by both arms.

Links and flow

At various points in this technique you can exit to mnemonics 25, 5 or 6.

Mnemonic 20

Shotokan movement - turn to back

1. Stand up face to back

2. Right hand out left hand under elbow

Burgar movement - pull and slap

1. Kamae

2. Drop left arm

3. Slap with right arm

My movement is more circular than the Shotokan version. I changed to the circular movement to make it a slap to the side of the head.

Oyo - defence against left hand pointing

1. Threatened

2. Trap the arm

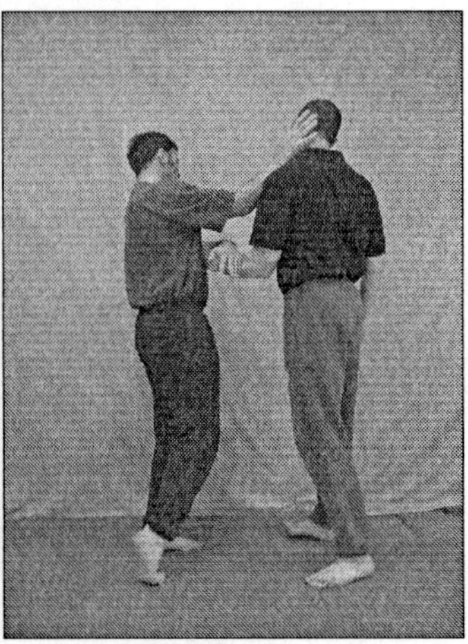

3. Slap

Ensure that when you trap the arm you slap at the same time. Trapping the arm means that even if he sees you about to slap it is hard for him to defend.

This technique is for use when the threat level is high and merits a pre-emption.

Henka

The opponent may remove his arm before you trap it - in which case slap anyway. You are committed to your technique and your mindset is on pre-emption.

The other main variation is that he may punch with his right hand. In which case you are going to go straight into mnemonic 3.

Measured

Measure	Comments
Proactive	Pre-emption is as proactive as it gets.
Keeps initiative	Once you have slapped you can go on to strike again or control using the arm you have trapped.
Maximises safety	If you feel you are in sufficient danger then pre-emption is the safest route.

Measure	Comments
Maximises redundancy	Not much redundancy built in. If you miss with the slap then you will have to move into other attacking techniques. Having the arm trapped does give a moment of redundancy.
Workable under influence of adrenaline	The target is a natural target within the tunnel vision zone.
Works with instinct	A round slap to the head is in line with instinct.
Maximises predictable response	Either you will have hit him in which case he will move off to his right or if you miss he will have rocked out of the way to his rear. In either case you can chase with punching and kicking.
Unbalances the opponent	No direct off-balancing other than if you hit him with the slap he should be off-balance.
Leads the mind of the opponent	Pre-emption is a good way to suddenly change the opponent's expectation.
Low maintenance	This is an easily maintainable technique.
Range realistic	Verbal confrontation range.
Simple	Certainly a simple technique.
Transferable skill	Transferrable to other round techniques.
Overall balance of kata	Only pre-emption for this situation.

Links and flow

Flow from this technique to any of the striking or throwing techniques.

Mnemonic 21

Shotokan movement - pull to side

1. Pull back

2. To the side

Burgar movement - push down and strike

1. Push left hand down

2. Right hand forward

3. And to the side

Oyo - defence against right hand pointing

1. Threatened

2. Push on his elbow

3. Strike to the neck or head

Again, like mnemonic 20 this technique is for use when the threat level is reasonably high and you feel a strong pre-emption is reasonable. The push onto the elbow should force him to drop his shoulder and turn slightly, taking his left hand further out of play.

Henka

The opponent may move his arm before you can control it. In which case go forward to strike anyway - that is where your mindset will be.

He may be punching with his left hand in which case you will be going directly into mnemonic 4.

Measured

Measure	Comments
Proactive	Pre-emptive, which is at the top end of the proactivity scale.
Keeps initiative	Yes, provided you flow into other striking, throwing or controlling techniques.
Maximises safety	Pre-emption is an excellent strategy to maximise safety. Also turning the opponent away increases the level of safety.
Maximises redundancy	There is little redundancy in this technique but it is over so quickly the real redundancy is in being able to flow to other techniques to follow on.

Measure	Comments
Workable under influence of adrenaline	Simple and direct, it targets the head which is in the tunnel vision zone.
Works with instinct	Striking like this is instinctive.
Maximises predictable response	Turning the opponent and striking the neck should turn the opponent away and cause him to bend slightly backwards.
Unbalances the opponent	The opponent should go off-balance to the back.
Leads the mind of the opponent	Pre-emption is an excellent way to change the opponent's expectation suddenly and thus lead his mind.
Low maintenance	Simple gross motor skill technique which therefore requires little in the way of maintenance.
Range realistic	Close verbal threat range.
Simple	Uses gross motor skills.
Transferable skill	Simple trapping and striking.
Overall balance of kata	Only pre-emptive technique for this scenario.

Links and flow

After this technique you should flow immediately into any appropriate striking, takedown or control technique.

Mnemonic 22

Shotokan movement - block to front and side, triple nukite

1. Cross hands.

2. "Double block"

3. Step forwards nukite

4. On the spot nukite

5. On the spot third nukite

Burgar movement - parry, cover, control, attack

1. kamae

2.Parry

3. Cover and check

4. Step forwards vertical hand strike

5. Vertical hand strike

6. Vertical hand strike

My movement and the Shotokan movement are almost identical with the exception of the target height and my focus on using the palm to strike.

Oyo - defence against two-hand push

1. Two-handed push

2. Parry across with the lead hand

3. Cover

4. Check

5. Strike

6. Strike

7. Strike

Henka

The width of your fence or kamae will determine how and where he can push you. If you stand with a narrow fence he will feel more like he can push your shoulders by going outside your arms. If you stand with a wide kamae he will see the opening to the centre to push your chest between your arms.

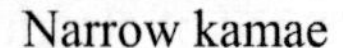

Narrow kamae

Wide kamae

1. Two-handed push outside a narrow kamae. Intercept his hands

2. And start striking

Measured

Measure	Comments
Proactive	Reactive technique in the first instance. The two-handed push (like the single-hand pushes) can be hard to see coming. However, if you are pushed and have re-established some distance you can induce him to push again simply by telling him not to push you again. From his point of view the push was successful and he has something to prove to you by another successful push.
Keeps initiative	If you get the first parry then there is a good chance he will be off-balance and you can then move in and keep the initiative.
Maximises safety	The technique takes you to his outside and his momentum will put him off-balance.
Maximises redundancy	Parts of the technique can fail and yet the overall technique can work. For example, it is possible that your right hand may get trapped on your chest instead of clearing the cover. However, because you are turning your body to the side and checking his arm with your left arm the technique can still work.

Measure	Comments
Workable under influence of adrenaline	The parry, cover, check sequence borders on a complex motor movement but is still simple enough to do under pressure. The strikes all go to the head in the tunnel vision zone.
Works with instinct	Turning attacking limbs aside and striking to the head are in line with instinct.
Maximises predictable response	Provided the parry works the results are predictable.
Unbalances the opponent	If the parry works and he has momentum coming forward then he will be off-balanced to the front.
Leads the mind of the opponent	When an opponent is off-balanced he first concentrates on regaining his balance.
Low maintenance	This technique does not take a huge amount of work to maintain at a workable level.
Range realistic	Reasonably close verbal / striking range.
Simple	The co-ordination of the parry, cover, check sequence is bordering on a more complex movement but overall the technique is pretty simple.
Transferable skill	Parrying, covering, checking and striking are all skills that appear elsewhere. The parry, cover, check is also used for other pushes.
Overall balance of kata	Only technique in the kata to deal with a two-handed push.

Links and flow

Flow to mnemonics 5, 25, 6, 8 or possibly the tail end of mnemonic 19.

Mnemonic 23

Shotokan movement - turn double-hand block

1. Reach up and spin anti-clockwise

2. Turn through 270 degrees

3. "Double block" to side

Burgar movement - turn hands down

1. Pull down with left hand, push up with right, hover left leg

2. Spin, leaving left leg to hover for a moment

3. Let the right hand lag behind a moment

Bring right hand down fast to catch up with the left. Drop down in stance

The timing of my movement is slightly different to the Shotokan and the raised left leg at the start is slightly different. Other than that the movements are identical.

Oyo - shoulder twist takedown

1. Pull the arm sharply down and push his shoulder away

2. Place your foot in front of his leg to trip him

3. To take him down

Henka

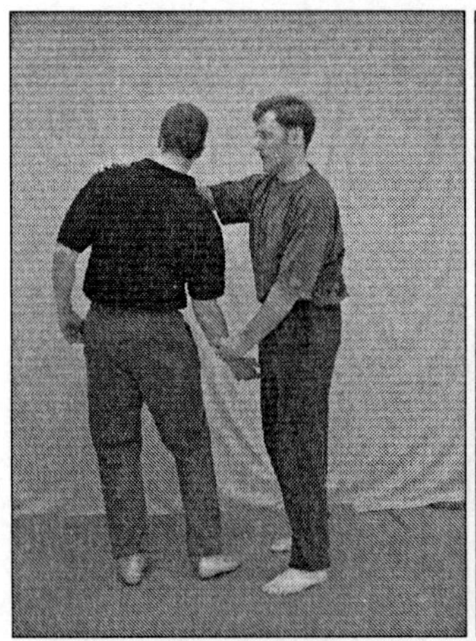

1. Turn his shoulders sharply 2. Press the back of his knee

Measured

Measure	Comments
Proactive	Yes, it is positive action from the moment you find this situation.
Keeps initiative	Once he is off-balance you can keep the initiative, even if he doesn't go down he will be off-balance.
Maximises safety	By controlling his arms it is hard for him to punch or butt you. Also by pulling him to the front it makes it hard for him to kick.
Maximises redundancy	The leg movement to trip is not entirely necessary to the technique.
Workable under influence of adrenaline	This technique is used after things have kicked off and you have gone to a standing grapple.
Works with instinct	Pulling in standing grappling is natural, however, the twisting movement is less so.
Maximises predictable response	If you can get him off-balance to the front he will try to regain his balance by stepping forward.

Measure	Comments
Unbalances the opponent	Yes.
Leads the mind of the opponent	Once his balance is compromised he will focus on trying to stay upright.
Low maintenance	This technique does require some practice.
Range realistic	Close / grappling range.
Simple	Reasonably simple but does need good timing.
Transferable skill	There are other twisting and spinning techniques within the kata so the skill is very similar and therefore transferrable.
Overall balance of kata	Only move in the kata that deals with the situation where you have grabbed his arms.

Links and flow

Once he is down you could follow with a lock, pin or escape.

Mnemonic 24

Shotokan movement - tate shuto, knee raise, punch

1. Step across

2. Knee up, cross arms...

3. and block tate shuto

4. punch

5. "Block" down to right side both hands open and palms upmost.

Burgar movement - hands extended, knee raise, punch

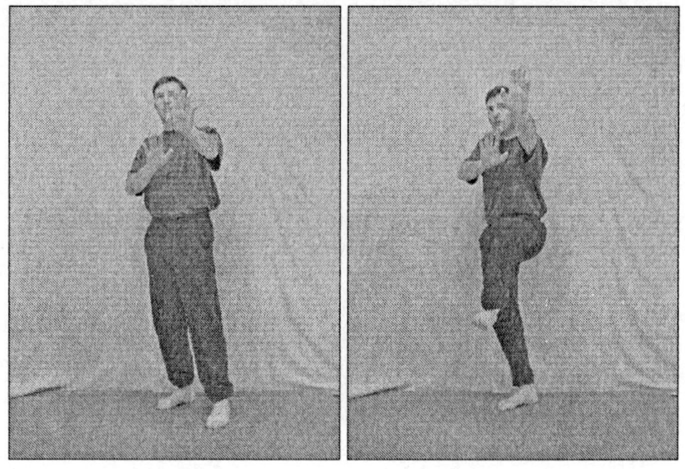

1. Kamae 2. Lift knee and reach out

3. Punch into the left hand 4. Grab 5. Hands down to side.

The only major change I have made here is to leave the left hand out and to strike into it which makes hitting a potentially moving target easier.

Oyo - defence against football kick

1. Kamae

2. Deflect the kick and check his momentum

3. Loop hand round the back of his neck

4. Punch

5. Grab chin and back of head

6. Progressively twist to throw

Note: twisting the head is dangerous and should be done progressively with the intent to throw rather than to injure the neck.

Henka

He could kick with either leg and will probably be following up with punching. Use the left hand to check any obvious punching. Once you have grabbed his head it will help to put in a few strikes such as a head butt or a knee to the groin before throwing.

Measured

Measure	Comments
Proactive	The first part of the technique is reactive but the aim is to be proactive by moving in, closing the distance to start hitting and to throw him down as quickly as possible.
Keeps initiative	If you gain the initiative then you are in a position to deliver numerous strikes and to throw.
Maximises safety	Does not really achieve this but is making the best of a bad situation.
Maximises redundancy	Not a huge score on this measure but there are numerous opportunities for multiple strikes.
Workable under influence of adrenaline	The technique is a reasonably instinctive flinch reaction and the grab and punch are inside the tunnel vision zone. Lifting the leg can be difficult under adrenal conditions.
Works with instinct	The movement is the second most natural flinch reaction to deal with a kick - the first being to drop a hand down to parry the kick.
Maximises predictable response	Not a good score on this measure.
Unbalances the opponent	Provided the leg block makes a sweeping contact with the kick - otherwise not.
Leads the mind of the opponent	Not a good score on this measure.
Low maintenance	This is an easy technique to maintain. The difficult part of it is in the timing.
Range realistic	Kicking range
Simple	Relatively simple to do although the timing needs to be right.
Transferable skill	Punching and head twist throw are skills common to others in the kata.
Overall balance of kata	Only defence against front kicks.

Links and flow

If he doesn't go down with the throw you can go into any of the techniques that work close-in.

Mnemonic 25

Shotokan movement - tate shuto, knee raise, punch

Step across

Knee up and "block" tate shuto

Punch

Burgar movement - two-handed pull, knee raise, punch

1. Step out and pull down with your arms (linked at wrist)

2. Knee up

3. Drop leg down, twist to the right pushing left shoulder out with hand as a hook

5. Punch into your hand.

I made a fairly large change to the kata here because I needed a close-in working technique and the movement in the kata was fairly close here.

Oyo - close-in work

1. Grab (strike with forearms and squeeze)

2. Knee

3. Pull to biceps or shoulder

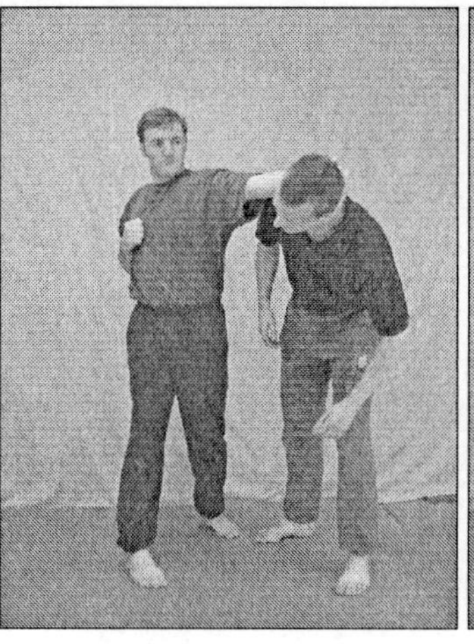

4. Bump him away using biceps or shoulder

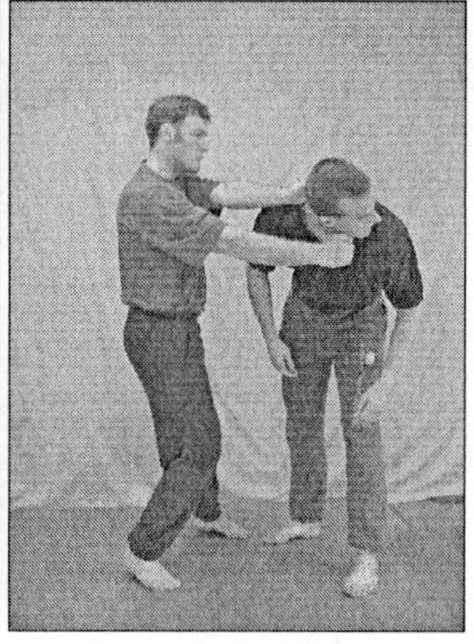

5. Punch

Henka

The angle of your pull can be varied.

1. Pull off to the side (left)

2. Knee to the groin

3. Push out with the shoulder and then punch

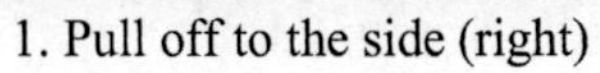

1. Pull off to the side (right)

2. Knee to the outside of the thigh

3. Shoulder bump to the back and then punch.

Measured

Measure	Comments
Proactive	If you look at the Links and flow sections of the other mnemonics you will see that many flow into this technique. As a result this technique forms part of a proactive chain.
Keeps initiative	After the strikes you can exit to any of the takedown or other striking techniques.
Maximises safety	Only insofar as it is a proactive technique.
Maximises redundancy	Parts of the technique can fail without compromising the overall effectiveness.
Workable under influence of adrenaline	This is an aggressive attacking technique which uses adrenaline as fuel.
Works with instinct	Grabbing the opponent and using the knees and then punching is in line with instinct.
Maximises predictable response	Causes the opponent to bend forward and then move his head laterally.

Measure	Comments
Unbalances the opponent	Being pulled forward and then shoved to the side has an unbalancing effect.
Leads the mind of the opponent	Only insofar as he is being pulled over and struck.
Low maintenance	Not a difficult technique - low maintenance effort.
Range realistic	Grappling range.
Simple	Grabbing, kneeing and striking are simple skills.
Transferable skill	Kneeing and striking are both transferrable.
Overall balance of kata	Only technique in the kata that works in at this close grappling range.

Links and flow

Exit point 1 - after the knee.

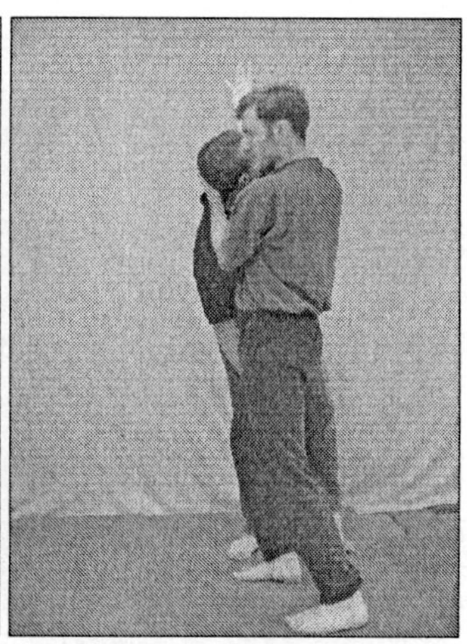

Transfer your grip and use the head twist of mnemonic 13

1. Exit point 2 - after the punch

2. Move round quickly twisting his shoulders as per mnemonic 23

Mnemonic 26

Shotokan movement - augmented backfist

1. Step forwards with the right foot

2. Circling the right arm

3. Vertical backfist

Burgar movement - circling hands, backfist

1. Cross hands, bringing right fist up

2. Circle right arm round

3. Vertical backfist.

Oyo - half nelson come along hold

1. Finger pointing (right hand)

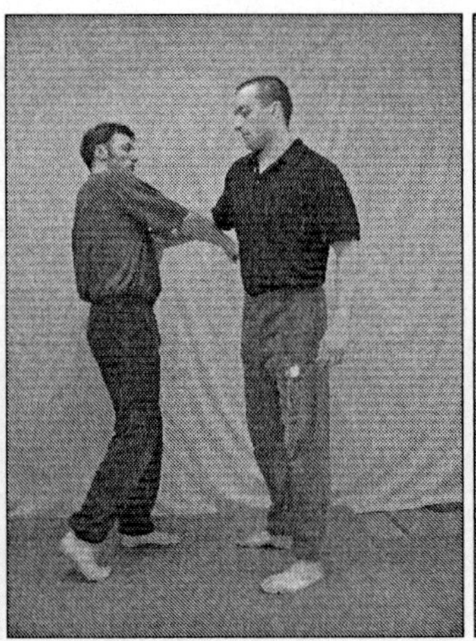

2. Strike the hand out of the way and hit the elbow up.

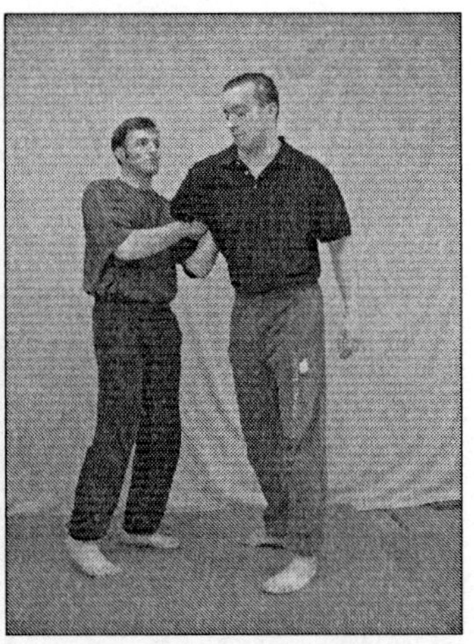

3. Thrust your left arm forward and behind his shoulder

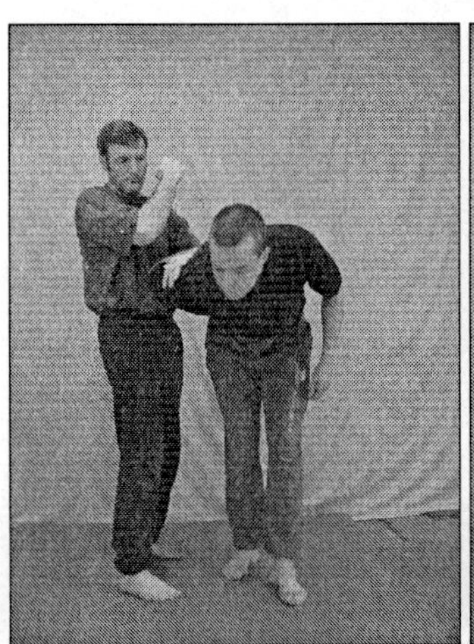

4. Push him forward

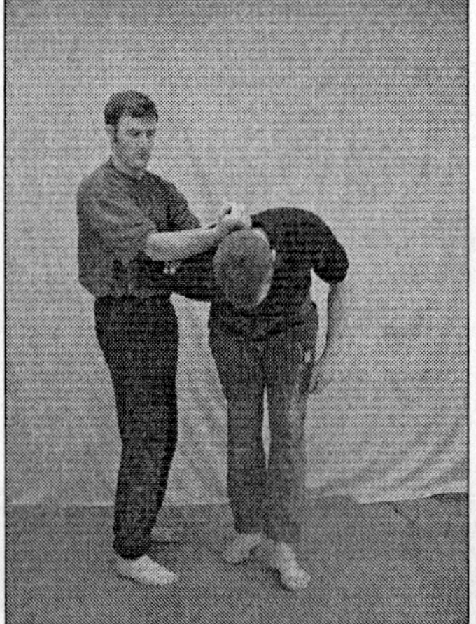

5. If he tries to stand up, rap him on the back of the neck.

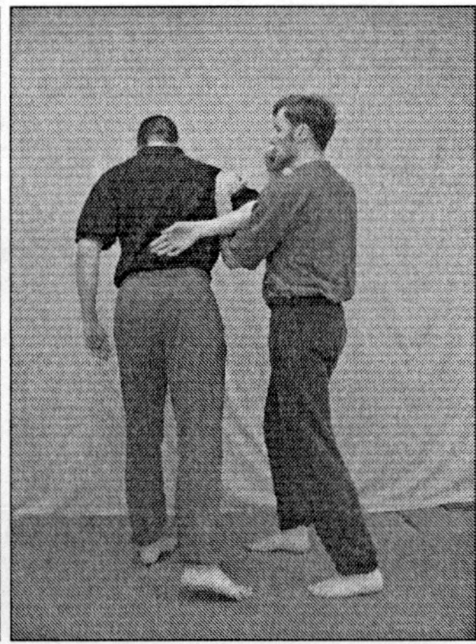

4a. Rear view of picture 4.

1. Left hand pointing

2. Press the hand to the side and push the elbow up

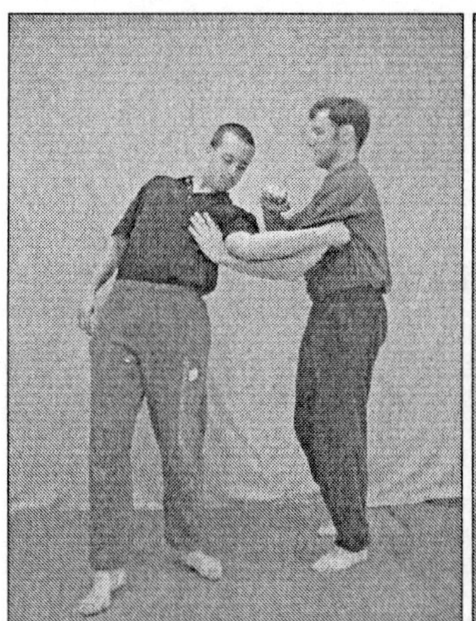

3. Push you left arm to his chest

4. Increase the pressure to bend him back

Henka

The two main variations are shown above.

Measured

Measure	Comments
Proactive	This is a proactive response to being threatened. It is more of a control technique than an all out pre-emption (as per mnemonics 20 and 21).
Keeps initiative	You have him in a hold and a plan for when he struggles.
Maximises safety	In both variants his non-pointing hand (i.e. The one that his most likely to punch) is taken out of play.
Maximises redundancy	If the hold does not go on, the strike is already on its way to his head. This strike can lead you into others.
Workable under influence of adrenaline	This technique is designed to cope with a lower-level threat than full-on. The level of adrenal pump is lower and so the more complex nature of the technique can be accommodated.
Works with instinct	Not a particularly instinctive movement.
Maximises predictable response	Each variant has a predictable response sufficient to know that the follow-on strike should hit an available target.
Unbalances the opponent	Each variant bends him either forward or back.
Leads the mind of the opponent	You suddenly go proactive, which should be a surprise to the opponent. This means that he has to focus on recovery and defence rather than attack.
Low maintenance	Fairly low maintenance.
Range realistic	Close verbal threat range.
Simple	Slightly complex but no fine motor skills required.
Transferable skill	Not really in common with other techniques in the kata.
Overall balance of kata	There is another pair of techniques for coping with this threatened HAOV but the other techniques are more highly pre-emptive and are for dealing with severe threat.

Links and flow

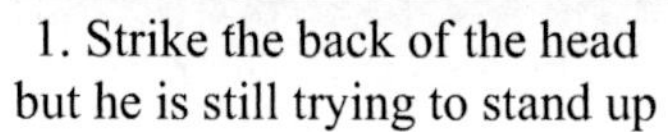

1. Strike the back of the head but he is still trying to stand up

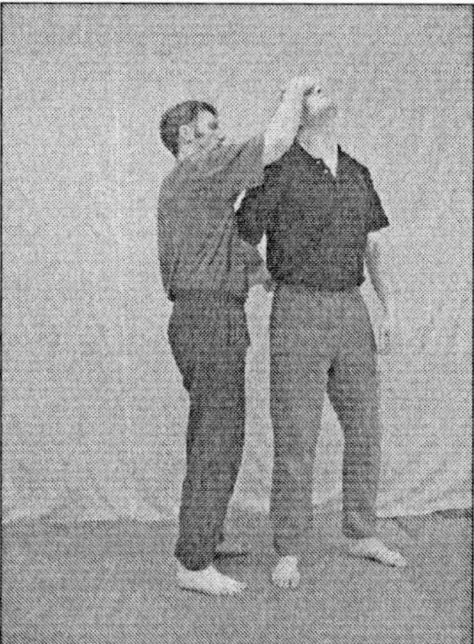

2. Move left hand to the small of his back

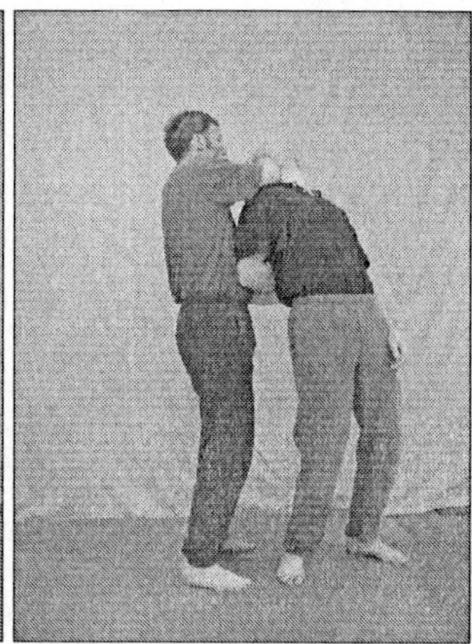

3. Force his head back to throw him down.

Mnemonic 27

Shotokan movement - step back hammer fist, step forward punch

1. Step back

2. Hammer fist

3. Step forwards with right leg and punch

Burgar movement - drop and withdraw, step forward punch

1. Stoop low and step back

2. Hammer fist position

3. Step forwards and punch

Oyo - defences against chancery head locks

Note that there are 4 ways that you can be grabbed in the chancery head lock. All four situations are taken care of by the same movement.

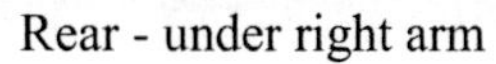

Rear - under right arm

Rear - under left arm

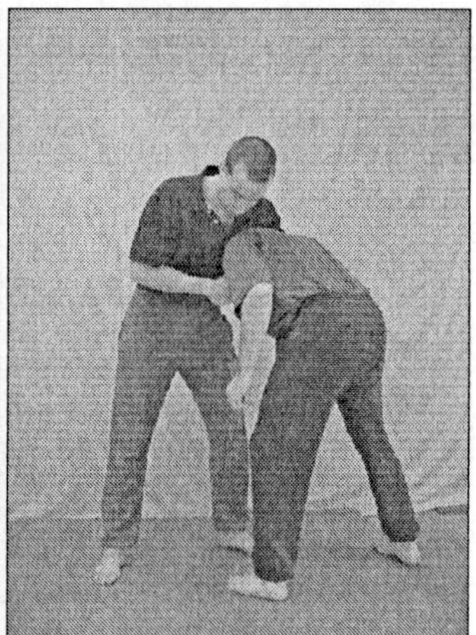

Front - under right arm

Front - under left arm

Rear - under right arm

1. You are to his rear and under his right arm

2. Attack his groin with your left hand

3. Shoot your left arm up to his head and create a gap to get your head out

4. Push him forward

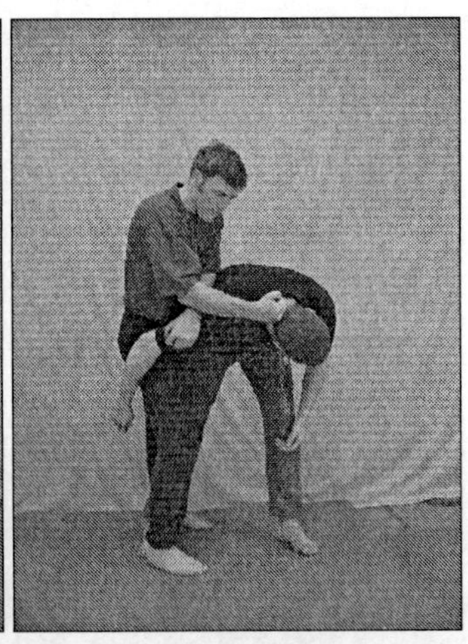

5. Punch

Rear under left arm

1. Rear chancery under his left arm.

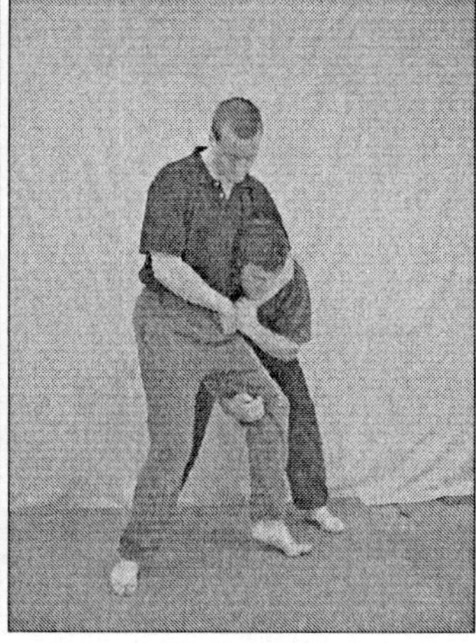

2. Attack his groin or inside of this thigh.

3. Shoot your arm through

4. Strike his thigh

5. Slip out and...

6. Punch

Front under the left arm

1. Grab his wrist whilst covering you chest to guard against a knee strike

2. Attack the groin

Once you have grabbed his wrist drop some weight into his left arm so that it "glues" his left leg down, which makes it difficult for him to lift his knee.

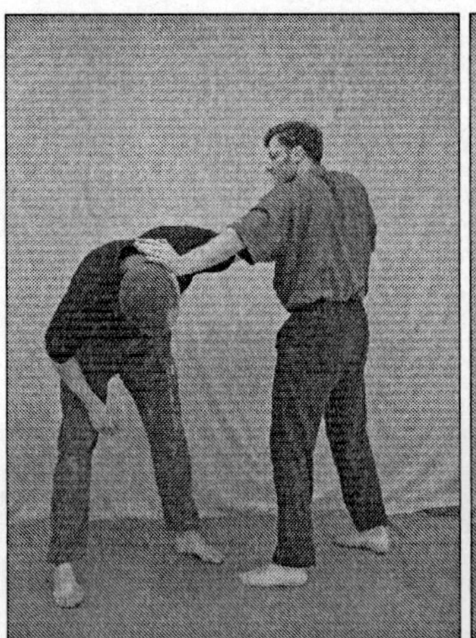

3. Slip out with your hand on his collar bone

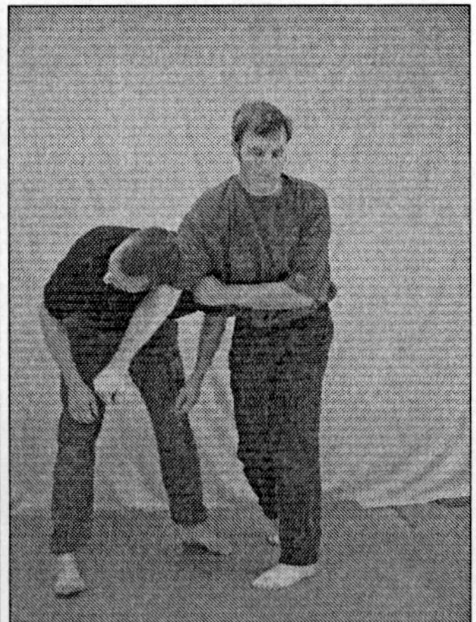

4. Punch

Front under right arm

1. Under his right arm. Grab his wrist

2. Attack the groin

3. Twist in and elbow his thigh

5. Slip out and...

6. Punch

Henka

The two most likely things to happen in this hold are that you will be punched in the face (in the rear holds) or he will use his knees (in the front holds).

Prevent the punch doing too much damage by covering your head

Put weight into the leg that he is lifting and use arms to protect yourself

Measured

Measure	Comments
Proactive	You are reacting to the situation but taking proactive steps to get out.
Keeps initiative	Once you are out, his is a poor position and you can strike repeatedly or throw him down.
Maximises safety	You cover the obvious targets which under the circumstances is the best you can do. Those defences can stay in place while you are attacking elsewhere to effect your escape.
Maximises redundancy	Only a medium score on this measure.
Workable under influence of adrenaline	This technique can be pretty rough and ready and may require some violent struggling to get out. Adrenaline fuels this type of activity.
Works with instinct	It is natural to struggle and strike when held like this.

Measure	Comments
Maximises predictable response	Attacking the groin or thigh should cause a slight loosening of his grip.
Unbalances the opponent	Various components unbalance him.
Leads the mind of the opponent	The pain compliance parts of the technique (provided he is open to pain) will help you to gain control. Otherwise the off-balancing components should shift his mind to maintaining balance.
Low maintenance	Not a difficult technique to practice.
Range realistic	Grappling range.
Simple	Pretty easy to apply.
Transferable skill	Not particularly transferrable.
Overall balance of kata	Only technique for escaping this head lock.

Links and flow

After the punch flow into any striking or throwing technique.

Mnemonic 28

Shotokan movement - hands front, dip head, hands behind, turn left

1. Face side, raise arms

2. Swing arms behind and incline body

3. Hands to hips

4. Turn to back with left leg

Burgar movement - hands to front, dip head, hands behind, turn left

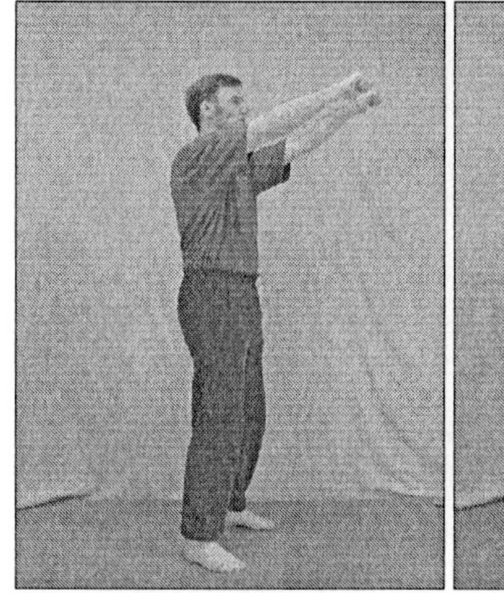

1. Raise arms to front 2. Drop hands to the side

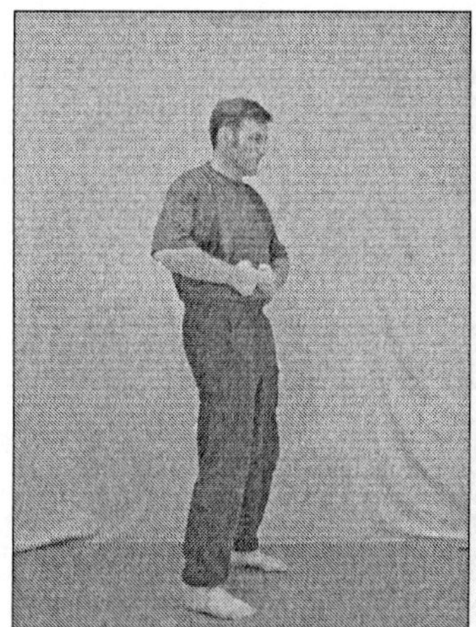

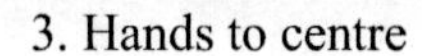

3. Hands to centre 4. Twist and drop to side

This movement gives us defences to all four combinations of bear hugs (front and back, under- and over-arm)

Oyo - defence against front under-arm bear hug

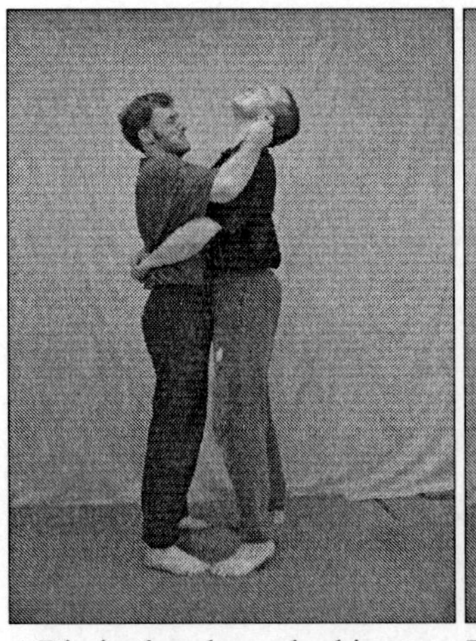

Dig in thumbs under his ear lobes

For more serious situations slap his ears

Most times you are not going to be just held in this position. Most likely you are going to be lifted off your feet and thrown down. You have very little time to work in.

Henka

Depending on the seriousness of the situation you can dig your thumbs in under his ear lobes towards yourself and upward at 45 degrees; this is very painful for him. Failing that you can slap his ears, or in very dangerous situations strike his neck.

You can follow any of these with strikes or kicks.

Measured

Measure	Comments
Proactive	You are reacting to the initial situation in a proactive way.
Keeps initiative	Once you are moving you can follow up with strikes and kicks.
Maximises safety	Best of a bad situation.
Maximises redundancy	Not a good score but there is not much scope otherwise.
Workable under influence of adrenaline	No complex motor skills are required and the target is in the tunnel vision zone.
Works with instinct	You are attacking the head.

Measure	Comments
Maximises predictable response	Most people will respond to the vital point under the ear by releasing their grip and jumping back.
Unbalances the opponent	No direct balance interruption.
Leads the mind of the opponent	If they are susceptible to pain compliance then they will attempt to remove the pain.
Low maintenance	Simple easy to practice and remember.
Range realistic	Close range
Simple	No complex motor movements.
Transferable skill	Not really transferrable to other movements in the kata.
Overall balance of kata	Only technique to deal with a front under-arm bear hug.

Links and flow

Flow to strikes and kicks.

Oyo - defence against front over-arm bear hug

1. Over-arm bear hug. Throw your head about to create some space and distract him

2. Force your hips back and your arms out to loosen his grip

3. Slip down and strike inside his thigh.

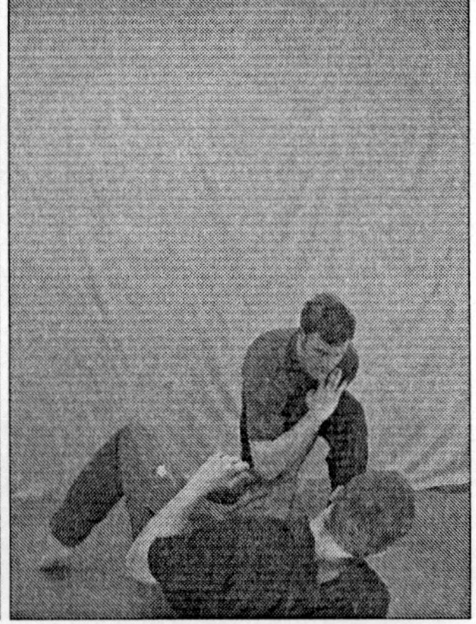

4. And pull on his ankle to throw him down.

Henka

His grip may be very strong and you may have to work some strikes inside before you have space to slip down.

Measured

Measure	Comments
Proactive	Reacting to the grab in a proactive way.
Keeps initiative	Once you have slipped out and hit his leg (regardless of whether or not he goes down) you can follow on with strikes and kicks.
Maximises safety	Not a good score on this measure - but under the circumstances it will have to do.
Maximises redundancy	Not a good score on this measure.
Workable under influence of adrenaline	Yes, adrenaline can fuel this type of struggle.
Works with instinct	Yes. Your instinct is to struggle free.
Maximises predictable response	Head butting to start will distract him and then forcing your hips back will cause him to lean forward slightly which helps to loosen his grip.
Unbalances the opponent	He should be forced forward to try to maintain his grip which unbalances him to the front. The elbow strike to the inside of his thigh should unbalance him.
Leads the mind of the opponent	His mindset will probably get stuck on maintaining his grip.
Low maintenance	Simple struggling technique.
Range realistic	Close range.
Simple	Simple struggling technique.
Transferable skill	Not particularly.
Overall balance of kata	Only technique to combat a front over-arm bear hug.

Links and flow

Follow with strikes and kicks, or if he is downed then escape.

Oyo - defence against rear under-arm bear hug

1. Strike the backs of his hands

2. Head butt and then slam your hips into his groin.

3. Drop keeping hold of his right arm and...

4. Throw

Henka

The main variation on this technique is that you may not unbalance him sufficiently to throw him, in which case you could slam him backwards. The other variation is that he may pull you down on top of him after the throw.

Measured

Measure	Comments
Proactive	Reacting to the initial grip in a proactive way.
Keeps initiative	Once you start your attack you can generally keep the initiative. However, sometimes if the throw does not work well then you can find yourself in a ground-wrestling situation which is not good.
Maximises safety	Not a particularly good score on this measure but needs must.
Maximises redundancy	Not a good score on this measure.
Workable under influence of adrenaline	No complex motor skills required.
Works with instinct	Not a particularly instinctive technique.
Maximises predictable response	The rear head butt and strike with the hips give a predictable response.
Unbalances the opponent	If the throw goes to plan then he is certainly unbalanced.
Leads the mind of the opponent	Your attack puts him on the defensive and he should get trapped into the mindset of holding on.
Low maintenance	This is not a difficult skill to maintain.
Range realistic	Close range.
Simple	Simple movements and skills.
Transferable skill	Not very transferrable.
Overall balance of kata	Only movement in the kata to deal with a rear under-arm bear hug.

Links and flow

If he is down you can strike, lock or escape.

Oyo - defence against rear over-arm bear hug

1. Over-arm bear hug

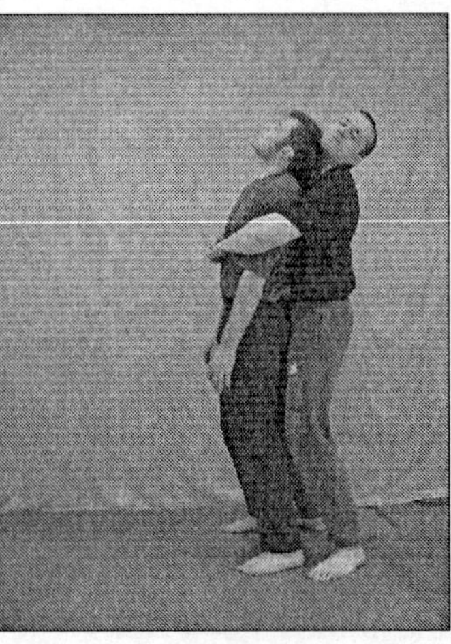

2. Force him to move his head

3. Slam your hips into his groin.

4. Grab is arm and

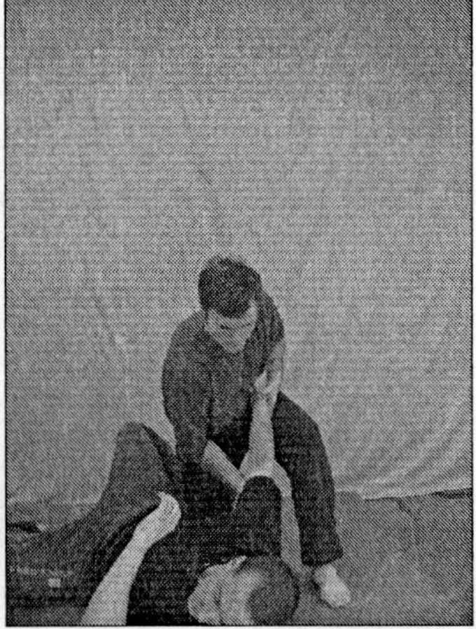

5. Throw.

Measured

The same measures as the under-arm rear bear hug apply.

Oyo - defence against running tackle

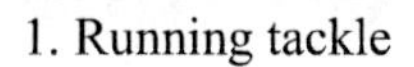

1. Running tackle

2. Shoot legs back and drop your weight on to his shoulders.

3. Force him down.

Measured

Measure	Comments
Proactive	Reactive technique.
Keeps initiative	You try to gain the initiative by taking him down and starting to get some strikes going.
Maximises safety	Under the circumstances, if you can stay on top of him he will find it difficult to get some strikes into you. Watch out for his friends though!
Maximises redundancy	Not a good score on this measure.
Workable under influence of adrenaline	Gross motor movements and survival mindset.
Works with instinct	Grabbing and holding on is an instinctive thing to do.
Maximises predictable response	If you get onto his shoulders he will fall forward.
Unbalances the opponent	Getting your weight onto his shoulders will unbalance him to the front.

Measure	Comments
Leads the mind of the opponent	Not a massive score on this measure.
Low maintenance	Not a difficult skill to maintain.
Range realistic	Grappling range.
Simple	Simple movement.
Transferable skill	No other comparable skill in the kata.
Overall balance of kata	Only defence for a running tackle.

Links and flow

Follow up with strikes.

Mnemonic 29

Shotokan movement - circle arms, raise hands, double-hand strike

1. Step forward to cat stance and circle the arms...

2. To block down to both sides.

3. Lift both wrists to "block" with the wrists.

4.Double-hand strike

5. Turn to face front

6. Push back. Then return to "ready" stance and complete with a bow.

Burgar movement - raise hands, kick, drop hands, double-hand strike

1. Raise hands to the front at eye level.

2. Right foot kick

3. Strike hands down to the side

4. Slide forward and strike with the sides of the hands

5. Turn with elbow low.

6. Push back with the elbow.

My movement and the Shotokan movement are mostly the same but I have changed the emphasis, which is put on different parts of the movement.

Oyo - defence against head butt with double lapel grab

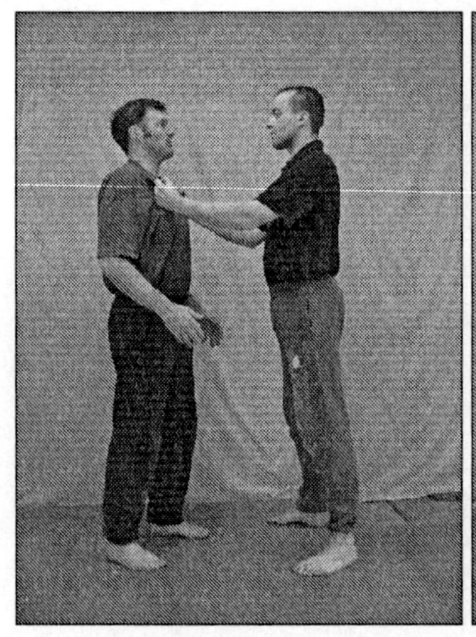

1. Double lapel grab possibly for a head butt

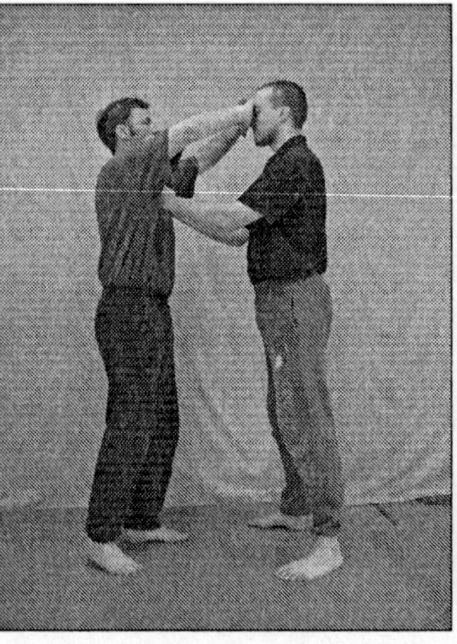

2. Cover his eyes (also stops the head butt)

3. "Under the cover of darkness" kick him in the groin

4. Slam down onto his upper forearms

5. Strike to the collar bones.

Henka

1. He hangs on to you (a possible natural reaction).

2. Go to the last part of the movement

3. And strike or throw him down or both.

Measured

Measure	Comments
Proactive	Covering his eyes gives you the chance to get proactive.
Keeps initiative	Once you have started going proactive you keep the initiative by continuing to strike.
Maximises safety	Covering his eyes also serves to prevent him from head butting.
Maximises redundancy	It doesn't matter if he hangs on or lets go, the technique can survive both outcomes.
Workable under influence of adrenaline	Simple movements. Lifting the leg can be more difficult under adrenal influence.
Works with instinct	Taking your hands towards his head and kicking low are natural movements.
Maximises predictable response	Covering his eyes will lead to momentary confusion. Kicking the groin will cause him to bend forward.
Unbalances the opponent	Yes, particularly if he holds on and you throw him down.

Measure	Comments
Leads the mind of the opponent	Covering the eyes of the opponent causes a moment of confusion. Before he recovers from that you have put him on the defensive.
Low maintenance	Simple technique to maintain.
Range realistic	Grabbing range.
Simple	Gross motor skills.
Transferable skill	The kick and the finish where he continues to hold appear elsewhere in the kata.
Overall balance of kata	Only technique that deals with a two-hand held out lapel grab.

Links and flow

If he is still on his feet you can flow to any of the striking and kicking or throwing movements.

Section 3 - Your Own Single Kata Study

This section draws together the theory of section 1 with the example of section 2, and gives guidance on how to structure and execute your own single kata study.

In this section you will find details about:

- How to set about studying a single kata on your own which includes building methods to deal with habitual acts, which are underpinned with habitual behaviours,
- You will see how to build a training regime around the kata, using the kata as the mnemonic device to facilitate optimal practice.

Planning and practising your own kata

When I first started my single kata study, it was no more than an interesting experiment to see what it would be like. I had no idea where I was going with it. Now looking back I understand that I did not take an optimal path to where I am now. Part of the objective of this book is to pass on some of my learning in order to give you the ability to cover the same ground in much less time. Below I have set out a study plan that can be used as a guide to studying a single kata. It is only a guide and if you just copy it verbatim then you will probably miss the point. The real victory is in making your own discoveries.

Planning

It is important to have a rough plan of what you intend to do. My plan was to get into deep bunkai for the whole of the kata and see where that took me. With hindsight, it was not a very sophisticated plan. Looking back, I can see what may be better ways to approach the subject. A habitual act of violence study route may be more fruitful and balanced.

Suggested sequences for single kata study

Below are two suggested staged progressions to a complete kata study. These are by no means the only ways to approach the subject but I suggest that they would be worthwhile paths to follow.

Path 1

1. List key HAOV

2. Prioritise the HAOV

3. Choose the kata to study

4. Break down the kata to find solutions to the HAOV

5. Refine the responses to the HAOV

6. Find linking and finishing techniques

7. Ensure there is an overall balance over the kata and that responses to scenarios are not duplicated

8. Practice the responses using the kata as a mnemonic tool

9. Drill the responses, links and finishing techniques using the kata as the key to your training regime.

Path 2

1. Choose the kata to study
2. Determine which HAOV each movement is designed to counter
3. Build a balance of responses to HAOV from the movements
4. Refine the responses to the HAOV
5. Determine the linking and finishing techniques
6. Practice the responses, links and finishing techniques using the kata as a mnemonic tool
7. Drill the responses using the kata as the key to your training regime.

Goal setting

Whichever way you go about your study, it is important at each stage to set goals concerning your next immediate step. Goal setting can be enormously difficult if you do not know what your ultimate destination is, and not all subjects in human experience should have an ultimate goal set. In single kata study you do not quite know where you will end up – which is all part of the self-discovery part of karate. Short-term goals in karate are easier to set and therefore at each stage you should get a clear understanding of where you want to get to on that step.

For example, on Path 2 above the first goal is very simple "choose a kata". The goal is very clear, how you go about it may not be so clear. Which one should you choose? Do you select a modern variant or spend time digging up a more ancient version that you think may contain more original movements? The how is not so important as having a clearly defined goal.

Choosing the kata

This is very much down to personal choice. Pick one that you like and that you think you will be able to work with for an extended period. Once you have chosen, stick with your choice and don't chop and change. The whole point of sticking to a single kata is to force you to study more deeply. If you get to a sticking point and decide to move on to another kata, then you will not make the discovery that was just around the corner before you gave up. It is very often the case that just prior to a significant breakthrough the going is the toughest. For those that can keep going the rewards are great. However, those that turn back or change direction don't achieve their goal.

Initial bunkai selection

In order to achieve some balance of bunkai (i.e. not having many techniques that deal with the same HAOV) you will need to make several passes through the kata. Initially just select the first applications that come to mind. Then go through the kata again and chose the best applications for each HAOV. Discard the others and re-research those movements to fill in the gaps on your HAOV list.

In order to determine the bunkai, use the analysis tools set out in this book about reverse engineering kata. In particular the use of the reverse-HAOV method is fast and relatively easy.

Refinement

Each technique must then be refined. For each technique apply the measurement criteria and ensure that they all make sense and stack up well against the criteria. Keep practising each technique and pressure testing each one in reasonable scenarios so that you can have confidence in each technique and you know that the measurement criteria are sensible and working to your favour.

Creating a training regime

In order to create a training regime you need to ensure that you are practising your key skills (habits) and that you are practising your techniques in both a relaxed environment, to build confidence, and in a pressured environment, to test that the skills are working for you. You must make sure that your training regime uses careful and methodical mental rehearsal skills, which have been shown to enhance performance considerably.

Drilling

Once you have designed your training regime it is essential to drill your skills, habits and techniques to the point of "unconscious competence". That means that you have practised them to the point that you do not have to think about applying them. At that point you can put those skills and techniques into a maintenance programme so that you do not have to spend so much time drilling them.

Building a training regime around kata

Introduction

Assuming you have done the bunkai (the analysis) of your kata and you now have a balanced collection of skills and techniques that form the core of a self defence system. Now you need to put them all together as a whole and practice them so that in some sense the whole is greater than the sum of the parts.

It is important to create a set of training exercises that train the required attributes and techniques so that at times of stress you act in the right, most advantageous way. As noted earlier in the book, as long as the skills you have practised are well aligned with your instinctive combative armoury then you will have the best chance of your training staying intact at times of stress.

The first point to note is that there are essentially two types of practice.

A) Those that you do alone.

B) Those that you do with a partner.

Because you are using the kata as your central mnemonic tool, both A and B above are essentially kata training, although most people would label B as kumite. The main focus of this book is dealing with the practice that you do alone, however you should be aware that you need to find a balance between solo and partner work. Both have their positives and negatives and only by finding the appropriate balance and practising mindful of the pitfalls of each will you optimise your training time.

Only you can determine what you really need to practice. It is your personal responsibility to decide how to structure your training.

Performance vs practice

If you have been used to practising only the performance of kata for many years (as you may well have done if you have reached nidan or above in traditional style) then you are going to find it hard to adjust to changing your practice. You will need to slow down and break up the kata so that you don't just run through from start to finish. You must practice each movement in isolation. Ideally you will put it into some kind of context or scenario. Remember, practice the content and not the performance.

Below are some areas that you should consider including in your training regime.

"Horizontal" vs "vertical" practice

Not only do you have to practice your techniques so that upon recognising situations you automatically apply them, but you also need to ensure that you are applying all of the appropriate habits in those techniques.

In NLP (Neuro-linguistic Programming) there is a concept of levels of competence as follows:

1. Unconscious Incompetence: this is where you are not aware of a skill that you don't have.

2. Conscious Incompetence: this is where you become aware of a skill but you do not possess that skill yet - you know you stink.

3. Conscious Competence: this is where you have acquired the skill but have to think about it in order to carry it out.

4. Unconscious Competence: this is where you have the skill and no longer have to think about applying it.

Step 1 takes no effort at all! Step 2 only takes a small amount of observation of someone who has a skill - we recognise immediately that we don't have it i.e. we become conscious of a new skill that we have yet to acquire. Step 3 comes after some practice of the skill in question, and only takes as much effort as is required to perform the skill under conscious control. Clearly this varies from skill to skill and with the ability of the practitioner. And, it is the fourth step that we want but how do we make the transition from 3 to 4? The answer at this stage is frustratingly unclear in terms of how to achieve this optimally, and until more research has been undertaken the only answer on offer is *practice* and then more *practice*.

The question is how to structure that practice for best effect. Currently, it is thought that isolating individual skills or attributes and practising them mindfully, and then moving onto another attribute or skill is an acceptable way to achieve the objective. Working on this premise you can implement a mental imagery / physical practice that I call horizontal vs vertical training (see the introduction to The Habitual Behaviours on page 73)

In order to do this, first decide if you are going to work habits or techniques and how much time you have available in each session. For example you might say you are going to work techniques, in which case you will work your way through your kata and for each technique you will work that technique once or more for each habit (its good to do a few slow, a few medium and a few fast for each habit). When you do each repetition you must be consciously aware of what it is you are trying to achieve. You many sweat a bit physically in these sessions but the level of mental fatigue will be high. You should be careful to think, before doing so, that your objective is clear for each new habit you move onto for each technique. Let's say that you spend about one minute per habit per technique. In my example of Gojushiho you can see that there are nearly 30 mnemonics with a larger number of oyo (more than 40 depending on how many combinations and henka you look at). There are (presented in this book) nearly 20 habits. That means that if you do a "complete round" i.e. you do all habits for all techniques, you will practice about 40x20 which is 800 combinations. You may spend nearly a minute per habit per technique which gives 800 minutes of practice - that is more than 13 hours! If you do an hour a day you could cover all of that in two weeks, with a well deserved day off at the end!

I've found that in practice I tend not to spend so long on each technique and so a whole round can be completed more quickly. Also, in practice you probably will not be able to put in the time if you are also practising at a dojo, and if you have any life outside karate, so maybe half an hour a day would be more realistic in which case you could do a complete round in a month. Whatever way you look at it, this is a pretty serious work load.

After a complete round you may want some variance, in which case you could work vertically rather than horizontally so instead of going through each habit per technique you could go through each technique one habit at a time. This [doing all habits for one technique at a time] is less mnemonically sound. However, doing all techniques for each habit is easier because the flow of techniques is more easily remembered: you just follow your kata.

Also, instead of doing complete rounds, you could chose to have a blitz on one particular habit or technique.

Free flow

The horizontal/vertical training method described above is primarily aimed at instilling the habits into each technique. That clearly is a worthy goal, however, it is also important to be able to flow from one technique to another spontaneously. "Spontaneity doesn't just happen!" This aspect of our training needs work, so how do we train the flow?

This training method requires that your mental imagery skills are advanced. You need to understand how the opponent's body will react to the attacks you are using on it. Not only that, but you need to understand the variety of ways that it will react in so that you can train to those eventualities. Gaining that understanding can usually only be achieved by hands-on practice although as you get more experienced you can quite easily determine the most likely outcomes.

For each technique in the kata you need to know the links in and the links out. What this means is that you need to know how you may get into a particular situation, which technique to use to get out of that situation proactively (leaving yourself in a better position) and then from that position which technique to use until your opponent is subdued.

To train this method simply go through each technique in the kata. Practice that technique and at the end of the technique immediately go into another technique appropriate to the situation you find yourself in, and keep going to the next technique until no further technique is required. This is why kata does not just contain responses to HAOVs. There are also techniques that deal with "in the thick of it" and the "what ifs".

Let's take an example sequence so that you can see what is required. The following sequence is shown with a partner so that you can better visualise what is required, but remember you should be doing this alone as well as with a partner. Remember, also, that you can do more in your imagination than you ever can in reality.

1. Parry the push

2. Cover and check

3. As you start to strike he punches with his left fist; jam it at the upper arm

5. Now flow to attempt this takedown.

6. He is off-balance and rolls out of the takedown

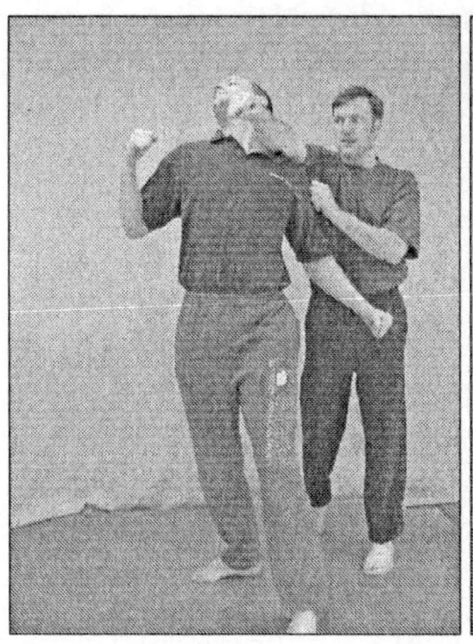

7. Grab him by the clothing and hit him

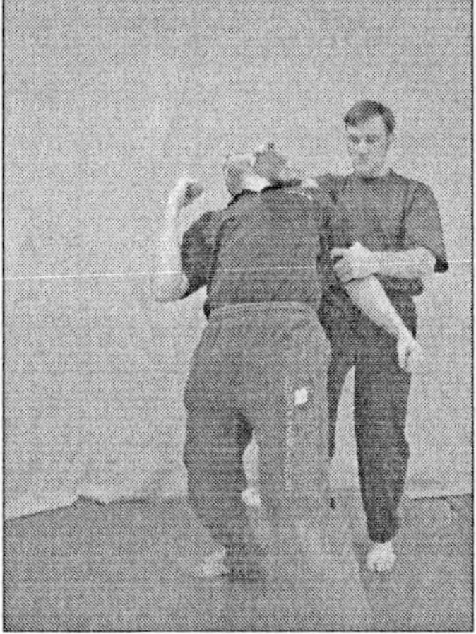

8. Kick his legs out from under him.

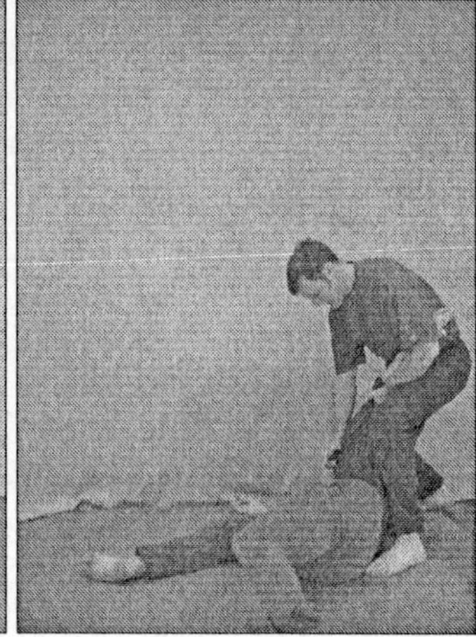

9. And punch as he goes down.

The above example shows flowing through several transitions upon the failure of the preceding technique (you will find all of these in the example of Gojushiho kata). Of course the previous technique may not have failed but you may still need to flow to another should the situation demand.

This flow training is a worthwhile training method. It is particularly good when combined with some random generation of the starting HAOV or situation (see below).

Using modern technologies to enhance the training regime

Heart rate monitors

Heart rate monitors have significantly reduced in price over recent years and can now be used in training. In particular, it is important to be able to gain control of your heart rate, and in order to do this you need to have some feedback as to what level it is running at. For example, an exercise to gain mental control over your heart rate is to imagine and act out high stress situations but during the high stress situation use an NLP trigger / anchor to calm yourself and reduce the heart rate to a more optimal level.

Random HAOV generators

I have mainly worked with audio (due to availability) but video would be a more useful media which I am actively looking into. Basically, a random HAOV generator spits out random HAOV at random intervals, and you must react to the HAOV and deal with it appropriately. I use a simple computer program to randomly choose a HAOV and read it out. Once the HAOV is read out it is important to build a mental image of it and then react and flow to resolution.

Clearly video (preferably to a large screen) would be better than audio. Naturally, a partner is best of all. A simple method that we use is to write the HAOVs onto small cards. The attacker shuffles the deck and turns over the top card (without the defender seeing). The attacker then uses that HAOV to attack. From the defender's perspective this is a totally random attack. (See possibility sets on page 44.)

Camcorder

The camcorder is now widely available at low cost and is an invaluable training aid. You don't need the latest tiny, advanced camcorder; a simple, minimally featured low cost analogue model will easily suffice. Simply set up the camcorder on a tripod and set it running to record your training session. Then watch it back after each set you do and observe carefully to pick up errors and areas for improvement. Then repeat the same set again so that you can use the feedback immediately.

Clearly using this tool you will spend about half your time watching your performance rather than actively practising, but you will find that it will lead to great improvement i.e. quality time over quantity.

Section 4 - Where To From Here?

This section is a sign-post which points the way to the future. If you have studied a single kata for a reasonable time period then you will have gained some insight into the past - the history of kata. By understanding the past, we are better able to deal with the future.

The Burgar kata hypothesis

People often ask me what I have learned through the study of a single kata. Certainly, I have learned many things but the key thing is very simple, and yet most traditional karateka will not be able to accept it. It is this: **that we should not be practising anyone else's kata.**

Noted karate researcher Patrick McCarthy states that kata are not a learning tool, rather, they are a culmination of lessons learned. This means that instead of learning the movements of a kata we should actually be learning individual techniques of self protection and then once we have learned them we should practice them. Putting them together in a sequence acts as a mnemonic device that allows us to recall the techniques and practice them. Thus, we create a kata that is the culmination of our learning and not the start of it. That personal kata then forms the basis of our individual training regime.

Karate is necessarily an individual pursuit. It is practised mainly for the benefit of the practitioner, although that practice may take place in a group setting. Others may benefit as a by-product of the practitioner training but that is incidental.

The primary goal of the karateka is to learn, practice and perfect a system of civilian self-defence to combat the habitual acts of violence (HAOV) that one may face in common scenarios of defence and to work in mutual confrontation situations. Again, this comes from the work of Patrick McCarthy who has compelling evidence to support the assertion.

Each karateka will have more than one teacher and influences in a lifetime of study. Even where a student stays with a single sensei for many decades there is always learning from other sources. Today, the vast majority of karateka have many influences and teachers, and therefore acquire a unique set of skills and knowledge along their path.

Given that the goal is to learn the skills necessary to defend oneself against HAOVs and in mutual confrontation situations, then clearly one must first identify the skills required, learn those skills and then practice them to a sufficient proficiency - or in NLP terms to a level of unconscious competence.

Given that you are necessarily pursuing a goal that is uniquely specific to you, there will be a set of responses and skills that you favour or find easiest to implement. These same responses and skills will not necessarily be optimal for everyone else although there may be considerable overlap.

Learning these skills is an ongoing process of continual refinement. A mnemonic system is required for the karateka to remember all of the skills and techniques, and to facilitate a structured regime of practice. In the past kata has been used as the mnemonic device as a matter of expediency (i.e. there was an insufficient supply of other materials like pens and papers, cameras etc. to use to aid the memory).[1]

1 Actually, even now we have many other mnemonic devices available there are few as good as kata for remembering often-used material such as a small number of self defence techniques.

The skills being learned are not unique to each student, however the combination of techniques and the associated skills that each karateka will utilise is unique to each - otherwise it would be sub-optimal (i.e. the student would be practising skills that would not work well for him compared to other techniques).

Therefore, if each person has a unique set of techniques and skills he will require a unique mnemonic to remember them. In other words, each karateka requires his own unique kata(s).

Therefore, ideally one should create one's own kata, which should be built up and modified over one's karate career. Remember, the only use of the kata is as a mnemonic device to facilitate a training regime; not changing it as new material is learned and integrated is reducing the usefulness of the mnemonic device. Therefore, it is part of the design specification of one's kata that it should change over time.

It follows that one must question the usefulness of *practising* someone else's kata.[2]

Practising someone else's kata is sub-optimal from two standpoints:

1. The mnemonic use is diminished compared to creating one's own mnemonic structure.
2. It will contain techniques that are not applicable to the practitioner.

Instead of teaching one's kata to students, one should be teaching them the fundamental skills relevant to those students. If one does not have the particular skills the students need then one should recommend a teacher who does. The other skill that students should be taught is how to construct their own mnemonic devices i.e. An individual's kata should die with him although the individual skills and techniques may have been passed to numerous other people.

Therefore, the question "Is there one magic kata that addresses all the HAOVs?" can be answered - yes, your own kata - if you have created it. Can you go out and learn a kata that addresses all the HAOVs? No, because learning someone else's kata would be sub-optimal - but it is easier!

Imagine this scenario:
Originally at time zero there are three karate masters. Each has their own kata that is optimised for each of them. They each compiled their own kata from learning self-defence techniques from various sources (say in Okinawa and China).

A student goes to each in turn and says, "Teach me what you know". Each master teaches his own kata because that is what he knows. The student then practices these three kata. He fails to understand that he should be putting in more learning effort himself to break out the lessons and build his own system. In effect, his system becomes a three sub-optimal kata system.

Time passes...

2 Note that I emphasise practising the kata as opposed to learning it. I believe there is a necessary process to go through learning something before one can reject it as inappropriate or not useful.

Now the student is a bit older. A new student comes to him and asks to be taught all he knows. The new student gets three kata from the first student and he also goes to visit a few other people who each give him a few more kata.

The new student now has a system with maybe nine kata. He should just be practising one - his own - but has not been told that that is the way it works, or the prevailing culture prevents him from doing so.

Time moves on and the original masters have learned more and have updated their kata to take the new material into account. They teach the new version to other students who do the same as the first student. The students of various generations are all doing different kata - who has the true version? Nobody does because the question is meaningless. Does this sound like anything familiar?

Let's put the above reasoning into context of some commonly-asked questions.

Q: Is there such a thing as a pure system, or are all karate styles simply amalgams of other systems?

A: There are no pure systems. In fact, the design specification of kata says that with each generation there must be a re-mixing and blending of what went before.

Q: Why do descendants of a particular teacher practice so many variations of the original kata?

A: The teacher's kata is evolving over a period of time. Students who study with him at any point get given the kata as it stands at that point in time. The teacher may not have communicated to the students that they are supposed to change the kata. In fact, given the culture from which sprang modern karate the opposite has happened. It is now taboo even to consider changing kata.

Q: The HAOVs that we face today have surely changed from those of old Okinawa. If you had to create your own two-man-drills and your own kata what would you include?

A: You need your own kata - one that addresses the goal of self-defence in your location/time/culture. Many of the movements would look familiar [to existing kata] because the human body does not change radically over just a few millennia and nor does the instinctive psychology. In addition, if I learn a kata from someone who lives in, say, Japan then much of the content may not be applicable to me i.e. the cultural as opposed to the instinctive differences. I must extract what is useful and put the rest to one side.

Q: If a wheel is well and truly lost then is it not a better option to reinvent one? If one has a comprehensive knowledge of the traditional wheel and its workings then one could reinvent one that surpasses the original in its effectiveness?

A: Yes I think we should be creating our own individual kata. The vogue over the last 10 years for reverse engineering kata bunkai is not a sensible use of time. I have been reverse engineering and modifying a single kata over the last 5 years - I do not regret doing that but I would not do it again. I now believe that that is not a sensible route to take. *However*, it may be that it is an important stage for many karateka to go through in order to mature the thought processes to get to the point where they are ready to accept building their own kata (particularly for karateka who are steeped in "modern tradition").

Q: Is there one kata that I can learn that addresses all of the HAOV already?

A: No - at least, probably not. You are a unique individual with unique requirements and a unique set of knowledge. Nobody stays with one teacher for an entire lifetime. Even if they do, they will have influences from elsewhere - especially these days where the population of available teachers is so much larger than in days gone by. That means that we individually can seek out teachers who specialise in the skills we require, and by using active (rather than passive) learning skills we can amalgamate the techniques and skills into our own practice regime.

Q: We know that teachers such as Higashionna taught a single kata to students but that the performance would vary from student to student. Why would this be?

A: The teacher might know immediately what would be good for the student to learn and what would not work. Why would he bother teaching the techniques that were not ideal for the student? Instead, he would teach what he considers useful for the student, who would end up with a different kata to his peers.

Q: Are you suggesting that we should be learning techniques from all manner of other martial arts and putting them into a personal context?

A: That is exactly the process that I am suggesting happened originally. You simply go out to find the best teachers to teach you the skills you need to reach your goal. Then you record and memorise them and then practice.

If we all agree that kata culminates lessons learned, we must ask the question, "why are we still practising other people's kata whose lessons are lost and we may not have learned yet"?

Where does all this leave us? I guess that most of the karate world will feel quite threatened by the notion of throwing away the kata that define their style and setting out on a journey of real deep learning rather than rote copying. Even now, for 99% of the karate world, the idea of changing a small movement or pose in kata is completely out of the question.

The idea of extracting the lessons from one's teachers and creating one's own mnemonic and practice regime is probably incomprehensible to most - it requires nothing short of a total paradigm shift.

How might this all fit with the modern practitioner? If we really believe that kata culminate lessons learned then we must reflect that in the way we learn, practice and teach. What should teachers be teaching? I believe they should teach the skills and techniques, methods of practice, appropriate use of mnemonic devices, and where to find people that can help the student further.

If the primary goal is not a civilian defence system but some other common goal, for example spiritual development or fitness - why could those ends not be served by the creation of one's own kata too? What would the difference be in outcome by practising someone else's compared to your own (provided they were both well constructed, of course)?

Finally, while we are questioning some of our foundations we have to ask the question "is kata still the best mnemonic device to use". Kata was devised in a time where writing material was less available, no photographs, cine film, video, digital cameras, audio recording devices, computer modelling and animation and computer databases, and multimedia. Understanding of mnemonics is now far more advanced since those days too. Kata has its advantages, certainly, but we should not ignore the changing times - is it time to put kata in the museum and use other mnemonic devices? Having carefully considered this question over a period of years I am firmly convinced that kata is the optimal mnemonic device for karate practice.

If my hypothesis is correct then we could conclude that:
Kata should not be passed from one person to the next. Fighting methods, skills, habits and techniques should be taught, and the karateka should build his own fighting system using appropriate mnemonic tools to facilitate practice.

References

This section is divided into two parts. The first gives a short list of books which, if they are not currently in your library, I would thoroughly recommend adding them and studying them carefully. The second part lists other work that I have also found useful in my study. This list is not exhaustive but should give you some places to look for further information. All three of the gentlemen who have kindly written forewords for this book travel extensively throughout the world, and you should organise for them to visit your dojo to get first-hand experience.

Highly recommended books / videos

Books

Pressure Point Fighting, Rick Clark, Tuttle, ISBN0-8048-3217-X

Rules of Combat, Vince Morris, ISBN 0-9539325-0-8

Streetwise, Peter Consterdine, Protection Publications, ISBN 1-873475-527

The Fence, Geoff Thompson, Summersdale, ISBN 1-84024-084-9

NLP & Sports, Joseph O'Connor, Thorsons, ISBN 0-7225-3671-2

The Naked Ape, Desmond Morris, Vintage, ISBN 0-09-948201-0

Videos

The Tegumi Renzokugeiko excercise, Patrick McCarthy

Powerstrike,, Peter Consterdine, Protection Publications.

S.P.E.A.R. System, Tony Blauer, Blauer Tactical Systems.

Other useful sources

Karate's Grappling Methods, Iain Abernethy, Neth Publishing, ISBN 9-780953-893201

Bunkai Jutsu, Iain Abernethy, Neth Publishing, ISBN 0-9538932-1-9

Bubishi martial art spirit, Translated by G. Alexander and K. Penland, Yamazato Publications, ISBN 0-9631775-1-6

Kill or Get Killed, Col. Rex Applegate, Paladin, ISBN 0-87364-084-5

Acupuncture, Trigger Points and Musculoskeletal Pain, Baldry, Churchill Livingstone, 0-443-04580-1

The Gift of Fear, Gavin De Becker, Bloomsbury, ISBN 0-7475-3835-2

Okinawan Karate, Mark Bishop, A&C Black, ISBN 0-7136-5666-2

The Alexander Technique Workbook, Richard Brennan, Element, ISBN 1-85230-346-8

75 Down Blocks: Refining Karate Technique, Rick Clark, Tuttle Publishing, ISBN 0804832188

Martial Arts for the University, Rick Clark, Kendall/Hunt, ISBN 0-8403-8107-7

Fit to Fight, Peter Consterdine, Protection Publications / Summersdale, ISBN 1-873475-42-X

Preventing face-to-face violence, William Davies and Neil Frude, The APT press, ISBN0-9520914-7-X

Advanced pressure point grappling, George Dillman & Chris Thomas, Dillman Karate International, ISBN 0-9631996-4-1

Kyusho Jitsu, George Dillman & Chris Thomas, Dillman Karate International, ISBN 0-9631996-1-7

Ryukyu Kempo, George Dillman & Chris Thomas, Dillman Karate International, ISBN 0-9631996-3-3

Get Tough, Captain W.E. Fairbairn, Paladin, ISBN 0-87364-002-0

First Strike, Sammy Franco, Paladin, ISBN 1-58160-018-6

1001 Street fighting secrets, Sammy Franco, Paladin, ISBN 0-87364-887-0

Karate-do Kyohan, Gichin Funakoshi, Ward Lock Ltd, ISBN 0-7063-1996-6

Karate-do Kyohan, Gichin Funakoshi, Japanese edition.

Tote Jitsu, Gichin Funakoshi, Masters Publication, ISBN 0-920129-16-1

Karate-do My Way of Life, Gichin Funakoshi, Kodansha, ISBN 0-87011-463-8

Karate-do Tanpenshu, Gichin Funakoshi (Translation by Patrick McCarthy), Ryukyu Karate-Jutsu Kokusai Kenkyukai.

On Killing, Lt. Col. Dave Grossman, Back Bay Books, ISBN 0-316-33011-6

The Biomechanics of Sports Techniques, James Hay, Prentice-Hall, ISBN 0-13-078494-X

Textbook of Acupuncture, Felix Mann, Heinemann Medical Books, ISBN 0-433-20312-9

Winning Without Drugs, David Hemery, Thorsons, ISBN 0-7225-2486-2

Sporting Excellence, David Hemery, Collins Willow, ISBN 0-00-218398-6

Small-circle Jujitsu, Wally Jay, Ohara, ISBN 0-89750-122-5

Shotokan Karate International Kata (vol 1 & 2), Hirokazu Kanazawa.

Biomechanics, Kreighbaum and Barthels, Macmillan, ISBN 0-02-366310-3

Tao of Jeet Kune Do, Bruce Lee, Ohara, ISBN 0-89750-048-2

Fists, Wits, and a Wicked Right, Marc MacYoung, Paladin, ISBN 0-87364-611-8

Floor Fighting, Marc MacYoung, Paladin, ISBN, 0-87364-716-5

A colour atlas of human anatomy, McMinn Hutchings Pegington Abrahams, Wolfe Publishing, 0-7234-1915-9

Advanced Dim-Mak, Erle Montaigue, Paladin, ISBN 0-87364-779-3

Dim-Mak, Erle Montaigue, Paladin, ISBN 0-87364-718-1

People Watching, Desmond Morris, Vintage, ISBN 0-099-42978-0

The Human Zoo, Desmond Morris, Vintage, ISBN 0-09-948211-8

Kyusho Secrets, Vince Morris.

You or Him?, Vince Morris.

Okinawa Kempo: Karate Jutsu on Kumite, Choki Motobu, Translated by Seiyu Oyata

Karate - my art, Motobu Choki (Translation by Patrick McCarthy), International Ryukyu Karate-jutsu Research Society.

Tales of Okinawa's Great Masters, Shoshin Nagamine (translated by Patrick McCarthy), Tuttle, ISBN 0-8048-2089-9

The Essence of Okinawan Karate-do, Shoshin Nagamine, Tuttle, ISBN 0-8048-1163-6

Best Karate (Series), Nakayama, Kodansha International.

NLP Workbook, Joseph O'Connor, Thorsons, ISBN 0-00-710003-5

I Thought You'd be Bigger, Kevin O'Hagan, New Breed Publishing, ISBN 0-9517567-7-X

Pre-emptive strikes for winning fights, Jamie O'Keefe, New Breed Publishing, ISBN 0-9517567-3-7

Ancient Okinawan Martial Arts 1, Patrick McCarthy, Tuttle, ISBN0-8048-2093-7

Ancient Okinawan Martial Arts 2, Patrick McCarthy, Tuttle, ISBN0-8048-3147-5

The Bubishi, Translation and analysis by Patrick McCarthy, International Ryukyu Karate-jutsu Research Society.

Clear Instructions to the Excellent Art of Wrestling, Nicolaes Petter, 1674, www.ejamas.com

A Bouncer's Guide to Barroom Brawling, Peyton Quinn, Paladin, ISBN 0-87364-586-3

Anatomy & Physiology, Seeley Stephens & Tate, Mosby Year Book, ISBN 0-8016-6685-6

Unante, John Sells, WM Hawley, ISBN 0-910704-89-9

Dynamic Aidido, Gozo Shioda, Kodansha, ISBN 0-87011-301-1

Sharpening the Warrior's Edge, Bruce K. Siddle, PPCT Research Publications, ISBN 0-9649205-0-6

Secrets of German Medieval Swordsmanship, Translated and Interpreted by Cristian Henry Tobler, Chivalry Bookshelf, ISBN 1-891448-07-2

The art of fighting without fighting, Geoff Thompson, Summersdale, ISBN 1-84024-085-7

3 Second Fighter, Geoff Thompson, Summersdale, ISBN 1-873475-66-7

The Pavement Arena, Geoff Thompson, Summersdale, ISBN 1-873475-11-X

Chimpanzee Politics, Frans de Waal, ISBN, 0-8018-3833-9

Natural Conflict Resolution, edited by Filippo Aureli & Frans de Waal, University of California Press, ISBN 0-520-22346-2

Peacemaking among primates, Frans de Waal, Harvard University Press, ISBN 0-674-65921-X

Athletic Ability and the Anatomy of Motion, Rolf Wirhed, Wolfe Medical, ISBN 0-7234-1540-4

Demonic Males, Richard Wrangham & Dale Peterson, ISBN 0-7475-3301-6

Index

A

B

C

D

Printed in the United Kingdom
by Lightning Source UK Ltd.
9495000001B